# TURNING TOTAL QUALITY MANAGEMENT INTO CLASSROOM PRACTICE

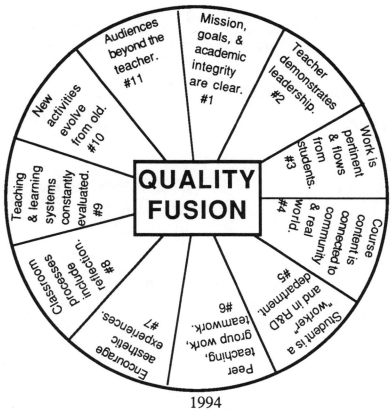

1994
Cornesky & Associates Inc.

1003 Ravenswood Drive
Anderson, SC 29625
Tele: 864.231.9780 or 800.388.8682
FAX: 864.224.2436
E-mail: TQM1BOB@AOL.COM

CORNESKY & ASSOCIATES, Inc., 1994

First Printing February 1994

Second Printing June 1994

Third Printing May 1995

Library of Congress Cataloging-in-Publication Data

ISBN 1-881807-05-3

**Cover design by Ms. Chris Silverthorn**

# About the authors . . .

**Margaret Byrnes** is a nationally acclaimed presenter and consultant in understanding the at-risk population and total quality management for classroom teachers. She is the primary author of *The Quality Teacher: Implementing Total Quality Management in the Classroom.* She brings a wealth of experience to these endeavors from the perspective of teacher, school counselor, agency counselor and vocational institute director. She is a member of the ASQC Education Division Curriculum Committee. Margaret is the editor of *Creating Quality K-12* Newsletter as well as a total quality management consultant specializing in K-12 schools. Her address is 1842 Bonforte Blvd., Pueblo, Colorado 81001; phone (719) 545-8821; fax (719) 545-1508.

**Robert Cornesky**, author of numerous books and articles on Total Quality Management, including *Implementing Total Quality Management in Higher Education, The Quality Professor: Implementing TQM in the Classroom,* and *Quality Classroom Practices for Professors* has over 25 years experience in higher education across the nation. He has served as the Dean of a School of Science, Management & Technologies at a comprehensive state university and as the Dean of a School of Allied Health at a health sciences center. Bob is the editor of the *Chronicle of CQI* Newsletter and an consultant specializing in total quality management educational institutions. His address is 489 Oakland Park Blvd., Port Orange, Florida 32127; phone (800) 388-8682; fax (904) 756-6755; e-mail: tqm1bob@aol.com

# CONTENTS

Table of Contents

Table of Contents

Table of Contents

# Introduction

The following is a total quality management-based procedure revolving around the Foxfire educational approach by Eliot Wigginton (1985). The Foxfire educational approach consists of 11 core practices from a 25 year old approach started in Appalachia; however, we have elaborated and modified it and **fused** it with the TQM principles of Dr. Deming and other quality experts—thus the title *Quality Fusion.*

"Fusion" has several very interesting definitions:

1) A mixture or blend formed by fusing. (We have literally "formed a mixture or blend" by fusing the total quality management approaches with the Foxfire educational approach.

2) A reaction in which atomic nuclei combine to form more massive nuclei, generally having some excess mass that is converted into energy. (We believe that we have created a reaction in which the teaching/learning "nuclei" are combined to form a more massive teaching/learning "nuclei" in which the excess teaching/learning experience is converted into meaningful activities and fun.)

*Quality Fusion* uses an educational approach that actively involves the students ("workers") in the learning system as they meet customer expectations, including parent, employer, and the instructor down the line. *Quality Fusion* evolved from our extensive training seminars and workshops for teachers revolving around our best selling book *The Quality Teacher: Implementing Total Quality Management in the Classroom* (1992). However, unlike the earlier book, *Quality Fusion* is developed for teachers who are partially trained and knowledgeable about TQM principles and approaches, but still want to apply the processes, tools, and techniques of TQM to their classrooms. For these teachers, we offer a technique that will maximize teacher and student successes while the teacher expands and develops more fully his/her experiences into her/his personal quality approach.

The processes within the *Quality Fusion* approach are meant to be modified to meet the needs of teaching and learning, however, modifications are not advised until you understand totally the principles and approaches of TQM. The *Quality Fusion* approach, the core of our initial teacher training program, involves eleven steps. When you first begin your journey of applying this approach into your classroom, we suggest that you use a **wholistic approach** to the following steps rather than attempt this in a linear sequence. The steps are listed below, and this book will devote a chapter to each point as we attempt to guide you on your quality journey.

## 1. The mission, goals and academic integrity of the class must be absolutely clear.

Each teacher should embrace state- or local-mandated skill content lists as "givens" to be engaged by the class. They should not only accomplish them to the level of mastery in the course of executing the class plan, but also go far beyond their normally narrow confines to discover the value and potential inherent in the content area being taught and its connections to other disciplines.

## 2. The teacher must demonstrate leadership.

The teacher's role is that of a coach, collaborator, and team leader, rather than boss. S/he monitors the academic and social growth of every student, leading each into new areas of understanding and competence.

The teacher's attitude toward students, toward the work of the class, and toward the content being taught must model the attitudes expected of students. The attitudes and values required of the students and teacher should reflect our responsibility in a democratic society.

## 3. All work must be pertinent and flow from the students.

Much of the work teachers and students do can best be done as teams and must flow from student desire and student concerns. From the beginning the work is infused with student choice, design, revision, execution, reflection and evaluation. Teachers are responsible for assessing and ministering to their students' developmental needs.

Most problems that arise during classroom activities are solved in collaboration with students. When a student asks, "Here's a situation that just came up. I don't know what to do about it. What should I do?" the teacher turns the question back to the class to wrestle with and solve, rather than simply answering it. Students are trusted continually, and all are led to the point where they embrace responsibility.

## 4. Course content is connected to the surrounding community and the real world.

The processes of connecting the content of all course work to the surrounding community and the real world engage the students in identifying and characterizing the communities in which they live.

Whenever students research larger issues like changing climate patterns, acid rain, prejudice, or AIDS, they must "bring them home," identifying attitudes about illustrations and implications of those issues in their own environments.

## 5. The student is not only treated as a "worker," but also as a team member of the "research and development" department.

The work is characterized by student action, rather than passive receipt of processed information. Rather than students doing what they already know, they must be led continually into new work and unfamiliar territory. Once skills are "won," they must be reapplied to new problems in new ways.

In a classroom run under such processes, students always operate at the edge of their competence. Therefore, it must be clear to them that a mistake is not a failure, but an attempt in innovation. They must realize that positive constructive scrutiny of those mistakes by the rest of the class will occur in an atmosphere where students will never be embarrassed. In essence, they must accept the principle that new knowledge is the result of "research and development" and that mistakes are part of the process.

## 6. Peer teaching, small group work, and team work are emphasized.

A constant feature of the *Quality Fusion* teaching/learning system is its emphasis on peer teaching, small group work, and team work. Every student in the room is not only included, but needed, and in the end, each student can identify his/her specific stamp upon the effort. In a classroom thus structured, discipline tends to take care of itself and ceases to be a major issue.

## 7. Students should have aesthetic experiences.

Teachers must acknowledge the worth of aesthetic experiences. They should model that attitude in their interactions with students and resist the policies and practices that deprive students of the chance to use their imaginations. From these experiences students develop their capacities to appreciate, to refine, to express, to enjoy and to break out of restrictive, unproductive modes of thought.

## 8. Classroom processes should include reflection.

The teacher and the students should set a time aside for reflection on a daily basis. This thoughtful time is to stand apart from the work and should be an essential activity that takes place at key points throughout the day. The reflection evokes insights and nurtures revisions in the classroom teaching/learning system. Since this is the activity that teachers and students are least accustomed to doing, the teachers will have to dedicate themselves to this undertaking.

## 9. The teaching/learning system should undergo constant evaluation.

The work produced by the students should be constantly evaluated for changes in skills, content, and attitudes. A variety of strategies should be employed, in combination with pre- and post-testing, ranging from simple tests of recall of simple facts through much more complex instruments involving student participation in the creation of demonstrations that answer the teacher challenge: "In what ways will you prove to me at the end of this class that you have mastered the objectives we have designed?"

Students should be trained to monitor their own progress and devise their own remediation plans, and they should be brought to the point where they can understand that the progress of each student is the concern of every other student in the room. Students work with teachers to develop a portfolio.

## 10. New activities should constantly evolve from the old.

As the year progresses, new activities should spiral gracefully out of the old, incorporating lessons learned from past experiences, building on skills and understanding that can now be amplified. The students should understand that the quest for quality work is never ending and that the finished product of one class is nothing more than a conclusion of a series of activities from which to start a new series.

The questions at the end of each class period, as well as at the end of each course, should be: "Now what? What do we know that we didn't know when we started out together? How can we use those skills and that information in some new, more complex and interesting ways? What's next?"

## 11. There must be an audience beyond the teacher.

Beside the teacher, the students should be recognized for their achievement by other audiences. This might include another individual, a small group, a community group, or other students, but it must be an audience the students want to serve, or engage, or impress. The audience could be a "customer" and may be either an internal customer (teacher), or an external customer (community group). The audience must affirm that the work is important and is needed and was worth doing—and it should, indeed, be all of those.

**Chapter One:** The mission, goals and academic integrity of the class must be absolutely clear.

## ESTABLISH A CLASSROOM MISSION

Deming's (1982) first point is: "**Create a constancy of purpose for the improvement of product and service ...**" In other words, focus, focus, focus! Unless you know where you are headed, how will you ever know when you've arrived?

A key word for point one is *constancy*. Constancy of purpose requires that you have a firmly established view of your classroom mission and that you adopt a long-range plan to implement it and to improve upon it through years of "research and development."

Without having a constancy of purpose, *i.e.*, a clearly defined mission statement and a plan to implement it, you will be driven by reactions to immediate concerns and you will have the tendency to move in wayward directions in order to satisfy the immediate needs of an "instant gratification" society.

Unless you and your students have a clear view at a very fundamental level of what the basic goals and academic integrity of your class are, both you and your students will have no map to guide your personal development.

The need for classroom mission statements might seem obvious, but seldom do we see them in classrooms around the country. Partly this is so because teachers have so little reflection time, spend almost no time discussing them in their teacher preparation program, and once out of university go immediately into a school.

Developing a mission is not as easy as it may seem. It essentially defines the purpose of one's work. What so many may take for granted is that very thing that apparently keeps many from being successful. If you don't know where you're going, you'll probably never get there because you won't have any idea where it is you want to go. Teachers without a clear mission statement have little or no idea what they desire to accomplish or what their purpose in the classroom is. If your mission is **to teach world geography** you may feel that you are being successful in spite of the fact that as many as 50 or more percent of all students are not learning. This, of course, is one of the oldest philosophical debates...if no one learns can one still claim to have taught?

7

If the mission is "to teach world geography," the teacher has no sense of purpose in the classroom. We must remind ourselves that schools don't exist for teachers to teach, but for students to learn. If this is the case, considering the above mission, that teacher has not viewed learning as the primary responsibility or constant purpose. This brings us to the need to understand fully one's place in the organizational scheme. It also presupposes that each person understands the role of everyone else within the system.

Teachers (and perhaps we need to consider changing that title to something more appropriate like **facilitator of learning**) absolutely must reconsider their function and move their focus away from teaching and towards learning. Quality teachers are leaders. They lead students and facilitate the learning process. The interaction between teacher and learner must be shifted so more responsibility for learning is placed on the student, and more facilitating is done by the teacher.

Teachers who view themselves as service providers often have less trouble with this concept. The teacher/student and supplier/customer relationship is depicted in Figure 1.1. Indeed, teachers do provide a service for students. They do more than that, however.

Teachers are the individuals who take an initial leadership role in creating the learning environment. As the year progresses, however, teachers increase gradually the leadership responsibilities of all students who are full partners in co-creating the learning experiences and establishing a learning environment where everyone can succeed. As the teacher exerts less control, and mentors students to assume leadership roles, students become more active in their own learning. This in turn leads to fewer discipline problems and a greater interest in learning.

Figure 1.1: Teacher/Student—Supplier/Customer Relationships.

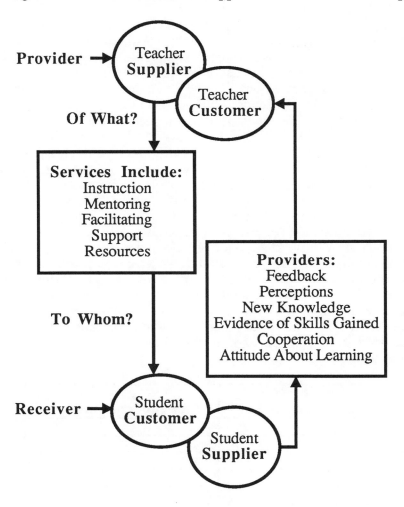

Let's assume the teacher has deliberated and determined his mission to be:

**To facilitate students' learning about the world they live in, the state, region, nation and international global community through the study of economics, geography, and world cultures so all students can thrive and survive in the 21st century.**

Carefully read this mission statement and reflect on it. How might it be improved? Is there anything about this mission statement that seems ambiguous to you? If you were to represent this mission statement in some other form, such as a drawing, what would it look like?

Mission statements are best developed only after considering your beliefs about students and their world. Since beliefs do drive you along towards your mission, give some thought to your beliefs. Be very honest with yourself and write them down. If you sincerely don't believe all students can learn, then don't write that down because your actions and interactions with students will give you away. Reflection such as this is not easy, but it is necessary to your future success as a quality teacher.

With your mission statement, reflect on your classroom processes and practices. In what ways do you support your mission, and in what ways do you impede progress towards the mission? Every action...every word...every look you give during the day must line up with your mission. This is much more difficult than it seems!  Do you occasionally fall into a trap and don't know how to get out of it? Sometimes we don't really recognize the mistakes we make until we give serious thought to our modus operandi and then write down our thoughts. Remember, there will be a tendency to revert to old coping skills when the going gets a little bit tough. Take time to reflect and complete the chart below in order to examine your processes and systems within your classroom that either support or impede your mission.

| Things I do that support my mission | Things I do that impede my mission |
|---|---|
|  |  |
|  |  |
|  |  |
|  |  |
|  |  |
|  |  |

## SELF-IMPROVEMENT PROGRAM

Deming's (1982) thirteenth point is: **"Institute a vigorous program of education and self-improvement."** Your next step is to reduce the behaviors that impede progress towards the mission and increase the supporting behaviors. It is a good idea to keep track of the impeding behaviors by creating a check sheet. An exercise that is helpful is to monitor your own actions, words, and looks every day for at least 15 days. Remember your beliefs. This exercise may help you uncover some subconscious beliefs you were heretofore unaware of, but that definitely affect your behavior in the classroom. Maintain it meticulously and it will provide a reminder of the traps that you fall into. By bringing that behavior into your awareness you can create an action plan for change. See the example below.

## DEFECT CHECKSHEET

| Day | Punished a Child | Screamed | Crabby |
|---|---|---|---|
| 1 | III | II | yes |
| 2 | I | III | no |
| 3 | IIII | II | yes |
| 4 | II | I | no |
| 5 | I | | no |
| 6 | III | IIII | yes |
| 7 | I | I | no |
| 8 | II | II | no |
| 9 | II | III | yes |
| 10 | IIII | II | yes |
| 11 | II | I | no |
| 12 | | | no |
| 13 | I | I | no |
| 14 | IIII | III | yes |

A step beyond this would be to note who is being punished and for what reason. It is highly probable that you have engaged in a power struggle with a certain student(s). If so, both you and the student(s) will be the ultimate losers. As long as power struggles are going on between students and teachers, no learning is taking place except that the students know how to "push your button." Examine your check sheet to determine whether or not you have been engaged in power struggles. The person who needs to take the first step in resolving power battles is the teacher, so do whatever you need to do to cease this struggle today!

On the days you indicated you were crabby, it might be helpful if you jot a note or two down indicating what happened that resulted in you feeling crabby. Perhaps you have hypoglycemia and are unaware of it, but realize if you don't eat regularly you lose control. Or, maybe there are some little annoyances in your life that seem to get bigger when you come to school. Can you do anything about these? For instance, if you are always late or come to school just "under the wire," perhaps you can rearrange your morning routine so you arrive a few minutes earlier to allow yourself time to get ready for the day.

Become aware of how you are treating the students you've punished. Do your actions fit into your mission? If not, then assess how you can give more responsibility for solving problems to the student so the power struggle doesn't need to continue. Continuously align your behavior with your mission statement. Any self-behavior that doesn't help you move the students toward the mission is an area you may wish to consider for your own continuous improvement. Just as you occasionally need help in realigning towards the mission, so will the students. Be patient with yourself and each student. Since we are all imperfect, we are excellent candidates for personal continuous quality improvement. Progress may be slow, but imagine how good you'll feel when you realize how on target you are towards accomplishing your mission.

## DEVELOP YOUR GOALS

Once you've developed your mission statement based upon your beliefs, it is time to make tentative goals for the year. Set the goals high enough so they will represent a stretch for you. Each year your goals should be based on continuous quality improvement from the previous year. Goals should be measurable and must fit in with the district goals and priorities (see "Discussion" at the end of this chapter). Yearly goals for yourself may be slightly different from the classroom goals that students help set. For instance, perhaps one of the district's priorities is to increase the amount of parental involvement in the educational process. One of your goals, therefore, will naturally have to do with parental involvement. However, the students' classroom goals will probably be more directly related to learning than their parents' role in their education.

## COMMUNICATE

Each fall, just prior to the start of school , it is very helpful (and a wonderful way to begin engaging more parents in education) to send home a packet of materials and to make telephone calls regarding your class to all parents/guardians.

### Packets

The packets might include:
- letter of introduction
- district vision, mission, and goals
- building mission and goals
- classroom mission, beliefs, and goals

- introduction to Total Quality Management (TQM)
- explanation of how TQM processes work in the classroom
- customer/supplier contracts (outlining expectations of each parent and teacher)
- list of district outcomes for the class
- opportunities for parents/guardians to volunteer in class and/or school
- training opportunities for parent/guardian volunteers

## Phone Calls

It is usually better to make phone calls to parents before school starts introducing yourself and letting them know you are looking forward to having their child in your class and that you'll be sending them some materials to better acquaint them with you and how the class will operate. It helps to get school off to a good start and leaves the parents feeling good about the teacher.  Remember that some parents/guardians did not have a very pleasant school experience, so whatever you can do ahead of time to set the stage for a friendly, arms around approach will pay big dividends later.

Using the Total Quality approach is so different that most parents will be confused if some effort isn't made to educate them immediately in TQM processes and continuous quality improvement.

## ACADEMIC INTEGRITY

Once you have established a classroom mission and goals that are  aligned with the building and district mission and goals, familiarize yourself with the outcomes required by the district pertaining to your grade level or content area. In fact, we recommend that the outcomes be displayed prominently in the classroom, and always carried close to you. It wouldn't hurt to have them listed, perhaps in some shortened form, on a 3 x 5 card that you can carry everywhere with you. The purpose of all this is to impress upon you the importance of the outcomes, especially in terms of your mission and hopefully, the way your work is assessed. It is far too easy to lose sight of the required outcomes. Quality teachers view outcomes as minimal standards and never as ultimate goals.

Be certain to provide students and parents with copies of the district standards. If you have information about state standards and/or national standards, we recommend you adopt the most stringent of all standards whether national or local. Go for the highest levels of learning, and refuse to accept the lowest as the student's best.

It behooves all teachers to survey parents to discover the best time for them to meet and then schedule one or more meetings to review the standards and what they means to their children. Explain how the classroom will operate and flow chart the learning process so parents understand how the classroom will function. Explain what their role will be in supporting their child's achievement. Explain your role in the process. Be sure to provide plenty of opportunities for parents to ask questions. This approach is different from their experience, so the importance of going through this communication process cannot be over-emphasized.

Students can and should be informed about what is expected of them during the coming month, marking period, semester or school year. Expectations (outcomes) can be clearly stated and explained to students so they understand, without reservation, what is expected. Learning experiences can meet one or more outcomes. In fact, some experiences may exceed 30 outcomes upon completion. Others may only cover one or two, but they may be critical.

The outcomes can be reached in many ways when students co-create their learning experiences by working with teacher to determine the way they will learn something. This makes a beautiful blend since the end result is very highly motivated students. The teacher's job becomes much easier since there are few, if any, discipline problems. Students become so much more focused that the problem with time on task simply means that there isn't enough time during the school day for students to accomplish everything they want to do.

With each learning experience, teacher and students together determine which outcomes will be achieved when the experience is finished. It may take some time for teachers to put all the outcomes on a chart, but the time is well spent since students can thereafter keep track of their own growth and mastery. Along the side of the chart, are listed the outcomes. Across the top, the teacher and students can fill in each learning experience. Prior to beginning, students and teacher together review the outcomes, and after determining which will be mastered for any given learning experience, the students marks each appropriate box. When the learning experience is complete and the teacher and student(s) assess it for quality factors, then each box is blackened. In this way, every student, parent, and teacher has instant access to the child's progress, and the information contained on the chart accurately depicts their skills. This approach takes all the mystery out of how much progress the student is making in any class. The following is an example:

| Outcome | Competency | Competency Elements | Know | Do | Change | Create |
|---------|-----------|--------------------|------|-----|--------|--------|
|         |           |                    |      |     |        |        |
|         |           |                    |      |     |        |        |
|         |           |                    |      |     |        |        |

## FINALLY

While we recommend tracking outcomes or standards, we want to remind you that the focus of the classroom experiences must remain on process and not the outcomes. Through the co-creation of learning experiences, learning can become such a joy for students and teachers alike that you'll undoubtedly discover that achievement will soar far beyond your original outcomes. We caution you not to dilute the process improvement techniques called for in continuous quality improvement. The whole idea behind co-creation of the learning experience is that students and teachers together determine the way(s) in which outcomes will be achieved. There are an infinite number of roads leading to the same outcomes, so allow yourself and the students to have fun while determining what road to take. Remember, not everyone has to take the same road. Students learn best in different ways, and there may even be instances when you have 6 or more different ways to achieve the end.

As the **facilitator of learning,** your role is to focus on the mission and goals you've established while assisting all students to achieve them. Punishment and other old coping patterns must give way to the idea of releasing control to students so they can become more responsible for their own learning, as you take on the role of facilitator and mentor.

Encourage parents and others to become involved with the students to increase everyone's level of excitement and interest in learning. Clearly state your expectations with parents as your primary suppliers, but also freely inform them of their rights as your customer.

By maintaining a clear constancy of purpose and by having a written mission statement and set of measurable goals you will be able to align all activities within the classroom towards success. In this way, using the continuous quality improvement model, you'll be able to work with students, parents, and others to build quality into every process within your classroom. By building quality into each process, the end result will be a much higher level of achievement for all students and you and they can experience the joy of learning!

## DISCUSSION

### Aligning School District Goals with Building and Classroom Goals

Constancy of purpose is the way Deming puts it. Focus, focus, focus! Unless you know where you are headed, how will you ever know when you've arrived? These seemingly obvious points, are less obvious to many teachers, principals, and central administrators who consistently refuse to align the district's mission and goals with what happens in the classroom. In fact, few schools around the nation make any attempt to align what goes on in classrooms with local, state, or national goals or standards. It is true that except for mathematics, the national standards as of January 1994 are not yet set, but how many schools have adopted even the mathematics goals and have engaged teachers in the professional development experiences needed to achieve them?

Another area sadly lacking in alignment is the America 2000 goals and state goals or school district goals. As Deming has been reported to say, so what that the governors have set national education goals. They are meaningless unless they also recommend a means to achieve those goals. Goals, like exhortations and slogans, do little or nothing except lower morale of the workforce because they cannot see how such goals can be achieved. Several major reports have recently been published stating that there is little hope America will achieve the national education goals in this century. In fact, one such report concluded that unless dramatic changes and complete systemic educational reform occurs, America will never achieve the goals in this century or any other. That is a very sad commentary on our school systems.

If we think about which former students are most successful in life, we can clearly point (either from personal or professional experience) to those who had clear goals and a focus (constancy of purpose). These students seem to stay on track and achieve success not only in K-12, but also as they pursue post-secondary education or employment. The students without any future goals or focus seem constantly to flounder, bouncing from one course to another without really learning much. Far too many students in the latter group float through high school doing minimal work and getting C's or D's by using their short term memory to take tests. If you were to ask these students to explain what they learned in the previous course or previous year, or perhaps even the previous semester they would be unable to do so. Yet, many of these same students are not singled out for special help maybe because they participate in an occasional school activity and rarely cause problems.

The illusion is that schools work for these kids! We suggest that these students (who may comprise as much as 70% of the entire student body) are not being properly served by the educational system. It is failing for them as much as if they were getting F's in every class. The difference is that students who fail in high school would not be considered at any post-secondary institution. Students who are floaters are often admitted into post-secondary institutions, some even receive scholarships, but all have trouble succeeding because they have been passive learners with little, if any, understanding of what study means. When we use the word "study," we refer not to studying for a test, but learning to be a reflective person who studies and ponders questions of life and how their learning experiences can be utilized. Students who flounder usually don't know what they want to do, have no idea of how to set goals, and, therefore, cannot resolve problems effectively. Their future is as cloudy as if their heads were filled with cumulous clouds.

To become effective, entire school systems must develop a vision, mission, and goals that are enthusiastically endorsed by all administrators, teachers, and support service personnel. In too many cases, school districts don't have a vision, mission, and goals. Is it any wonder that these systems are fragmented, with squabbles between buildings and teachers over resources and space? Futhermore, many teachers have no knowledge of the district vision, mission, and goals. If they don't know where the district is headed, how can anyone know what his/her own job is? How can one fit into an organization when no one has properly educated that individual about the organization and where it is headed? Impossible?— yet it happens year after year after year.

Another pertinent issue is how school districts without a vision, mission, and clearly stated goals can think about evaluating teacher performance when they don't even know what their purpose is. It is folly for school district administrators to pretend they can evaluate teachers adequately if there is no plan spelled out within which the teachers are expected to operate.

On the other hand, we have interviewed many teachers and discovered that few of them have a personal mission statement or personal and professional goals. Frequently, we hear, "Well,

I know my mission is; I just can't put it into words." This is a crucial point, and one not to be taken lightly. Each teacher should be informed of the district's vision, mission, and goals. There should be yearly training for teachers, administrators, and support personnel to discuss the district's plan and then to set the building plan. Each building's plan must align totally with the district plan; otherwise, chaos will reign throughout the district and the likelihood of meeting district-wide goals will be nil.

Furthermore, once teachers are fully informed of the district plan (we hope that central administration doesn't determine the strategic plan in isolation, but with full participation of teachers, students, and the community) and have helped set the building plan, each can begin to reflect on a classroom mission statement and establish yearly goals. This type of planning requires full engagement of a cross-section of all stakeholders, time to reflect and give thoughtful consideration of each aspect of the plan, a willingness to set goals that are measurable, plus an agreement on the means to achieve the goals. This presupposes that teachers, administrators, and support personnel are willing to suspend any notions about evaluation and contract issues and assume responsibility for the achievement of the goals as measured by the agreed upon outcomes.

The use of measurable goals is a wonderful way to get any assessment out of the realm of the subjective and into the objective realm. Data collection can be relatively simple, take little time, and still yield valuable information. Used properly, data, agreed upon by everyone, that measures progress towards meeting the building and district goals is the least biased way to assess performance.

Long gone are the days when we can rely on the subjective reports based on a few days of observation by the principal or department chairs. It is obvious that these evaluative measures have done nothing to improve classroom performance insofar as achieving the district's mission and goals is concerned. Indeed, we suggest that school districts not only provide ample training for administrators, teachers, and support personnel in a self-assessment procedure based on the Malcolm Baldrige Quality Award Criteria, and connect the self-assessment directly with achieving district and building goals. The Baldrige Award Quality Criteria call for data in the form of charts and graphs to support improvement trends rather than the traditional anecdotal reporting now used.

In her forthcoming book *Weave Quality into Your Schools* (1994, in press), Margaret Byrnes combines Hoshin Planning with teacher self-assessment. She suggests that if teachers are asked to assess themselves and the results used as a tool for punishment, there is little hope that they will be honest. On the other hand, if there was a system in place that allowed teachers to self-assess using criteria that depended on data, pre-determined collaboratively with key stakeholders, they would feel free to seize the opportunity to create an action plan directly focused on achieving district goals. As it stands now, many teachers believe they are victims of a subjective evaluation that is neither equitable nor fair.

ΛΛΛΛΛΛΛΛ

The following is a checksheet tool to help the teacher to implement the **Quality Fusion** technique into their classroom.

Step 1:   The mission, goals and academic integrity of your class are absolutely clear.

√   Established a classroom mission statement.
√   Developed personal goals for the class.
√   Communicated mission and goals to parents/guardians.
√   Aligned classroom mission and goals with those of the school district and the school.

## Chapter Two: The teacher must demonstrate leadership.

The teacher's role is that of a coach, facilitator, collaborator and team leader, rather than boss. S/he monitors the academic and social growth of every student, leading each into new areas of understanding and competence.

The teacher's attitude toward students, toward the work of the class, and toward the course content must model the attitudes expected of students. The attitudes and values required of the students and teacher should reflect our responsibility in a democratic society.

Leadership addresses issues of commitment to Quality. It (leadership) provides the driving force behind the quality movement. Therefore, in order to lend credence, you must implicitly and explicitly understand what a Total Quality Classroom "looks" like. Without such a clear and thorough understanding it is impossible to recognize those practices and processes which are helpful and those which are harmful. Traditional teaching and classroom management styles do not allow for such an examination since they are based on the teacher as manager rather than the teacher as leader.

Let's define Total Quality and how it works in education.

Total Quality is:

- a management theory;
- a guiding light that ceases to blame others for organizational problems;
- customer driven and focused;
- a style of leadership that empowers others to analyze root causes of organizational problems and assist with building Quality in to avoid recurring problems;
- a "do it right the first time" approach;
- a proven method for lowering costs and saving jobs, thus staying in business;
- a data-driven decision-making approach to satisfying the customer first, last, and always; and
- a theory that recognizes that everyone wants to do a good job, and that problems within the organization are mostly due to faulty processes and systems that keep everyone from being successful.

Figure 2.1 shows how TQM works in the classroom.

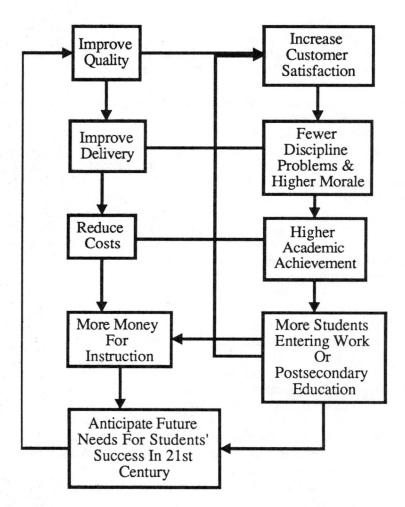

Leadership for Quality emphasizes empowerment of workers and focus on customer satisfaction. Quality leaders also seek to inspire and lend support to suppliers (parents and previous teachers) that they too may bring Total Quality to their classroom. The combination of all these efforts demands one assume a strong leadership role. While Total Quality seeks to strengthen the breadth of decision making and empowerment, it does not diminish the necessity for a depth of leadership from the chief executive (teacher) that allows such a breadth to happen. In other words, while power is spread throughout the classroom, there remains the need to stay focused, set priorities, and maintain the highest standards.

The strength and commitment of the leader (teacher) is the key to quality. At the same time, a quality leader must relinquish many previously held beliefs and actions that are associated most clearly with more traditional management styles. To make things more complicated, there are no "instant" pudding approaches to quality leadership. Like everything else about the quality movement, one's leadership role evolves and becomes more refined as the workers (students), suppliers (previous teachers and parents) and customers (students, subsequent teachers, colleges and universities, employers, and parents) provide valuable, indeed irreplaceable, feedback that allows the leader (teacher) to grow while the organization (class and school ) moves towards quality. Remember, within the classroom, the teacher assumes the role of top leadership, and, therefore must find ways to empower the students and others (parent volunteers, aides, etc.) to become partners in the improvement process.

## DRIVER OF THE SYSTEM

**Leadership** is the first category of the Malcolm Baldrige Quality Award criteria. It is also known as the "driver" of the total quality system, for without it, all else fails. It may also be the most difficult and diffuse to decipher because it seems to imply several things. One is that the leader must be strong. That might appear to be in direct contrast to the entire concept of empowering workers. However, Deming, Crosby, Juran and other Quality experts all agree on the importance of leadership for quality. One cannot ignore its significance. This means that as a quality teacher, you will want to take time to give shape and distinction to your own definition of quality. Not only must you understand what quality is; you will have to be able to articulate it in words that students, parents, and colleagues can understand. Remember, age appropriate language is important if the quality statement is to have any meaning to your constituents. Teaching first grade requires that you find a clear and simple way to state what quality means so that when you disseminate the statement all students can understand. According to one's level of teaching, the formal statement of quality should be the same for students, teachers, parents and the administration. If the school has a quality statement, then it must supersede each teacher's.

For example, Primeo Academy's (fictitious name for a non-graded school for students age 12-18) mission statement is:

**To prepare students with the highest quality knowledge, skills and abilities necessary to become responsible and productive citizens in a global community.**

Teachers within this school articulate their quality statements within the context of the school's statement. A math teacher might have as her/his Quality statement:

**Quality work is defined by the ability to reason, to use and understand logic, and to work together to apply the mathematical concepts learned to real life situations.**

Throughout K-12, it is assumed that great care will be taken to prepare a quality statement, and then to articulate it to students, parents, and colleagues. Like your classroom mission statement, this can be a time consuming process, but consider that it is the foundation for all that you will be doing within the classroom. Unless each of the participants understands what you are seeking, how can you expect them to take an interest in following your lead?

Leaders who have no followers are leaders of the wind—leaders of nothing. One cannot say that one is a leader unless there is a group of willing followers. Avoid the temptation to "rush" into the curriculum and the urge to cover the first chapter fearing that something awful will happen. This is what we call the Chicken Little syndrome. These are teachers who believe the sky's a' fallin' if they are not keeping up with the curriculum. Unfortunately, these habits are often a result of misguided, traditional teacher evaluations and/or faulty thinking about the teaching/learning process or the curriculum. It is exactly this rush to "get started" that has been at the root of teaching and learning failures for years. Joel Barker, futurist and author of the *Future Edge: Discovering the New Paradigms of Success* (1992), speaks of the failure of our educational system to deliver on our promise to all children of our country because of the disparity between action and rhetoric when answering the "why" question. Indeed, many students do not see any connections between the real world and school.

David Langford, Candace Allen, and other pioneers in quality teaching have learned that students need to understand "why" before they become interested in "how." The 'why' question strikes at the heart of leadership. One simply must resist the urge to dive into the curriculum in favor of allowing students to understand and gain for themselves clear, straightforward answers to 'why' they are in this class and 'why' it is necessary to learn this content matter. In other words, students need to know how the information and skills gained in the class will be helpful and meaningful to their lives now and in the future. We elaborate on this point in Chapter Four.

Quality teachers recognize that this level of understanding flips the motivation factor from external to internal. Successful teachers are experts at getting the students to recognize the basic worth and meaningfulness of any subject matter. David Langford and others give this process as much time as it takes, generally 3 to 5 days, but it may require even more time and energy. Undoubtedly you will have to revisit this question more than once during the course of the school year. Clearly, a quality teacher does not consider this wasted time, but rather building the necessary foundation upon which a quality classroom can stand. Proponents of quality teaching faithfully go through this process since in the end, students achieve more by the end of the year than in a traditional setting. Like so many things in life, it requires a leap of faith.

**WALK-THE-TALK**

From the beginning, your leadership must reflect quality in every way. This is easier said than done, and once you begin your quality journey, you will be reminded daily how difficult, albeit exciting, it is. In short, there is no substitute for your displaying quality about every aspect of yourself or your actions both in and outside the classroom. You must "walk-the-talk."

Training students in quality begins before you ever enter the classroom. It begins with your commitment to becoming a Quality Teacher, and it never ends. Students will test you and your commitment, often going to great lengths to try to trap you. Recognize this as normal human behavior and maintain your sense of humor, admit your mistakes, and thank the students for their reminders. Throughout the process, gain the trust and respect of students through communication. This is why it is so important to clearly understand what quality means to you. Anything less will surely leave you confused, frustrated, and disillusioned

Persistence is a vastly underrated human trait, but a very powerful habit. In fact, most successful people will rank this trait as one of their best. Maintain your quality vision, and at the same time be willing to alter the quality plan upward (never downward) as the organization (or your classroom) bumps against outside factors that require flexibility. Take the posture that each time the students test your commitment to quality, they are giving you a gift. That gift is a constant reaffirmation of your belief and conviction that Total Quality is the way to higher academic achievement.

In fact, leadership for quality will begin to permeate everything you are and do. When you adopt a customer focus, you'll find yourself looking at all your activities and commitments from a different point of view. As a customer to many, you'll find yourself asking: is this quality? Once that happens, then you can be sure that you are well on the way to adopting a leadership role rather than boss manager role.

With the customer focus, and clearly defined ideas about what you want and expect, you will be able to align all classroom activities towards meeting your goal. Is the goal to have all students succeed at learning within your classroom? If so, then analyze all your classroom processes to determine if each process is in tune with your goal. If not, you have a critical determinant for a continuous improvement project.

Many enterprises now have mission statements posted in conspicuous places for customers to view. It amuses us that the local post office had its mission (customer focused) posted on the wall, where customers could easily see and read it until Thanksgiving. On a trip back to the post office during the Christmas rush, we noticed it had been taken down. It made us wonder whether the post office was only customer focused when it was not rushed. This would be funny if it weren't typical of so many enterprises.

Either you have a quality mission with a customer focus or you don't. You cannot change according to the time of year. For instance, two weeks before school gets out in June, you cannot dispense with your commitment to quality for fear the students will "get out of hand," or by thinking "I still have so much to cover." Your leadership commitment must be vital, strong, and totally focused at all times. Panicking at the end of the semester or year will not result in students' doing any more or any higher quality work.

The need for the leader to stay focused cannot be understated. Quality leaders demonstrate through actions what they are about. Having a written statement about quality, and then saying things that drive in fear will confuse students and parents alike. Not only is it important that your actions and statements be focused on quality, but also your personal appearance. People recognize those individuals who "walk their talk" rather than "stumble their mumble" to be the true leaders. Quality is not something that relates simply to what we do between 8 AM and 3 PM each day.

The need for teachers to become quality role models has never been greater, particularly in those areas where poverty is highest. It is an obligation of every teacher to be a role model, but the Quality Teacher sets continuously higher standards of excellence for himself/herself as well as for the students. Anything less will confuse students, making it more difficult for them to recognize quality and far less able to reach it.

The Quality Teacher becomes more involved, rather than less involved. S/he makes time to speak about quality at every opportunity and points out quality wherever possible. One's presence at PTO/PTA meetings, community meetings or functions, or faculty meetings sends strong messages to external customers and suppliers. In fact, these are viewed as important opportunities to keep the organization focused on quality. Through this type of involvement communities will awaken to the need to assist in creating Quality Educational Learning Communities.

A Quality Teacher aligns every aspect of his/her work with the stated mission and goals. Along with this alignment comes a need to study and understand how students learn. Quality leadership is predicated on an understanding of Deming's system of profound knowledge. Profound knowledge holds the key to unlocking the secret of quality for teachers and other leaders. Often a lack of understanding of **Profound Knowledge** (see below) is what is missing from leaders who attempt to build quality into their organizations only to have the organization fail. Profound knowledge is so important that the entire theory of quality management is wrapped around it.

## PROFOUND KNOWLEDGE

Deming's system of profound knowledge appears simplistic but is very powerful. It holds that in order to bring total quality management principles and processes into the organization (in our case, the classroom) one must have a thorough understanding of four concepts, namely, 1) an appreciation for a system, 2) statistical theory, 3) theory of knowledge, and 4) psychology. Let's examine these points briefly.

- **Appreciation for a system**
  - > Education is a system with many sub-systems and processes within the subsystems.
  - > The school district is one large system.

> Each level (elementary, middle, and high school), no matter how many buildings, represents a sub-system within the larger system.
> Each building is a sub-system of that sub-system. For example: Martha Washington, John F. Kennedy, and Lincoln Elementary Schools are each a sub-system within the Elementary sub-system of the School District system.
> Each classroom is a sub-system within the sub-system of the building.
> The school district is a sub-system within the state department of education.
> Within each system there are numerous processes that make up the system. Some processes that make up the classroom system are the teaching/learning process, attendance procedure, tardy procedure, clean-up process, discipline, evaluation/assessment, etc. In short, everything that is done within the classroom is a process.
> Deming and other quality experts agree that anywhere from 85-95% of all problems within an organization are due to faulty processes and systems. Management controls the system (*works on* the system), and, therefore, management must be responsible for taking the lead in changing it. Teachers are managers of the classroom and as you can tell from the short list of classroom processes above, it is true that management (teachers) control the system. Therefore, *understand that adopting a systems view means the focus is on improving processes —not results.*

You may be saying, "In our district I am evaluated on results and, therefore, must exert all my energy to making certain the students learn what the district and curriculum dictate." Don't confuse the issues of process improvement with student achievement. What Deming would say is that inspection at the end (such as a test, the end of a grading period, or the end of the year) is simply too late to discover there was a process flaw that kept everyone from being successful. Quality must be built into every process before high quality results can follow. Quality classrooms focus more on process improvement while setting high quality expectations, and have found that indeed results do follow. The fear comes from not being able to "see" instant results. We suggest that this may be one area where you'll have to demonstrate a leap of faith and *believe it is true* because total quality management and systems thinking have saved many

Fortune 500 companies from financial ruin. Now TQM is mandated for U.S. hospital accreditation, and it has proven effective for those teachers who have taken the leap.

- **Statistical theory**
  - > Quality experts agree with Deming that the use of data is critical to know what action to take for process change. So often when data is not used, management tampers with processes not knowing the real problem(s).

In many respects, the fear of statistics and use of data when working within a system that deals with people has led to the further demise of our educational system. For example, over the years educators and consultants have suggested a variety of educational reform remedies that would purportedly transform the system into a workable one where all students could succeed. Some of these ideas were: tracking, pull-out programs, gifted and talented programs, and ability grouping. Other more recent attempts include outcomes-based education, whole language, cross-curricular approaches, team teaching, and middle school teaming. However, none of these was predicated on the use of data to determine whether or not they indeed would resolve root causes of problems. Other efforts, such as the gifted and talented, and ability grouping within the classroom, are still being debated in some sections of the country, while outcomes-based education approach is taking a great deal of criticism from the religious right.

The important thing to think about when pondering any of the above and the other reform efforts that are not mentioned is this: *Have they created systemic reform in education that has led to higher academic achievement and success for everyone?* The answer is simply NO! One reason is that none of these efforts has employed a systems approach and second, none has employed data and statistical theory to make decisions about what and how to change.

Understanding statistical theory means that you must understand the concept of variation. You should learn what makes a system stable and unstable. You should know the "common causes" of variation (and how they are often mistaken as "special cause" variation), and the special causes of variation (and how they are often mistaken for common cause variation). You should understand how improper tampering with the system can create bigger and more difficult problems than if had you done nothing.

In education, a fairly common cause of poor learning is student boredom, yet it is often treated as a special cause. Common causes are those things that regularly recur due to normal statistical variation of the system. Student boredom is probably one of the biggest contributors to students' unwillingness to complete homework, do assignments, and to read, yet many believe it is the student's problem and not a process problem. As a consequence, no action is taken to collect data, discover root causes, and implement an action plan for reducing boredom.

Special cause variation might include:
- A high absentee rate due to a flu epidemic,
- The football team scheduled to play in the state championship game, and
- The first snowfall of the year.

In order to fully understand the processes within the classroom, you will have to become familiar with simple statistical tools. They are not difficult to learn or understand and even elementary students can perform most of them. The more difficult statistical tools (control charts) can be made very simple through the use of computer software. Without the data, statistical tools, and a clear understanding of how to use them for process improvement, it is impossible to assume that you can optimize any of the classroom processes.

- **Theory of knowledge**
  - > Theory of knowledge is another way of answering the question "how do you know?" We know that when management changes one process, it generally has ripple effects throughout the system. You can begin to realize how important it is to have a thorough understanding of systems theory, and how crucial it is that you begin to view your job through a systems lens.

  - > The quality experts use this example to help clarify theory of knowledge. If you took apart one model of each automobile produced and discovered the very best transmission, the best ignition, the best brakes, the best steering, etc. and analyzed what made them the "best," you could probably document it. But, if you attempted to put each of these "best" parts into one automobile you would soon discover that the car wouldn't run. That is because the sum of the parts does not equal the whole. It is the way the parts interact with each other that creates a synergy that makes the car run.

Therefore, in thinking about education and the classroom specifically, we must remember that it is the way each of the processes interacts with the others that creates the quality classroom. Recently a second grade teacher told us that she was unhappy with the way her students were moving between the learning centers and also how they were using them. She didn't think that they were optimizing the use of their time or learning. Being a newcomer to quality principles, she decided to let the students know what she was thinking about and asked for their help. Indeed, the students became excited and worked very hard for about two hours. When they were finished, the classroom looked and felt very different than it had before. The students were enthused about their creation and eagerly got to work.

Another second grade teacher came to visit and she, too, got very excited about what she saw and decided to replicate the changes in her classroom. Three days later the same two teachers were talking and the second one was complaining, saying that the changes she made were the most ridiculous thing she'd done and how everything in her classroom turned into chaos and confusion and that the students were not working. She acted as if the first teacher were to blame for her problems.

In truth, what the second teacher failed to consider is that it was the students' response to their needs that recreated the first classroom into a dynamic, exciting learning environment. The first teacher had empowered the students to assist in creating the learning environment and by so doing was energizing them to focus on learning and not other things. The second teacher tried, much like the automobile example mentioned above, to take what she considered "best" and place it into her classroom, not thinking about how changing one thing could affect the rest of the classroom processes.

Another example is in the use of coercion. Teachers who employ coercive tactics, even if it is with one or two students, alter the learning environment for everyone. Where fear is entrenched, people simply cannot do their best. Classrooms based on fear (of grades, discipline, ridicule, humiliation) are not places where students maintain a high interest or are eager to take educational risks to optimize their learning. These classrooms may be quiet places, but are places where no one reaches his/her potential, not even those students who may be rule governed and want to please the teacher.

The theory of knowledge means that management has a complete understanding of the impact of change on the system.

This places the burden on management (the teacher) to engage in a Plan-Do-Study-Act (PDSA) cycle prior to making any change.

- **Psychology**
  - \> Management must understand people and their needs. This means that we recognize five basic needs of people. They are survival, love/respect, power, fun and freedom. Every human behavior is based on satisfying one or more of these needs. A good source of information about need satisfaction is Dr. William Glasser's books: *The Quality School* (1990) and *The Quality School Teacher* (1993).

  - \> If you don't pay attention to these needs, then neither students, parents, or colleagues will respond in ways that optimize the efficiency and effectiveness of your classroom and/or school.

Assuming they've got their survival needs met, the over-riding need for most students is for love/respect. When you think about it, isn't that the one thing that you need most? Often we hear teachers complain that they, like Rodney Dangerfield, don't get any respect anymore. When you attend faculty meetings, do you have a real sense that others listen to you and respect your work and what you're attempting to do? When you think of the students, can you honestly say that you respect each one? If not, then be certain that your attitude and behavior towards those you don't respect will be very different from the ones you do respect. Give yourself a reality check. On what basis do you withhold your respect? Do you really know the student(s) or do you just know something about them from classroom behavior and observation? We suggest that unless you really know someone (and that comes from caring enough to develop a rapport) then you cannot begin to understand what motivates their current behavior.

Notice that the other needs include power, fun, and freedom. You might want to give yourself another reality check. How much power do the students in your classes have right now? Do they have any decision-making power? If so, who has it—everyone or only some of the students? How much fun do you and the students have in class? How do you define fun? What about freedom? Do students in your class(es) have any freedom or must everyone do the same thing at the same time in the same way?

We've gone round and round with district administrators who believe that school should not be considered "fun," but a serious place of work. This is an issue that lies at the heart of the concept of pride in workmanship. No one takes pride in doing repetitive, dull or watered down work. Students who are engaged in this kind of school work view it as drudgery and may even begin to view school as punishment. On the other hand, students who have the opportunity to tackle real life issues in a meaningful way (see Chapter Four), and then report results to a governing body (see Chapter 11), will be more likely to take great pride in their work and see the joy of learning. Fun comes in many forms. It does not mean that one has to sit and giggle all day. There is a great deal of fun in knowing that you've accomplished a very difficult, skill stretching task, or in creating new knowledge and reflecting with wisdom on your work (see Chapter Eight). Joy in learning comes from having fun in the process and knowing that you've accomplished something worthwhile. Pride in workmanship is crucial to optimizing learning.

A basic belief of the psychology category of profound knowledge is that everyone comes wanting to do a good job. Perhaps this is reason for another reality check. Do you believe that every student comes to school wanting to do a good job, and that faulty processes keep everyone from being successful? This is what quality classroom teachers believe. We've found this concept to be a difficult one for many to accept. Clearly the presenting behaviors of some students might lead us to be duped into thinking otherwise, but having worked with at-risk students for over 20 years and having children of our own, we realize that behavior rarely has to do with the child not wanting to do good work. Yet, responding to the symptoms is what most often gets teachers into trouble and provides a classic example of how faulty processes within a system keep so many students from becoming eager learners. As a result of outward behavior symptoms, many teachers react with coercion, behavior modification, and other tactics that never resolve the root cause of the problems and rarely engage the student as an active, eager learner.

Motivation of students occurs when:
- They feel respected,
- The teacher provides many experiences for classroom decision-making,
- The learning environment is free of fear, and
- Learning experiences are meaningful to students.

Pride in workmanship comes from creating products that are meaningful and have a greater audience than the teacher. Students who are given roles of equal partners with their classmates and teachers rarely have a need to engage in anti-social behavior and nearly always will accomplish far more academically than anyone previously thought. Motivation must be internal, never external. The carrot and stick approach, rewards of stickers, pizza parties, T-shirts or even leather jackets never result in optimizing the classroom achievement. Instead, you'll forever find yourself in the cyclone of having to find bigger and better rewards as the previous ones lose their effectiveness.

> Students won't do anything well unless they want to want to do it. Teachers may think they have won with students when they cajole, intimidate, or use coercive tactics, but those students will never do quality work.

In essence, the four aspects of Deming's system of profound knowledge are the foundation upon which your understanding of total quality classroom management must be based, especially when you fuse TQM with the principles of the Foxfire approach. Study each of them, engage in study groups to get in depth about your thinking on each piece. Quality management theory does not stand on any one, two, or three pieces of profound knowledge but is rooted in the synergy that exists among all four. We caution you not to think that you can "pick and choose" those aspects of quality that appeal to your current way of thinking. If you do attempt to bring quality to the classroom in this fashion, you will be disappointed in the results and you will become frustrated thinking that the "quality stuff" is no better than any other fad to systemic reform.

## QUALITY BY FACT, OF PROCESS, AND BY PERCEPTION

Each quality leader examines quality from at least three different perspectives. Each one is important and we must learn to recognize the worth of all three. Each asks a different question of management.

- **Quality by fact**—Does the product (of the learning experience or service) meet the specified requirements?

- **Quality of process**—Does the process and/or system produce the product or service as intended?
- **Quality by perception**—Are the customer's expectations met?

Each of these poses an important question for teachers. First, quality by fact. Indeed, does the student's work represent quality and does it meet the specifications? This presupposes that teachers, the district, and students all have a clear understanding of the specified requirements. This goes for every learning experience the students engage in. In later chapters we will examine ways to determine this in detail. Second, quality of the process. The question is: "Does the process allow every student to achieve the learning outcomes intended or are there process flaws?" Last, quality by perception is a major issue in education today. Many people believe that our educational system is substandard, including those schools and classrooms where students are doing excellent work (and there are many). In many instances we have to overcome the negative attitudes or perceptions of these customers. This is akin to what the U.S. automakers have had to do with respect to Japanese- and German-made automobiles. As long as the public perception was that cars made by U.S. automakers were substandard, their sales slumped. No matter how good the quality, the public refused to buy American believing that foreign cars were better. Notice that the auto companies have gone out of their way to dispel those perceptions. They have not ignored them because public perception is reality. If your customers believe you have an inferior product, then you will have to deal with this as if it were reality, because it is reality for those customers. In education, we must not only build in quality by fact and process, but we must also deal with the quality by perception issue. You cannot ignore it.

## TEACHING AND LEARNING STYLES

Recognition and understanding don't always translate into action, so care must be taken to integrate one's personal preferred teaching style with other teaching styles. Many students have asked, "Why do they give us that learning styles stuff if they don't use it?" Using different teaching styles can be difficult because many of us were reared in an educational system that focused on one method over the others, typically the lecture method. There are some who believe we ought to go back to "the good old days" where teachers 'taught' and kids sat quietly and 'learned' it. These individuals say that the system worked then, therefore, we should go back to it. In actuality, that system was not effective. The differences between then and now include the disparity in socio-economic levels of the student body, the rapidly changing job market towards technology and away from unskilled laborers, and the global economy to name a few. Years ago, students who couldn't cope in school simply left and were able to find jobs (e.g. in mining, on the assembly line, or as railroad workers) that paid enough to provide for their families. Today, life is infinitely more complex, and most individuals have to complete some post-secondary education in order to thrive.

Imagine a physician who returned from the grave after 100 years and observed an operation. S/he would realize that some sort of healing process was being performed, but s/he would also know that s/he could not take the place of even the nurse. To further illustrate, imagine a manufacturer who returned after 100 years. S/he would not be able to comprehend the production processes now using robotics and statistical process control methods. By the same token, a teacher who returned after 100 years would see little difference in how the students were being taught and s/he would not feel uncomfortable in most classroom settings. Just as times have changed in industry and medicine, educators must realize the need for change in classroom strategies.

## LEARNING EXPERIENCES

Leadership in a quality school or classroom presupposes a recognition of the need for additional schooling and applied learning, and focuses one's attention on preparing students for such an experience. It is no longer satisfactory to assume that your class and/or K-12 schooling can be the end goal for any student. In fact, Deming's thirteenth point is: **Institute a vigorous program of education and self-improvement.**

A quality leader maintains high expectations and uses whatever empowerment methods are necessary to gain student and parent commitment to achieving them. In addition, the quality leader recognizes that having high expectations is not enough; one must know how and with what means one can demonstrate and help students achieve them.

This may pose a dilemma for many teachers today since an often heard cry is "it takes so much more time and energy." True, quality teaching does take more time, especially in the beginning; however, these activities you devote yourself to are very different from those in a traditional setting. For instance, a Quality Teacher pays careful attention to the need to show students examples of quality work. Students, especially those at the secondary level who have not experienced quality work, will have little idea of what it looks like, let alone know how to accomplish quality. This is especially true of individuals who have previously struggled within the traditional top-down boss management style classrooms. Students with parents who don't value education, who are undereducated, or who quit school are especially vulnerable in a quality system. These are the students we must focus on, however, since they are also potential drop-outs and a potential drain on society. This point, perhaps more than any other, makes a very strong case for school systems to adopt a Total Quality approach. Prevention is so much less expensive in time, money, and energy than remediation, and once students get beyond 4th grade, other factors (e.g. sexuality, drugs, etc.) come into play and can sabotage school experiences.

## LEARNING STYLES

The ability to create initial learning experiences for students that accommodate a variety of learning styles is essential for a quality classroom. Then, to achieve greater knowledge and understanding (wisdom, if you will), it is essential that the teacher be able to lead all students into becoming co-producers of additional learning experiences, each one building upon the preceding and accommodating each student's preferred approach to learning. This represents a paradigm shift away from the traditional.

In effect, a Quality Teacher provides the leadership that allows each student to create and successfully carry-out learning, while providing assistance through mentoring, facilitating and coaching the learning process. The designated outcomes for each learning experience are established and agreed upon by all; however, the actual way in which the outcomes are reached can be left to the discretion of students and/or teams of students. All this takes place within the broad framework of the curriculum, but allows for individual differences, student empowerment, and internal motivation.

As the teacher provides more leadership to move the entire class towards quality, students become interested and feel less threatened, and the "need" to know will have become firmly established. This is a critical point for a quality teacher. Questions about the curriculum scope and sequence are sure to be raised by parents, colleagues, administrators, and school boards. We are not suggesting that you do away with curriculum, but rather to get the teachers and students together to define the learning experiences that align to the desired outcomes specified in the curriculum. This means that "canned" curricula and textbooks with designated assignments, tests, chapter questions, etc. should be phased out of the quality classroom, perhaps to be used as reference materials. These should be replaced by experiences that are co-produced by students while the teacher provides leadership in defining the broad category of what is to be learned. Traditional thinking that all students must experience learning in the same ways to achieve desired outcomes will be replaced when teachers develop quality leadership approaches to learning.

## CONTINUOUS QUALITY IMPROVEMENT (CQI)
It is imperative to recognize that leadership cannot be sustained without on-going education. Thus, it is as important for teachers to maintain a high degree of continuous improvement as for students. Continuous improvement comes from reading, attending conferences, seminars, and workshops about quality as well as about one's discipline; keeping active in professional organizations; visiting other schools and classrooms; and communicating with one's internal and external customers. Engaging in Total Quality obligates the individual to continuously seek out opportunities to provide quality leadership to students, parents, and colleagues. Evidence of these activities should be included in assessing teacher's leadership skills. It is impossible to become a quality leader within the school setting without giving ample time to a thorough understanding of Total Quality principles and processes for one's personal life too.

Actually, it is impossible to believe that anyone could claim to be a quality leader and not have TQI principles and processes permeate every aspect of their life. Upon getting involved in Total Quality, one begins to think differently about everything. This leads to a change in response to external events. Quality seems to be the measure with which everything is judged, whether it be a relationship, service, or product reliability. A Quality Teacher seeks ways to influence others to adopt quality standards. Some obvious ways to do this are through presentations, example, and a willingness to share information and ideas. Another, perhaps less obvious way, is to become a better listener. By being an active listener, you send a signal to others of your desire to understand their point of view and their needs. As Covey (1989) says, seek first to understand, then to be understood. Once you know this, it becomes easier to seek synergism through collaboration and agreement on alternative (win-win) solutions.

Quality teachers have an obligation to share their knowledge and leadership with others, but care must be taken not to assume an "air" of superiority when expressing it. Inviting others into your classroom and being open to their ideas, concerns, and suggestions will speak mountains of your leadership and knowledge of quality. Sensitivity and patience will be your "friends" as you spread the Quality word.

The classroom leadership role you assume will determine your success as a quality teacher. Indeed, imagine a classroom where:

- everyone is engaged in meaningful, ability-stretching learning experiences;
- every student knows how to use quality improvement tools to analyze and resolve problems;
- every student knows how to make the classroom run more efficiently and effectively and how to do his/her job better and works on improving everyday;
- every student is eager and willing to share information that will help improve the learning experience for everyone;
- every student makes over 25 suggestions for process improvement during the course of the year and 95% of the suggestions are implemented;
- students work eagerly to resolve real world problems to improve the quality of their life, the life within the community, and the school;
- all students know what is expected of them and that they far exceed the expectations of their parents, the school district, and the community;
- students and teachers work collaboratively to create a learning environment totally free of fear;
- students and teachers experience the joy of learning together daily; and
- students work together in teams and each student contributes to the learning experience.

These are some of the possible results from creating a quality classroom.

## QUALITY IS NOT A SILVER BULLET

Using total quality management principles within the classroom is not a quick fix to the myriad of problems we have in schools today. The **Quality Fusion** technique we are describing is based on using statistics and data to make decisions. It takes time to engage in the Plan-Do-Study-Act cycle, but by examining each process for root causes of problems, you can eliminate them forever as you build quality into the teaching/learning system.

A word of caution. You will experience the euphoria of rapid improvement shortly after beginning your quality journey, then things will flatten out. When this happens what you're really discovering are the problems underlying the surface problems. Each layer of problem that you uncover will expose another, then another, and another. Each will be more difficult to resolve than the first. But, these are the heart of systemic problems, and the reasons why previous reform attempts have failed.

One high school teacher we know made rapid gains, going from over 45 percent failure rate to less than seven percent in just one semester of implementing quality. What she discovered is that many of the students were unable to read and, therefore, couldn't grasp the meaning of words or the context within which they were used, and simply didn't understand the material. She discovered this after engaging in a cause/effect diagram for one learning experience and was so surprised that initially she didn't know how to approach the problem. To date, this remains an issue and one that involves the entire system beginning in the elementary school. When, and if, her school district determines to implement quality management principles district-wide, she is ready to take this issue and pose it as a continuous improvement project with a cross-grade level (*i.e.,* cross-functional) team of teachers to engage in the P-D-S-A cycle.

Please be patient when implementing quality. The underlying notion is continuous improvement of every process, and that means that you forgive yourself and the students when mistakes are made. If everyone focuses on continuous improvement, then you can drive a good deal of fear out of the classroom and remain on track. What we suggest is that you remember these things:

- mistakes are opportunities for continuous improvement
- quality is not a silver bullet;
- quality is a life-long journey—you'll never get there and be able to quit;
- quality is elusive and continues to get better, thus the never-ending journey; and
- quality is what gives us a sense of pride in workmanship.

Create a quality classroom NOW!

ΛΛΛΛΛΛΛΛΛ

The following is a checksheet tool to help the teacher to implement the **Quality Fusion** technique into their classroom.

Step 1:   The mission, goals and academic integrity of your
          class are absolutely clear.
          √   Established a classroom mission statement.
          √   Developed personal goals for the class.
          √   Communicated mission and goals to
              parents/guardians.
          √   Aligned classroom mission and goals with those of
              the school district and the school.

Step 2:   You are demonstrating leadership.
          √   Developed a definition of a total quality classroom.
          √   Walk-the-Talk about quality.
          √   Understand Deming's system of **Profound
              Knowledge**.
          √   Use a variety of teaching styles.
          √   Have a CQI program for self and for my students.

## Chapter Three: All work must be pertinent and flow from the students.

Most of the work teachers and students do is best done as teams, flowing from student desire and student concerns. From the beginning the work is infused with student choice, design, revision, execution, reflection and evaluation. Teachers are responsible for assessing and ministering to their students' developmental needs.

Most problems that arise during classroom activities are solved in collaboration with students. When a student asks, "Here's a situation that just came up. I don't know what to do about it. What should I do?" the teacher turns the question back to the class to wrestle with and solve, rather than simply answering it. Students are trusted continually, and all are led to the point where they embrace responsibility.

## BREAKDOWN BARRIERS—DAY 1

Once school begins, start working with the students to establish a mission statement they can understand and "buy in to." This essentially answers the WHY question for students. Often students don't know why they are in class, or why they have to learn something. If students don't know the answer to the WHY question, they most likely will not be eager participants. This is true for all of us. If we know why we are asked to do something, and agree with it, then few will resist doing it. We elaborate on this principle in another chapter.

The importance of the WHY question becomes more real with Deming's example of washing the table. If someone (such as a teacher) tells a student to wash the table, the reason for doing that is extremely important. For example, if you should wash the table because we are going to perform surgery on it then you'll use certain materials to wash it with, and scrub it to be sure it is clean. If you should wash the table because we are going to eat on it, then you know immediately how clean it needs to be.

In another example, let's assume you are swimming and someone yells at you to get out of the water. You don't know WHY they are asking you to do that, and so your first inclination is not to do it. How quickly or determinedly would you react if he yelled:

- some storm clouds are coming!
- it is time to come in and eat!
- a swarm of jellyfish are headed your way!
- sharks!

Can you see how important the WHY question is?  And, yet how seldom do teachers take time to answer this question adequately for their students?

Many students (young and old) simply will not participate unless they understand the relevance of anything directly to them. These individuals may be the ones you've noticed who are reluctant learners. Perhaps you've even called them unmotivated. However, just the opposite is generally true. Students who know the relevance or the WHY of any learning experience are internally motivated and eager learners.

Some teachers have a tendency to answer the WHY question by responding with some version of "you'll need to know this when you grow up." That doesn't work for too many students, and especially not for those who need more immediate pay-off. If you haven't considered answering the WHY question, do it now in anticipation that your students will ask you later. Even if they don't, as one of your early activities the first week of school, take the opportunity to ask them WHY they are in your class.

It usually stuns students when teachers ask them questions like that. However, the responses you'll get will tell you a great deal about the way you'll need to work with the class, and even with certain students. In response to the question: WHY ARE YOU HERE? a teacher may get a range of answers from:
- my parent/guardian made me come
- so I can get good grades and go to college
- so I can get an 'A'
- because it is safer here than on my street
- because I can eat here
- because I want to be a doctor

Obviously, you'll want to continue asking WHY until students respond with something about learning. Once they realize they are there to learn, your motivational battles are over. In fact, you cannot motivate students to do anything they don't want to do. To get students beyond the range of answers listed above, you'll want to ask "why" to each of their responses. For instance—If the original answer is "So I can get an 'A'"—ask why do you want/need an 'A'?

## STUDENTS AS PARTNERS

There is a good deal of empirical evidence to suggest that when students have the opportunity to co-create learning experiences with their teacher, a higher level of interest, motivation, and achievement results. Given this, it is important to recognize the paradigm shift for teachers away from top-down control to full partnerships with students.

While the concept of partnering with students may seem foreign, it is in fact a perfect melding together of notions about teaching and learning. That is, we learn best when we believe the task fulfills a need, is achievable even though it may represent a quantum leap, and will be fun. Anything short of that generally leads to boredom, disinterest, and resistance. Teachers long ago discovered how disastrous the combination of these can be as measured by student apathy, disruptive behavior, and complete resistance. Teaching is impossible when students are bored, uninterested and resistant. Short of taking a hammer and banging knowledge into a student's head, there is virtually nothing a teacher can do to "make" someone learn.

If this concept is so obvious, why do so many teachers resist changing the instructional format to include students as full partners? One idea may be that we teach the way we were taught, and to date very few schools are using the students-as-full-partners concept. Therefore, what is being suggested is an entirely new and different way for teachers and administrators to work.

One could also make the case that administrators, school boards, and the public are often more interested in a "quiet, orderly" environment even if it means that students are passive recipients of information and facts that will be outdated within five years. The whole notion of students as partners in the learning experience is perhaps even more foreign to this group. One answer to this barrier may be that teachers and students engage in massive educational efforts with administrators, school boards, and parents.

Increased student achievement, fewer discipline problems, and increased attendance speak louder than words, and teachers who are dedicated to making schooling pertinent for students may want to open their doors for parents and others wishing to "see" what makes total quality classroom special. Parents **will** notice when their children are eager to go to school that something is different. Children who come home from school happy, eager to share the day's activities, and whose enthusiasm for learning spills over into after school hours will surely win over even the most resistant parent.

Consider this view:

# THE STUDENT AS CUSTOMER

"Quality should be aimed at the needs of the
customer, present and future."
W. Edwards Deming

### STUDENTS WHO ARE

| SATISFIED | UNSATISFIED |
|---|---|
| • will be more secure | • will be irritable |
| • will work harder | • will not engage fully in learning |
| • will achieve more | • will give up easily |
| • will not pose discipline problems | • will resist working with others |
| • will want to help others | • will create more discipline problems |
| • will feel good about school | • will dislike school |
| • will sense a need to learn | • will dislike learning |
| • will be cooperative | • will not be very cooperative |
| • will be more focused | • will have less hope for the future |
| • will have hope for the future | • will be unwilling to risk new things |
| • will have fun! | |

## TEAMING IS A KEY TO QUALITY

One of the first steps is to gather the class around you in the fall and talk about the concept of teaming. Thus you are setting the stage for the entire school year by letting the students know that each of them is vital to the group and that each is important and has special gifts and skills that others do not have. Include yourself in this discussion and as being a part of this team effort. Set a warm, friendly, arms around, classroom climate right away.

Begin the conversation about valuing each other with the fact that there are times when each individual will need help from others and how important it is to know that we all agree to be helpers. Draw some examples from your own school experiences and then ask the students for examples. Small children may surprise you with the expertise they have already accumulated in this regard.

From third grade up, you can engage them in conversation about teams—what makes a great team, what makes a poor team, etc. Draw examples from baseball, football and basketball. Most youngsters can identify or have some ideas about teamwork. Perhaps one of the best, and least complex examples of the team concept can be drawn from basketball. For instance, if one player is an excellent shooter but never passes the ball, is the team likely to win many games? If all players can pass the ball, but never shoot the ball, will the team win? What if one of the players always passes the ball to his friend and never to the others? What if the coach plays favorites and never lets the other people play? Will this result in a great team? How are the other players likely to feel about the coach and/or the "stars" of the team? From questions like these, you can easily stimulate discussion about what it takes to have a great team.

You would like the outcome of any discussion about teaming to have the net result of having all students look to each other for help when they require it and to be supportive of each other. An important concept is that everyone in the classroom become 'response' 'able' in any given situation. That is, there is a need for everyone (including the teacher) to work towards helping move the class forward by not interfering with others' ability to learn, as well as to respond to classmates when they need help. Students can then determine ways in which they can help each other and what inappropriate behaviors might be. It is most helpful when teachers play a "back-up" role in this kind of discussion, using gentle guidance but allowing the students to fully participate. Encourage everyone to engage in the process. At the same time be alert for signs that may indicate one or more students might try to become classroom bullies. As you spot these "red flags," find a way to bring them into the discussion.

Of course, these and all classroom activities must be developmentally appropriate for the age level of your students. Be careful, however, not to assume that children can only "do this much" or "understand this much" because of their age. For years, adults have determined that students could learn only a given amount, and that became the standard for getting an 'A' grade. We know now that those were artificial standards imposed on students and limited by the thinking of the adult making the decision. Indeed, in schools where these limiting thoughts are not present, students (at all ages) achieve much more.

Beginning in fourth grade complications begin to surround conversations such as these. This is because in traditional schools some children have already had many failing experiences causing them to begin giving up. At this age, also, we see major behavior changes, and the downward cycle to drop-out is underway. If not physically dropping-out, many of these students will simply begin emotionally dropping-out. Then too, is the pecking order students engage in. Trends are obvious, and as children get older, the methods they use to ostracize each other become more vicious. Surnames, size, physical maturity, gender, race, religion, poverty, parent/guardian configuration, type of home or place can all be a reason for children to pick on each other. Once this begins to happen, the problems for the "picked on" child dramatically increase. Of course, in a quality school or classroom this kind of behavior would simply not be tolerated, nor practiced by students, teachers, support staff, or administrators. What is done about this will impact the way students interact with each other, the students' energy level, and the ability/eagerness to engage in teaming activities. Again, depending on age, one must be careful to structure the conversation so no one is hurt.

**Ask the students for their suggestions about groundrules for engaging in class discussion.** Depending on the age of the students, they may come up with 30 or more ideas and suggestions. As the leader, pare the list down by asking students if they would agree to combine one or more suggestion until you are left with one or two. (The **nominal group process** (NGP) is a good tool to use in this exercise and is described in the appendix. Other useful tools to identify and rank problem processes and systems in your classroom are shown in Table 3.1.) Most, if not all, will come under the heading of "respect."

| Table 3.1: Several extremely useful total quality improvement tools to identify and rank problem "processes" and/or "systems" in classrooms. |
| --- |

**Affinity Diagram**
- Used to examine complex and/or hard to understand problems
- Used to build team consensus
- Results can be further analyzed by a **Relations Diagram**

**Cause and Effect Diagram (Fishbones)**
- Used to identify **root causes** of a problem
- Used to draw out many ideas and/or opinions about the causes

**Flow Charts**
- Gives a picture of the processes in the system

**Force Field Analysis**
- Used when changing the system might be difficult and/or complex

**Histogram**
- A bar graph of data which displays information about the data set and shape
- Can be used to predict the stability in the system

**Nominal Group Process**
- A structured process to help groups make decisions
- Useful in choosing a problem to work on
- Used to build team consensus
- Used to draw out many ideas and/or opinions about the causes

**Pareto Diagram**
- Bar chart that ranks data by categories
- Used to show that a few items contribute greatly to over-all problem(s)
- Helps the team identify which processes/systems to direct their efforts

**Relations Diagram**
- Helps the team to analyze the cause and effect relationships between complex issues
- Directs the team to the **root** causes of a problem

**Systematic Diagram**
- Used when a broad task or goal becomes the focus of the team's work
- Often used after an **Affinity Diagram** and/or **Relations Diagram**
- Used when the action plan needed to accomplish the goal or the task is complex

Your work is not complete yet, as you'll need to solicit from students their understanding of "respect." Don't assume that everyone understands it the same way. Find a creative way to give examples of what respect is and isn't, such as: if you push Sally's books on the floor is that being respectful? What if someone comes up and slaps you on the shoulder and says "Hi, buddy." Is that being respectful? What does respect mean in terms of classroom discussion...or team discussions?

As the class works through this exercise, keep in mind that the flow of this class is going to be very different from any the students (or perhaps even you) have experienced before. When the group has established the ground rule(s), you can proceed to the discussion about teaming. This conversation (for the older students) is likely to make some nervous and others may not want to participate. In some instances, middle or high school students might be more comfortable first discussing this in pairs. Some students will share their previous negative experiences with teams with a friend that they might not share (at first) with the group. The lack of trust between and among students and teachers will be a major factor in determining the overall success of the class. Take it slow, but be persistent. Teaming is such an important life-long skill and one that needs to begin in early elementary. If it hasn't, then you must find a way to weave the team concept into whatever grade level or class you are teaching.

Trust among students at middle- and high schools will develop very slowly. Trust among students and teachers will also develop more slowly, especially with students who have had negative school experiences. We recommend engaging in some trust activities as a way to begin driving fear out of the classroom, but some teachers resist the idea. True, trust doesn't come overnight or after one trust activity, but it can be developed through persistence and maintaining a gentleness, yet diligence, for all students to respect each other. If students mistreat each other, immediate steps must be taken to put a halt to it. This can be done simply by stopping the classroom activity and saying something like: "Class, I'm having trouble with the way people are being treated. Let's review the class rule(s) for a minute. Is it respectful to treat each other this way?" Words to that effect, calmly spoken will accomplish two things: (1) protect the students who are being mistreated, (2) send a strong, clear, consistent message that you are serious about this **respect** business. It doesn't make sense to point fingers, lay blame, get emotionally upset, etc., because those things stir all kinds of emotions among students and rarely succeed in accomplishing the goal.

Let's assume you work with high school students and at least 2 or 3 of them refuse to participate in team activities. The only way to reinterest them in the educational process and in working with their classmates is to develop the trust that obviously was lost in prior years. Many times these students have been ridiculed or picked-on by their classmates so they fear working with them in a team concept. Who could blame the student who has been ostracized for not wanting to work together? The other problem might be a "gifted" or eager to please student who has either had group experiences in which s/he did all the work while other group members did nothing or so little that the entire group was penalized. In either case you may encounter resistance from parents who do not want their child working with other students.

The process of gaining these students' trust is a slow one. It begins by having the students share some previous experiences with the class. We find it always helps if the teacher can share some personal experience that affected attitudes about group work. Sometimes that kind of personal sharing is the thing that can unlock student resistance. You might start by first explaining that you know sometimes group work is perceived as too difficult or non-productive, and in some previous years it may have gone awry, but it is a necessary skill for success in the work force of the 21st century and/or for getting along in families or other groups, therefore, one that will be practiced in this class. You cannot force students to work together, but by continuously focusing on process improvement and improving the classroom culture, most if not all, will eventually come around.

## CHOOSE YOUR PARTNER
One approach is to allow each student (either at middle or high school) to select one person they wish to be partnered with on a 'more or less' permanent basis. Give students some direction about selecting a partner that they can focus and stay on task with. In some cases, their best friend might not be the best selection. Critical partners become teamed with another set of critical partners for the learning experience. Jobs within the team are established, but cross-training is important if anyone becomes ill and is absent. At the end of the learning experience team evaluations are completed and debriefing takes place between the teacher and each team.

The teacher's role is to assist with leadership skills, particularly for the team leaders. It helps if everyone in the team understands that the team leader's role is not to do all the work, but that it is important for the leader to assist everyone else in completing the task. Sometimes students (at all ages) who are eager to please, possess leadership skills, or are more knowledgeable about the subject get excited and/or frustrated that the work is progressing too slowly, so they feel compelled to do it alone. Other students, if given the opportunity, would probably choose to take a lesser role. Teachers must be aware of any and all situations as they arise.

## STUDENTS AS PROBLEM SOLVERS

Another approach to teaming is to share a problem-solving model with the students. This means that each team understands that (just like in the real-world) there may be times when people don't communicate properly and the job isn't getting done. In this case, as in all others, the group has to take responsibility for resolving any problems. Thus, the teacher's role changes from boss-manager to mentor and facilitator. Students (even first graders) can and should be responsible for working through any classroom problems.

One way to approach this is to educate students about the five step problem-solving model. The model consists of:

Step 1 - State the problem;
Step 2 - Separate fact from fiction (distinguish any "feeling" kinds of assumptions from the facts);
Step 3 - Brainstorm solutions (without judgment);
Step 4 - Consider the consequences to each solution (without judgment);
Step 5 - Make a decision for change and keep track of the results.

Classes who are taught this model, and where it is regularly practiced, are more successful at staying focused on the task and get the "job" done with minimal problems. These are classrooms where students function quite nicely while the teacher is working with an individual or one other team. The students do not require constant adult supervision. In fact, the more students practice their own problem solving, the more empowered they become thus leading to greater self-confidence and sense of responsibility for their own behavior.

Students from grade two or three and beyond certainly can understand this model and can follow the model from a sheet of paper. It helps to have the students write down how they have gone about resolving each problem. Individual students and/or teams can use this model equally well. While it takes longer to teach the very young student this model, they can and do respond well to it. It is much more effective than asking students *what* they did wrong or why they did something. It is also without blame or shame and brings students together to resolve problems. Very young students might need adult help to remember the five steps and/or to remember their response(s) to each. Perhaps an older student or an aide can assist. Teaming is not nearly as effective when teachers have to become involved in resolving problems that crop up between students and/or with the learning experience.

Other ways to engage students as problem solvers include the use of quality improvement tools such as the Fishbone or Cause/Effect Diagram, Relations Diagram, and the Force Field Analysis—these and other tools and techniques are described in the appendix. The following is an example of how even second graders can use a Cause/Effect Diagram:

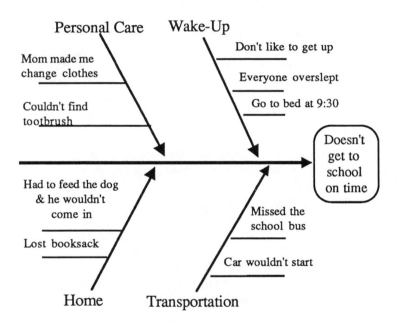

Imagine the lively discussion that could be generated from the aforementioned comments on the cause-and-effect diagram.

## STUDENTS AS AGENTS OF DECISION-MAKING

Another issue that frequently comes up is that student's don't know what they want or need to learn, and that if given any decision-making power, will choose to play rather than "work." Accompanying this issue is one of age. At what age can we expect youngsters to be able to help make decisions about their learning? It seems both these, as well as the other issues surrounding this question, all come back to identifying one's beliefs. Since beliefs drive behavior, if we believe that some students are "too young" to take responsibility, then we create a situation where they have no options. On the other hand, if we believe that at an early age (even pre-K) children do know what they want to do and what they need, then we can begin organizing the classroom so they can become full, active partners in the learning process.

It is often evident early in the child's school experience which children are raised in homes where they are given choices as toddlers. As youngsters gain experience in making choices, they become more self-confident and eager to cooperate. Indeed, this is the key to motivation. Children will be motivated to want to do things only after they have experienced some degree of efficacy in making decisions. Teachers who struggle with students who are "not motivated" might want to review their lesson plans and other materials to discover how often and when students were engaged in any decision-making. If there has been none, it is almost assured that students will be passive, disinterested, or resistant. Far too often these symptoms are mis-read and the student will be labeled as "not motivated."

## WHAT IS QUALITY?

One of the first steps in working with students of any age is to discuss the question of quality. What does quality mean to them? Can young children discriminate between quality toys and those of lesser quality? Can they also specify factors that are involved in their notion of quality? The answer, even with kindergartners, is a resounding YES! Not only can young children understand the concept of quality, they are eager to tell you. In fact, it can be a game. Suggest to students that they are employed by a large toy manufacturer to determine which toys are the best. Several toys can be displayed before the children. It makes sense to have at least two choices of each such as: two trucks or two dolls. Selected toys should be those that can be distinguishable in a variety of ways. For example, a Tonka™ truck vs. a plastic truck. You might ask the children the open-ended question at first: Which one would you choose and why? Then, you might structure the questions so the children can begin to discriminate and determine what elements the Tonka™ truck has that makes it more desirable. Examples might include a better paint job...the paint doesn't chip off very easily; the wheels are secured very well; the material (metal) it is made of is stronger than the plastic, etc.

Try to get them to recognize the difference between quality and "features." Perhaps the plastic truck has bright decals on the sides ("features") which may make it initially more appealing, but engage the students in a conversation about sturdiness and see if that makes a difference.

As students mature, you can structure this conversation around the material things in life that have particular meaning to them. For instance, older elementary youth might be very interested in games. Several games could be selected for them to consider for quality. In this case, one of the additional questions might include something about the rules–understandability of the how the game is played, and whether it is fun. Athletic equipment might be another option for this age. We personally would stay away from clothes since some students might become offended. You might look at cars, telephones, CD players or other things that also elicit high levels of interest among our youth.

This exercise is important for beginning school, however, because much of what happens later will be determined by the introduction to quality that you have suggested during the first week of class. Let quality become the classroom standard by introducing quality factors right away. Use the language of total quality management (TQM) theory to help. Even very young students can understand TQM if properly addressed.

In fact, if there is a company in your region that manufactures goods and/or food, write and ask them if your class can become quality testers. This keeps interest in quality high and gives students the feeling that they are performing a vital service. Whether it is taste testing tortilla chips and salsa, or testing the quality of toys, this experience can make a life-long impression on students. Imagine all the possibilities of doing something like this as a school (if not classroom). Students not only can run the quality tests, utilize quality improvement tools such as Pareto charts, check sheets, run charts, and control charts, but they can also write reports, give presentations, testify at public forums, etc. There is no end to what students can accomplish, even at a young age. Working in cross-grade-level teams, students who participate in the above exercise would be impressed with the importance of "quality" for the rest of their lives.

If the above option is not available to you, why not write or call several publishing companies to ask if your students can review new materials prior to publication. Though these companies hire editors, they may find this an interesting approach. If this doesn't work, why not write to the nearest publisher's clearinghouse for copies of books that haven't sold and have the students review them and mail the results of their findings to the publishers.

Whenever you engage students in this kind of study, and provided you wrap it around a quality framework, the interest levels will remain high. What is meant by a quality framework? Simply put, the students have to understand what quality is, and how it will be determined. In the manufacturing world the standards would be set by the quality control department most likely according to ISO 9000 standards (internationally set manufacturing standards that form the basis for much of the global economy. Many world-wide corporations insist that their suppliers meet ISO 9000 standards prior to purchasing their goods. At present, no such standards are set for education, although there has been much discussion about that recently.)

## WOW FACTORS!

It is necessary to explain quality factors (also known as the WOW factors). This is begun when students begin to evaluate the toys for quality. One might ask: What makes this truck (or doll, CD, car, etc.) WOW!? What are those things about it that really stand out and when you see it or hear it play, you want to say WOW!? In other words, identify those quality factors that you believe set this apart.

One might put this in context, too, for students using other examples: if you were to describe the world's greatest chocolate cake, what about it would make you say WOW!?

Students might mention such things as:
- rich, chocolate flavor,
- moistness, and
- thickness of layers.

Quality factors or WOW factors are measurable. They are product specifications, and as students gain this concept they learn that quality factors are product specifications for each learning experience. These are the elements that will ultimately determine whether or not one has achieved quality. Thus, in the final analysis the quality factors are the elements that determine whether a student or team has completed his/her learning experience satisfactorily. Students quickly learn that the only acceptable outcome of any learning experience is quality.

The next obvious question is what has to happen to (or go into) the product (or learning experience) to create quality. In our example, the question becomes how to tell someone how to create the "best" chocolate cake in the world. Working in teams, allow the students to decide and come to consensus within their team about the necessary ingredients, amounts, size and type of pan, oven temperature and baking time. If you use this example, please be certain to tell the students that a box cake mix does not work. This cake must be made from scratch. Explain to the students that they are creating **operational definitions** for making the "best" chocolate cake in the world. In other words, they are setting the parameters (ingredients, temperature, mixing processes, etc.) that they think will end up with the "best" chocolate cake in the world. In other words, if anyone were to bake a chocolate cake, following the operational definitions would result in the "best" cake . If the operational definitions are not followed carefully, then the results will be less than the best.

Students and adults seem to enjoy this exercise. As each team determines its ingredients, have students write them on the board. Then compare. Ask the question, if each team made a cake using the listed ingredients would all the cakes turn out the same? If not, would any or all of them meet the quality factors previously decided upon? If you have access to a kitchen, it would be fun to experiment with this farther and have each team bake their cake using the amounts and ingredients they listed. After the cakes come out of the oven, all of differing sizes and taste, explain the concept of variation to them. Then ask again, for a group consensus on those things that would contribute to making the "best" chocolate cake in the world. Once you have consensus on that, either have each team bake another cake or bake one cake for the class. When it comes out of the oven and has cooled, ask students to be the judge for WOW or quality.

By going through this process, students can quickly grasp the significance of the P-D-C-A cycle, variation, operational definitions, and quality factors. Consequently students start school learning about quality and something about quality management principles. This sets the stage for quality learning experiences and achieves it in a way that is both entertaining and fun yet makes the point very clearly.

**PERTINENT WORK**
What is pertinent work and how can it be achieved in any classroom? Pertinent work must include learning fundamentals, but it is the "how" that can be negotiated and collaboratively determined by students and teachers. For example, when teaching reading to kindergartners or first graders, the teacher might introduce a wide-variety of learning "pods." These pods represent themes upon which a holistic approach to learning

proceeds. Why "pods?" Pods are nature's way of expanding life through providing a house for future life forms (seeds). Inside the pod are innumerable opportunities for growth. As children and teachers begin to view the pod for what it really is, they can begin to recognize the wonderful opportunities for learning contained therein. In schools and classrooms, pods can encompass every academic arena and lend themselves to expansion and growth. That is, learning experiences can grow upon each other, and the possibilities are almost endless. Even very young children get excited about the possibilities, and their enthusiasm spreads to each other, the teacher, and parents. Some examples of learning pods might include:

- The Old West
- Dinosaurs and Cave Men
- Neighborhoods
- Pets
- Detectives

The teacher's role is to research the media center for materials relating to each of these suggestions, identify some additional sources for information, check out the city, town, or region for interesting human or physical resources, brainstorm some activities for each, etc. Teachers also need to talk to students, pre-school teachers, and parents throughout the year to discover student interests. Teachers can also engage in research by walking through any toy store to familiarize themselves with the latest in toys for the appropriate age. Often toys can be used to increase learning. Doing this kind of "homework" is different from writing daily lesson plans and still means that the teacher will be prepared to provide leadership to a class.

While we are going to allow the students to select the pod that interests them the most (we recommend that you offer several suggestions but allow students the opportunity to make additional ones), this approach does not mean that certain district, state, or national outcomes can be ignored.

Let's assume the students chose the detective pod for their first learning experience(s). This is a wonderful way to operate any classroom because of the children's natural curiosity. Come to class prepared to provide some "seed thoughts" for the children about what this pod might mean, and how the class and/or individuals or teams might pursue different learning experiences. We recommend that you begin by asking the children what a detective is and what a detective does. After fully exploring that, expand their thoughts by asking if they think scientists are detectives. What about doctors? Dentists? Farmers? Engineers? Animals? Soldiers? Teachers? Students? You get the idea. In a real sense this is like a kaleidoscope. It expands your thinking and creates continually changing patterns to create new thoughts and ideas. This is the heart of being a life-long learner.

For example, an elementary class might begin by doing some research at home. You might ask students to list what they know now and what they'd like to know. Explore with the students how they can get information, whom they might ask, and when they might begin their research. This could include such scientific skills as observing, counting, classifying, and charting things. One class decided they wanted to learn more about the television habits of classmates' families. The group agreed on a list of programs most thought they or family members watched. The list included: Oprah, Cartoons, News, Cheers, Donahue, and Sesame Street. Students were divided into teams and each person agreed to keep track for a two week period of the television shows their families watched. With the returned information teams of students could compare television viewing patterns between families. They planned to follow this up by investigating the newspapers and magazines their families read. The results of one student's (Shaletha) efforts are documented as follows:

Shaletha's two-week record of the number of times her family watched the TV shows from the list generated by her classmates.

| TV Show | Mom | Dad | Shaletha | Sonny | Henry | Total |
|---------|-----|-----|----------|-------|-------|-------|
| Oprah | 10 | 0 | 4 | 0 | 0 | 14 |
| News | 6 | 9 | 0 | 0 | 0 | 15 |
| Cartoons | 1 | 3 | 8 | 9 | 10 | 31 |
| Cheers | 4 | 8 | 7 | 10 | 9 | 38 |
| Donahue | 0 | 0 | 0 | 0 | 0 | 0 |
| Sesame | 0 | 0 | 2 | 5 | 6 | 13 |
| Total | 21 | 20 | 21 | 24 | 25 | 113 |

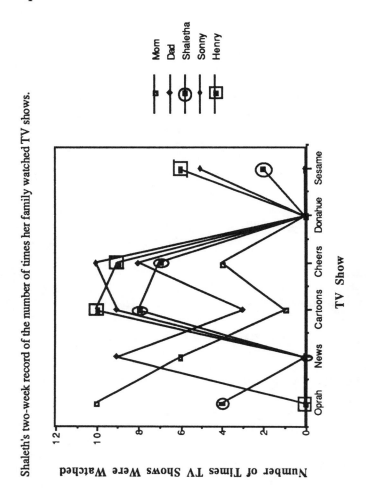

Shaleth's two-week record of the number of times her family watched TV shows.

Once you've got students thinking differently, create some initial experiences that make the point quickly and are not too difficult, but will keep the children's interest high. You might want to demonstrate (selecting some children to help) one of these activities, but then using centers around the room and with the children in small groups, allow each to solve one of the "puzzling" activities you created. When everyone has had a turn, have them show the class how they did it. Then, you might let students take turns trying their luck with other activities.

To avoid chaos and potentially unsafe situations, you'll have to be certain to go back to the rule(s) that the entire class has agreed to for safety. Small children often forget safety in their eagerness to participate, but in keeping with the arms-around, warm, friendly classroom climate, it makes sense to maintain a low-key approach to discipline. Children generally respond positively when they think people (adults) love them, and it is important to fill the classroom with positive and supportive actions.

You may have discovered already that a signal works best when things get too rambunctious. One signal that works fairly well is a flick of the light switch, if that is what you've agreed upon as a class. At first, you may find yourself flicking the switch often; however, as time proceeds and the children gain a sense of classroom expectations you'll have less need. Indeed, ideally you would give all the children permission to flick the switch when they feel that things are too chaotic for them. This takes some time and patience but can be a very powerful lesson for everyone in respect and caring for others.

After the initial experiences a natural follow-up is to have children go home and interview their parents or guardians. They might ask each such questions as: Do you ever have to be a detective? How do you find things when they are lost? Can you remember any particular time when you were a "detective?" These kinds of experiences are valuable for children and their families. First, it engages the parent/guardian in the child's education right away. Second, it lets you know that the children were interacting with at least one adult. The next day the children can share their detective work. You might also ask them if they've ever lost anything and how they went about finding it.

## CREATE INTERDISCIPLINARY ACTIVITIES

The next step is to prepare some kind of classroom experience that will encompass interdisciplinary activities and relate directly to the specified learning outcomes. Children, even the very young, need to know what is expected of them. Learning outcomes can be specified in words that children can understand and placed on a chart so they can keep track of their own learning. As with the cake experience, review the following with students:

- **Why are we doing this?** The reason must be compelling for everyone, otherwise they will not "buy in" and will resist, thus creating other problems within the classroom. The WHY question becomes the mission statement. In the case of the cake, the WHY question might have been answered: **We are going to bake the best cake in the world to celebrate the birthday of the person we love the most!**

We recommend that the mission for each learning experience be written collaboratively with students and teacher and posted in the classroom. It can also be written and provided to parents, along with the quality factors and operational definitions.

- **What are the quality factors (WOW) we will look for–how will we know this is the best cake in the world? How will we assess our results?** Limit these to the top 2 or 3 factors. Be certain to work with the children so everyone understands that these are the ways their work will be judged and that once they achieve the quality factors, they can move on to other things, but that everyone must reach quality. Here you can emphasize the importance of working together. This will be discussed in detail in another chapter. As students progress, a quality factor you might want to routinely include is cycle time. That is, how much time will be given to any learning experience? A quality classroom seeks to continually improve the learning experiences while reducing cycle time. Thus students advance more rapidly in a quality classroom.

- **Create operational definitions. If you were going to tell someone specifically how to create the "best cake in the world", what would you say?** What are the key elements or ingredients that are necessary to achieve the "best?" Young children will need more guidance than older students. Begin by seeding the list with one or two obvious elements and then allow the students to come up with more. You'll need to guide them through this, particularly when first starting the continuous quality improvement process. If the students don't come up with all the elements (or learning objectives) then you can add to the list by stating that you are a part of this group, too, and you know that the district has certain guidelines that must be followed. For that reason, you are adding these elements. Generally, especially with older students, the list generated by them is far beyond the district requirements. Once this is fully developed and understood by all, post this along with the mission and quality factors.

## ELIMINATE CONFUSION

Prior to beginning any learning experience then, students are given a copy of the Mission, Quality Factors, and Operational Definitions. This **eliminates any confusion** that might arise about the assignment or requirements. The same information is posted in large letters on the classroom wall.

By reaching into your own experiences, you might be able to plant thought seeds of creativity for learning experiences. Begin with something exciting and not too complex, but that everyone can relate to and that meets one or more of the district outcomes. The detective theme can be used all the way through K-12 in greater amounts of complexity.

Recently, **National Public Radio** did a lengthy report on how the garment industry generates vast amounts of pollution every year. Esprit™ has recently been involved in creating garments from organically grown substances and using recycled yarns. They are also engaged in collaboration with the manufacturers of metal buttons to create buttons that do not put any pollutants into the air or water. This was an entirely new and different way of thinking about pollution. It never occurred to us that the very clothes we wear were creating other problems for our planet.

Is this something that students could get interested in? Some yes, some maybe not, but wouldn't it be fascinating for them to explore, do research, testify, write papers, etc. to the garment industry or their suppliers? Wouldn't it also be fascinating to study the economics of this issue and how it might affect the local economy as well as the state, region, or national economies? Also, what if the garment industry continues using manufacturing methods and materials that pollute our air and water? Will the future be different for these children? Another interesting idea might be to study the effects of wearing chlorine bleached garments on the body. Perhaps there are no ill-effects, but might this be interesting to students? Is this kind of assignment pertinent? Definitely.

The learning outcomes that an be generated from the above question(s) are limitless. Imagine the reading, writing, research, speaking, listening skills involved. Imagine the data gathering, charting and graphing, statistical analysis and other mathematical skills that can be learned. Imagine the scientific discovery methods, problem solving, critical thinking, and new knowledge possibilities. Students can create brochures, write newspaper articles, hold press conferences, lobby their state and national legislators, and testify before public groups. They may even want to team up with a national organization interested in saving the planet. With an interdisciplinary approach, students can learn a phenomenal amount, maintain a high degree of motivation, achieve far beyond expectations, and maybe most important, they will feel empowered that they've done something significant; that the assignment was not merely "work" from a textbook, but truly significant.

When the assignment is completed, and the quality factors are met, students and teacher debrief. Here is one example of a simple debriefing form after a learning experience.

---

<u>How Helpful Were These Resources?</u>

Class  _____          Semester  _____
Period  _____          Project  _____

For this learning experience, we used the following resources:

| | |
|---|---|
| Lecture | Field Trip |
| Textbooks | Video |
| Library books | Computers |
| Discussion | Other |
| Newspaper - Magazine Articles | |

Please rate each on how much it helped you complete the learning experience:

    E = excellent, couldn't have completed it without it.
    G = good; was a big help
    O = okay; didn't help much
    <u>W = waste of time; was no help whatsoever</u>

| | RATING | | | |
|---|---|---|---|---|
| Method | E | G | O | W |
| Lecture | | | | |
| Textbooks | | | | |
| Library Books | | | | |
| Discussion | | | | |
| Articles | | | | |
| Field Trip | | | | |
| Video | | | | |
| Computers | | | | |
| Other | | | | |

What suggestions do you have for improving this learning experience?

---

When students have completed the debriefing sheet, the quality leadership team or teacher can collate the responses by using the debriefing check sheet. This information can improve all subsequent learning experiences. In the example below nearly 38% of all students rated the lectures "okay", while an equal percentage rated them good or excellent. In cases like this, the teacher would want to pursue with the students what was helpful and what wasn't. Many of us personify our work and become defensive when students or parents offer criticism or make suggestions. We caution you to resist doing that when you ask students to help. If you ask and they are honest, which is what you hope for, then don't become defensive. Ask for help and be grateful when it comes. In this case the lectures appear to require some alteration to become more effective for all the students.

The same example shows that over 41% of students think the textbook is a waste. Nearly 45% were lukewarm about the worth of the textbook. This response indicates that reading and references to the textbook should be kept to a minimum, no matter how "good" you or the district think it is. If the students view it as a waste of their time, they will simply refuse to do the work required or will do it minimally. Most especially, don't ignore what the students have said. They will continue to view you with goodwill as long as they can see that their suggestions are being taken seriously and changes are being made.

Keep the classroom mission statement in the forefront of your mind throughout these experiences. Remember that every action taken within the classroom should support the mission statement and goals. Hone in on your constancy of purpose like a laser beam, and there is no way you cannot succeed.

## Debriefing Check Sheet

| Method | Excellent | Good | Okay | Waste |
|---|---|---|---|---|
| Lecture | 5 | 6 | 11 | 7 |
| Text | 2 | 2 | 13 | 12 |
| Library Book | 7 | 9 | 13 | 0 |
| Computer | 10 | 12 | 5 | 2 |
| Discussion | 10 | 14 | 4 | 1 |
| Articles | 13 | 15 | 1 | 0 |
| Field Trip | 20 | 9 | 0 | 0 |
| Video | 13 | 11 | 3 | 2 |
| Other (letters, phone calls) | 25 | 4 | 0 | 0 |

Other ways to debrief after any learning experience are discussed in another chapter. The above method is helpful to teachers as they proceed on their own continuous improvement journey.

## WHEN PROBLEMS OCCUR IN THE CLASSROOM

More traditional teachers become uncomfortable when problems arise within the classroom. However, by focusing on the process rather than the outcome, the entire class can come together to resolve almost any problem. Generally when students are encouraged to resolve their own problems, the result is far superior and more long-lasting than if problems are resolved from other sources. This is an important issue for quality teachers and one that totally requires the belief that all students want to do a good job, but that it is the system that keeps them (and the teacher) from being successful.

Let's assume you do believe that all students come to school wanting to do a good job. One day you realize that the students are not making effective use of the learning centers that you spent so much time organizing. They also do not move from one center to the next very easily. These things are slowing the learning down, and the concern is that each day seems to become more chaotic. This provides a wonderful opportunity for the class to participate in creating its own learning environment.

In such a case, the teacher draws all the children around and expresses some concern about the situation. Then the teacher turns the problem over to the children by saying that since the centers exist for them, obviously they are missing some key elements that the students deem necessary. With a student as leader, the class brainstorms other ways to organize the centers, the materials they need to accomplish their work, and ways to move about the room more efficiently. Amazingly, students as young as second grade were able, within a relatively short amount of time, to reorganize, state their needs, and make recommendations for improvement. The teacher implemented all their recommendations and the situation immediately improved.

Just as important as the above situation was to the teacher, so was it to the students. These kinds of experiences help students learn to resolve problems that affect them and their ability to accomplish their work. The benefits of taking time to move through an exercise like this are invaluable. Students become empowered, more active in their education, feel better about themselves, and believe that they have some control over their lives. These are life-long benefits and lead to students who are willing to take greater educational risks because they believe someone listens and respects them. These are powerful ways to work with children of all ages.

At the secondary level, there are many similarities. When the learning process breaks down, when students become uninterested in the assignment or activity, these are wonderful windows of opportunity for teachers. Seize the day!! Without fear, allow yourself the opportunity to see what happens when students are asked for their input. Many teachers are afraid that older students will run roughshod over them and take over the class. On the contrary, students don't want to take over the class! In fact, most of them are so puzzled by this, that they do not believe that any teacher would really want to know what they think. Some secondary students in fact, have been so brainwashed into believing they are expected to be passive that they resist getting involved. Teachers needn't worry that anarchy will result.

A caveat to the above comments perhaps is in order here. Students who have been treated with respect and trust will want to help teachers and will be more willing to become active participants. Those who have been treated with disrespect and distrust on the other hand, will likely seize any opportunity to sabotage the teacher's efforts whether they are top-down boss-like or facilitative. It stands to reason then, that eliminating biases from your thoughts and behaviors is a key and critical element in establishing a quality classroom.

## FINALLY...

Quality classrooms are distinguishable in several ways. Teachers engage students continuously in co-creating the learning experiences. Work that is assigned has meaning to the students and real-world connections. Each learning experience grows upon the others and results from students and teacher debriefing and analyzing the previous assignment before creating the next.

Teachers in quality classrooms do not resolve problems in isolation but they work together with students, knowing that the collective wisdom of the group is much greater than their own. Students become empowered, more self-confident, eager life-long learners who care about the class as a whole and are willing to assist others as needed.

Responsibility for learning rests with each child, the teams, and with the class as a whole including the teacher. Everyone contributes to expanding the thinking of the group and works together to create exciting, efficient learning experiences.

ΛΛΛΛΛΛΛΛ

The following is a checksheet tool to help the teacher to implement the **Quality Fusion** technique into their classroom.

Step 1:  The mission, goals and academic integrity of your class are absolutely clear.

- √ Established a classroom mission statement.
- √ Developed personal goals for the class.
- √ Communicated mission and goals to parents/guardians.
- √ Aligned classroom mission and goals with those of the school district and the school.

Step 2:  You are demonstrating leadership.

- √ Developed a definition of a total quality classroom.
- √ Walk-the-Talk about quality.
- √ Understand Deming's system of **Profound Knowledge**.
- √ Use a variety of teaching styles.
- √ Have a CQI program for self and for my students.

Step 3:  All work is pertinent and flows from the students.

- √ Broke down barriers on day one by establishing a classroom mission statement with the students.
- √ Having students co-create learning experiences.
- √ Stressing the importance of teamwork in problem solving and decision making.
- √ Defined quality and what it means.
- √ Created interdisciplinary learning activities.

# Chapter Four: Course content is connected to the surrounding community and the real world.

One of the most common complaints students have about school work is that it lacks relevance to their lives and world. When interviewing students about their future, it is rare to hear any say that they believe what they are learning in K-12 has any relationship to their future career plans. Worse, when students have no plans, no goals or dreams, the curriculum has no meaning to them. From experience as adults, we all know that when presented with something that we are not interested, there is no incentive to learn about it. No matter how much someone tries to convince us, if we cannot imagine that it will add any value to our lives, we simply reject it. Occasionally, someone with great influence over us can persuade us to give "it a try." Sad to say, that is rarely the case between students and their teachers. An excellent teacher may be able to persuade some of the students to become involved because s/he works so hard at making "it" interesting. However, far too many teachers become burned out using this tactic, while far too many students still see no added value to the subject matter. Thus, we are left with teachers viewing students as unmotivated and not interested in learning.

If we carefully examine this phenomena, however, a different picture emerges. It is human nature to continue learning. Humans are very complex. We spend our days learning new skills and abilities that we believe will bring us respect, love, survival, happiness, and fun. As we grow and develop, we learn to act and react to outside influences (usually significant others) who give us feedback on our behaviors. The need to love and be loved, and the need for respect become the core of what drives our behavior. Thus, by the time a youngster reaches school age, behavior patterns are well established, based on the reaction of parents/guardians, grandparents, siblings, etc. These are the people we are heavily invested in wanting to please.

As we get older our willingness to do things simply to please others sometimes wanes, especially if other needs are more pressing. An example of this is the need for respect. If we feel that we are lacking in respect, then we often seek out those individuals and/or groups that will respect us for what we are. As children grow into adolescence, a sense of disrespect within the acceptable culture often leads youth to seek gangs, cults, and the like.

Students don't lose their enthusiasm for learning—they simply lose their enthusiasm for being told what to learn, when to learn it, how to learn it, and where to learn it. Young children who appear unmotivated at school are seldom couch potatoes who do nothing but vegetate in front of the television. They are often very active learners outside of school, but are not afforded the opportunity to learn in ways that meet their preferred learning style. In fact, we penalize children with learning styles that are a mismatch with our preferred teaching style.

The interesting thing about teaching and learning styles is that you may be teaching, but some children are not learning because it is like a foreign language if they are not tuned into your style. Sadly, these children get farther behind and are often punished for something over which they have no control. These are the children who have so many failure experiences by the end of third grade that they are stripped of their self-esteem and are left floundering in a world that does not make sense to them. They feel really bad until they eventually give up trying. Hence, these children and youth are totally misunderstood by their teachers and are often labeled as unmotivated. Once this happens, teachers give up on students who have already given up on themselves.

What looks like a unmotivated student  is really a student who has been denied the right to learn in ways that are interesting and exciting to him/her. We believe there is no such thing as an unmotivated learner. But rather many students are no longer motivated to be compliant in a system that does not recognize their worth as individuals. One glance at students when they are out of class reveals that they are continuously learning. Unfortunately, many are learning behaviors and other things that society wishes they wouldn't.

One thing is very clear. Youngsters start kindergarten eager to learn. By the time they reach the third or fourth grade, some say they hate school. In middle school we find more students unwilling or unable to abide by coercive rules and a curriculum that doesn't meet their needs. Acting-out behaviors increase and absenteeism increases. At the high school level, these students are branded as trouble makers, or at least unmotivated and lazy. They respond to a system they view as uncaring by not caring since it hurts less that way. High school students make a very strong statement that the system has failed by virtue of their behaviors. Absenteeism, tardiness, disrespect for adults, rebellion against rules, failure to do required assignments, failure to dress for physical education class are all expressions of dissatisfaction with the system.

This may be a radical thought and one that makes many educators angry. But think about it from the eyes of the teenager who is caught in the system that doesn't respond to his/her needs. Imagine that you are the teen-ager who has had her/his self-esteem whittled away by going to school (required by law) and receiving failure and/or sub-standard messages repeatedly. You've probably been scorned for not performing well on tests that measured things that were of no importance. Perhaps, you've become isolated from some students because someone deemed you belonged in remedial classes which were filled with kids like you. Over time, you became depressed and disillusioned with school. What you thought at age five would be a wonderful and exciting adventure turned into a nightmare. If this student were you, would you wake up every morning and be eager to return to a system that made you feel sad and bad about yourself? Probably not!

## WHAT IS THE ANSWER TO THIS COMPLEX PROBLEM?

If you have a sense that students are not responding enthusiastically to an assignment that you have poured your heart and soul into, then the first thing to do is ask the students to analyze the problem for you. Approach it from the perspective that you need their help since you cannot figure out why they are still unresponsive to the wonderful assignments.

Here is an example of how one high school social studies teacher approached this problem. Candace Allen, a ninth grade social studies teacher from Centennial High School (grades 9-12, total student body approximately 1200, school district population of 18,000, approximately 51% Hispanic, 48% White, and 1% African-American and Asian) in Pueblo, Colorado, reported that over 45 percent of all students were failing. Mrs. Allen had approximately 32 students per class; about half Hispanic and half white with abilities that covered the spectrum. She tried everything, including giving them a learning styles inventory. Ms. Allen is considered one of the finest teachers in Pueblo and was both puzzled and concerned by the results she was getting. She was concerned about the high failure rate (which had remained fairly constant for the past 10 years) and she continuously tried to make the course more interesting and the assignments more fun. She concluded that indeed it was the case that there are just too many students out there who don't care and are unmotivated. Just as Candace was about to give up, she heard about total quality management.

Here is the story of Candace Allen's earliest beginnings with quality.

Ms. Allen had prepared a World Geography assignment that she thought the students would love. They were to work in small groups, research one of the Eastern European countries, and answer a series of questions regarding its people, customs, topography, trade, and government. Each group was to present a written response to the questions and an oral report summarizing what they'd learned. Phase two of the project was to create a new government (a utopian government for that country) and project what would happen in the future to it. At first the students were excited, but after about three days their interest waned. That is when Mrs. Allen decided to use a **Cause/Effect Diagram** (she called it a Stinky Fish Diagram) with her class(es).

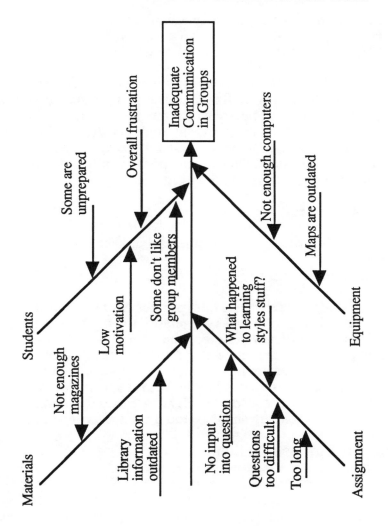

Inadequate Communication in Groups

Overall frustration

Some are unprepared

Not enough computers

Maps are outdated

Some don't like group members

What happened to learning styles stuff?

Low motivation

Students

Not enough magazines

Library information outdated

No input into question

Questions too difficult

Too long

Equipment

Materials

Assignment

**Results of Student Teams Brainstorming Solutions to "Stinky Fish Discovery"**

**Team 1: Questions too difficult**
**Students had no input**
**Too many questions**
**Library resources not adequate to answer all questions**

*Solutions:*
• Make sure students know the meaning of words used (like capitalism, socialism, etc.)

- Let students have input into question design
- Have fewer questions and make those few count
- Make sure library has needed material

NOTE: Mrs. Allen had the same students in Government class the semester before. She assumed that because they had been tested on the vocabulary words that they understood them. Despite the fact that most of the students did well on the vocabulary tests the previous semester, it became apparent that they did not understand the meaning of the words and therefore couldn't effectively carry-out the assignment.

## Team 2: Overall frustration
*Solutions:*
- Keep using your little assessments, but keep trying to listen to us.
- Make projects not so **BIG**!

The students felt that this project was overwhelming particularly because it had two phases to it. There were 26 questions to answer even before they could begin creating a utopian government and projecting into the future. The questions were also so overwhelmingly complex (albeit good, thoughtful questions) that the students had no prior experience with any assignment like it. The leap from eighth grade to this ninth grade class was overwhelming and they could not see any end in sight.

## Team 3: Low motivation
*Solutions:*
- Since we don't necessarily want to be in World Geography, you really need to make sure students see a need for stuff.
- You gave us a learning style inventory, so why not do more things that hit one of the styles.
- Keep asking us how we're doing

The first problem was that the students didn't understand the need to study World Geography. No one had bothered to answer the WHY question for them. They didn't have any affinity for the course of study and really didn't see how studying the world could possibly affect them. Mrs. Allen did ask the students to complete a self-assessment at the end of each day answering questions like: how are you coming, do you need additional help, etc. Because the students were scattered all over the media center and she was moving from group to group, she assumed that the self-assessment would alert her to any problems the students were having. She did not consider that the students felt that she wasn't "hearing" them, which was the real problem and why they asked her to keep asking how they were doing.

Last, though Mrs. Allen had given the students a learning styles inventory, this assignment did not seem to have any accommodation to differences in style. The students felt betrayed and believed that if she was really interested in accommodating their learning styles then all the assignments should reflect such concern.

## Team 4: Not enough group input into deciding on project
*Solutions*:
• You work too hard Mrs. A.
• Let us decide more.

Students all appeared to like Mrs. Allen. She has utmost respect for her students, works very hard, listens to them, and has all the qualities of an excellent teacher. Because of her good rapport with students she was able to get more out of them than most teachers in her school, although as you can see, it wasn't enough to maintain their interest or motivate them to try harder. In essence this group of students told Mrs. Allen that they wanted a voice in what the projects were going to be, and that if she would allow that to happen, they would be more interested and probably learn more.

She had never considered letting students have a say in creating assignments and after twenty-plus years of teaching this was an entirely new concept. This team really was addressing the issue of *control* of the classroom. Instead of reacting negatively to this suggestion, Mrs. Allen decided that she had virtually nothing to lose by allowing her students to help her co-create learning experiences from this day forward.

## Team 5: Some are unprepared
*Solutions*:
• Don't let them (the students) get so far gone
• Students help them

This team had an interesting view on what was needed to resolve the issue of some students being unprepared. Their first response indicates they were feeling abandoned by Mrs. Allen. This dependency on the teacher exists in classrooms where there is no empowerment of the students. Indeed, they felt that unless she **DID SOMETHING** that all would be lost; and in fact some students did simply give up feeling so overwhelmed at the magnitude of the assignment.

Their second response demonstrates a glimmer of hope. The students recognized that somehow they could help each other, but they clearly didn't know how or what to do. Mrs. Allen could be very helpful in this regard if she were to train the students.

### Team 6: Too much time spent on this project
*Solutions:*
- Fewer questions that are better worded would help
- Set guidelines for stuff that is due each day
- Get rid of some of those questions!

By the time Team 6 reported, it was clear that students felt the assignment was overwhelming. The questions were written without any clear understanding by the students, although Candace believed they were concise and easy to understand. Since she had not asked for input from the students they never had the chance to tell her what their perspective was. Clearly there were too many, too complex questions, and students were left feeling defeated before they began.

The students were also feeling adrift in a sea that didn't make sense to them. The assignment had no meaning for them, and they could not even begin to imagine how studying Eastern Europe might affect their world or their lives. The only reason for them to complete this assignment was to please the teacher.

The assignment called for them to work for a time in the media center answering the questions, but with no intermediate checks or check-ups to see how they were progressing. This was considered too "loose" for too many of the students who were used to having very tight restrictions placed on them and to report back to the teacher often. They were uncomfortable with this level of trust that Mrs. Allen had placed in them to finish the assignment on time.

### Team 7: Library resources aren't good enough
*Solutions*:
- Get more computers!
- Make sure the computerized encyclopedia is working
- Have more magazines
- Get newer maps
- Don't assign questions we can't find the answers to!

Another common complaint was that the resources were simply not available. Obviously some of these resources are out of Mrs. Allen's control, but she had put in an acquisitions order to the school media specialist for the purchase of more magazines (and gave suggestions for which ones to order). The map issue was more complex due changing world conditions.

Mrs. Allen did not consider whether or not the media center had materials available that would enable students to answer the questions and that was an omission that, if considered earlier, would have encouraged her to alter the questions. It was one critical piece that dramatically affected the student's ability to successfully complete the assignment.

As a result of the above experience, Mrs. Allen was determined that she would follow-through and allow the students to assist her in making the decision about how the class could run more smoothly and bring students back into the learning process.

## COLLABORATIVE DECISION: TEACHER AND STUDENTS

1.  Next time teacher will actively let students help choose and design the final product boundaries

2.  Teacher will seek student views on questions to be used as exploratory tools based more on where they really are as opposed to where I think they should be or are. The teacher will make certain the resources needed to answer the questions will be easier to find.

3.  Projects will be shorter, with less coverage of abstract concepts.

4.  Be sure all styles of learners are addressed.

After coming to these conclusions, Mrs. Allen still had to determine what to do about the second part of the assignment. she decided to ask the students: **What Shall We Do About Part II?**

The class decided which questions not to cover and to get Part II over with ASAP!

At this point, the students were very perplexed by Mrs. Allen's approach. They had never before had a teacher ask them what they thought about an assignment, and quite frankly there was something so different about it that they weren't sure how they felt. Mrs. Allen realized she would have to tell them what she was learning about and how she felt it would make her classes better for everyone, including herself. She began with a brief historical overview of Dr. W. Edwards Deming and his quality management theory, how he was rebuffed by U.S. companies, and the role he played in rebuilding Japan after World War II. What follows is a basic outline of how Mrs. Allen began training her students in total quality principles.

## Beginning Total Quality Training for Students:
1.  Tell the Deming Story and Japanese Experience
2.  Express the **basic principles of TQM in education**:
    - all kids want to learn and can learn and can be a part of the planning process
    - educational output can be improved if you focus on the process rather than the product
    - the product will improve as an outcome of process improvement
    - following TQM leads you through little steps of continuous improvement
3.  Ask the students to help brainstorm *things that keep them from being interested or motivated* in school. Here are typical responses:
    √  it's boring
    √  teachers don't know what kids care about
    √  teachers think they're all hot
    √  Subjects are all so planned out and they've been the same for 20 years
    √  the classes (like social studies) seem the same year after year
    √  teachers don't always know what's important
    √  too much reading
    √  too many worksheets and busy work
    √  students don't care about stuff they don't know about like socialism
    √  nothing is ever fun
    √  we have to be quiet
    √  too much other stuff gets in the way - like home, peers, etc.

## IMPLEMENTING STUDENT SUGGESTIONS
The Teacher:
- took each criticism (from the Stinky Fish Diagram) and showed how it could be solved by the 4 TQM principles.

- then read the "solution" (the 4 pledges) for the next project; asked for additional suggestions from the class—there were none; asked for and got a unanimous show of hands for "agreement with the changes," thus demonstrating commitment on the part of everyone in class.

- read the "solutions" for finishing the Project:
4th period - reasonable deadline.
5th period - agreed on following:
> Part I ends today
> Part II ends Thursday

## EVOLUTION OF A TQM APPROACH TO WORLD GEOGRAPHY
Teacher:  **Constancy of Purpose**
Prior to the above experience:
> **To have students achieve a 'good'  grade in World Geography**

**Focus:  On Outcome**
**Method**: Asked students who were being successful what worked for them.
**Results**: Some students participated fully...others became uninterested, ...most never fully participated.

Teacher:  **Constancy of Purpose**
Post this experience:
> **To improve the learning process so all students can achieve success in World Geography**

**Focus: Discover flaws in the learning process and establish a continuous improvement project to build in quality in the first place**
**Method**: Fishbone chart, giving all students an opportunity to identify problems with the process
**Results**: All students became interested in making the class better.

Each was empowered through teams to brainstorm ways to improve.

This heightened interest and participation and a sense of helping each other so the class could achieve success.

Students had fun!

---

### Testimonial from Mrs. Allen

"The neatest thing happened! All of the groups worked well today, though some people haven't prepared any research data and are requiring extra time in the media center. The 'behind' ones are helping each other get data. Some groups will finish early so they will be allowed to work on their map enlargements in the media center."

"The kids had fun projecting into the future in Part II. Lots of laughter and they had lots of questions for me. I became a 'resource center.' Some were saying that they wanted Part II to get over so they could go to Part III."

"So, even though the fishbone exercise indicated severe process problems, the processing of the problems seemed to make kids more willing to finish the project in good spirit."

---

By the end of the semester, Mrs. Allen had these results to her experiment in bringing total quality improvement principles to the classroom.

---

### Pre-Total Quality Management
### 40% failure rate

### Post-TQM
### Only the chronically absent failed

## More testimony and reactions from Mrs. Allen

Some students who had been failing all subjects turned completely around and as a result of this approach in ONE class, began to do better in all classes. At least 2 students with across the board F's, did not fail a single subject at the end of the year. One of these individuals is now talking about going to college.

Once students understood the NEED to LEARN, there ceased to be a motivation problem.

"What is so amazing is that all the students were active learners, all were interested, and for the first time, all were seeking more information about world geography. The transformation was simply amazing!  I would never have believed it."

Not until the students began to make the connection between the environment (**their suggestion for how to focus the world geography class**) and the different types of economies did they become totally engaged in this learning experience. In the earlier activity, the students were simply told to select one of the Eastern European countries to study. There was nothing that could have possibly hooked them into this learning experience, unless they had relatives living there or were first generation immigrants from one of the countries. Unfortunately, that was not the case in Mrs. Allen's class.

Indeed the student who posed the question, "What is socialism and so what?" was surprised when Mrs. Allen responded by saying, "that in socialistic countries there are no choices; that the tennis shoes you wear would probably not be available to you, but there would be one kind on the shelves and everyone would have to wear the same thing." That got the entire class engaged in a discussion of what it might be like to live in a country where choices were limited. Some thought it would be better and others not. What that issue did accomplish was to engage the students in the process of bringing world geography to their world.  It was a springboard for them to consider the environment and how countries pollute, what types of government create the best environment, etc.

## HOOK THE LEARNING EXPERIENCE

It is absolutely crucial to hook every learning experience to the student's world. You can do this three ways:

1) Based on the required and recommended student outcomes, have students consider ways they would like to learn so you can co-create the learning experiences together.
2) Interact with colleagues and create a cross-curricular approach to learning, thus making each learning experience meaningful to the students.
3) Be prepared to answer the WHY question, as it relates to why students need to learn your subject matter and be certain to ask students WHY they are in your class.

Elementary teachers are much better at engaging in cross-curricular activities than middle or high school teachers. Years ago when whole language became an accepted way of approaching learning, these teachers began creating thematic units. It makes sense to approach learning holistically rather than piecemeal as it most often is presented from about 5th grade on.

For example, have you ever encountered (except in school) a math problem that was just a series of numbers completely unattached to "something?" Think about the folly of teaching this way. Mathematics and the logic underlying it should become a part of all education, not just reserved for 25—50 minutes per day. In Mrs. Allen's world geography classes, can you imagine any place for incorporating mathematics into the course? Once considered, the possibilities seem endless. The same can be said for communication skills, science, and even physical education.

Have you ever considered how much physical education relies on the principles of physics, geometry, and kinesiology? Yet, are there many attempts to integrate this into the "academic" side of school? Interestingly, we consider book learning to be academic, but applied knowledge is often viewed as vocational. Without application, what is the lesson to be learned?

Even Shakespeare and other masters' works can be taught so that there is meaning for each student's life. The classics are the author's way of problem resolution dealing with situations that are still happening to students today. Humanity is still fraught with inequity, and there are abundant examples throughout the great works of literature.

Therefore, whatever your subject matter, your curricular interests, your grade level, work from the supposition that it can be brought to the student's world, and thus increase their motivation to learn and at the same time decrease discipline problems.

---

**Doing more of what you've always done will get you more of what you've always gotten. The question is: Are all the students being successful and are they all internally motivated to do high quality work?**

ΔΔΔΔΔΔΔΔ

The following is a checksheet tool to help the teacher to implement the **Quality Fusion** technique into their classroom.

Step 1:  The mission, goals and academic integrity of your class are absolutely clear.
√  Established a classroom mission statement.
√  Developed personal goals for the class.
√  Communicated mission and goals to parents/guardians.
√  Aligned classroom mission and goals with those of the school district and the school.

Step 2:  You are demonstrating leadership.
√  Developed a definition of a total quality classroom.
√  Walk-the-Talk about quality.
√  Understand Deming's system of **Profound Knowledge**.
√  Use a variety of teaching styles.
√  Have a CQI program for self and for my students.

Step 3:  All work is pertinent and flows from the students.
√  Broke down barriers on day one by establishing a classroom mission statement with the students.
√  Having students co-create learning experiences.
√  Stressing the importance of teamwork in problem solving and decision making.
√  Defined quality and what it means.
√  Created interdisciplinary learning activities.

Step 4:  The course content is connected to the surrounding community and the real world.
√  Demonstrated the connectedness between work and the real world.
√  Asked the students to analyze the learning assignments.
√  Began TQM training for the students.
√  Implemented student suggestions on how best to improve the learning system.

**Chapter Five:** **The student is not only treated as a "worker," but also as a team member of the "research and development" department.**

Traditionally in K-12, the teacher has had the responsibility for creating all assignments based on the scope and sequence of the curriculum in keeping with district approved learning objectives. Teachers have spent an inordinate amount of time creating daily lesson plans and unit plans. Most often the curriculum and sequence is determined prior to the start of the school year and in many districts curriculum review is on a seven year cycle. Is it any wonder that we have created a monster with passive learners where many students adopt a "come on, I dare ya' ta' learn me!" attitude? These students have realized the name of the game in traditional settings.

The rules of the game vary slightly, but can be generally characterized as:

Monday—read the chapter

Tuesday—answer the questions at the end of the chapter

Wednesday—see a video or movie relating to the chapter

Thursday—discuss the chapter

Friday—take a test (which, for too many teachers, has been prepared by the textbook companies.)

More progressive teachers do vary their lesson plans and attempt to make the subject matter interesting; however, far too many still adhere to something like the above example. For some reason elementary school teachers have been most receptive to new ideas and creativity. Middle school teachers are somewhat progressive, while high school teachers have become boxed into their subject matter, partly because of scheduling but also because their paradigm of high school is that classes are separate entities with little or no reason to interact with colleagues. The middle school has included teaming, but only a few are also using an interdisciplinary approach to learning. A more typical model is that teachers are teamed for homeroom, and in that, they have common planning time to discuss a common group of students, but rarely do they truly function as a team with curriculum wrapped around the pod idea, where the lines between content areas are so blurred that it becomes a holistic experience for students and teachers.

The paradigm shift is so dramatic that teachers, administrators, and parents all have difficulty conceptualizing what a quality school or classroom would be like. The basic problem is that everyone was schooled in a very traditional way, and grandparents were schooled the same way, too. Unless each individual can jump out of the box of thinking about school, the tendency is to continue to re-create a failed system.

One fallacious argument that we often hear is that we should go back to the good old days, focus on reading, writing, and arithmetic and reinstitute strong discipline policies, and everything will return to "normal," which is perceived to be "better." Perhaps we should spend a minute thinking about the good old days and expose the myths of education to date.

MYTH 1: Back in the thirties, forties and fifties public education provided everyone with a high quality education.

The world was different in the middle part of this century. Families were mostly intact, and mother didn't work outside the home. There were a number of "juvenile delinquents," however, who did not fit in at school. These were non-conforming students and/or very bright students who were bored by a rigid, dull curriculum. Disruptive students were expelled or dropped out of school and were immediately able to obtain good paying jobs in mines, on railroads, or in factories. Neither business nor education was interested in having the worker or student do anything but follow orders. There was little attempt to remediate these students to keep them in school.

Some people did get a solid basic education. However, even these students were not allowed to exert creative solutions to problems. The lucky ones were able to enter post-secondary institutions, but these generally were reserved only for the wealthy or powerful white families. For most students graduation from high school was the end of their formal education.

MYTH 2: If it worked then, it can work today.

The world is very different today. No longer do the majority of students come from two-parent families. Neighborhoods and churches seldom are organized to fulfill the role of "protector and policeman " that they played in the first half of the century. Television, video recorders, cars, drugs, and violence have combined to create a different world. We live in a culture that is based on instant gratification and the quick fix.

Lastly, in the global economy that makes this nation interdependent with all other countries of the world, the menial labor intensive workforce just doesn't exist to the same extent it did even 10 years ago. Today's youth face a world that is totally alien to people over 45. The leading manufacturers are looking for a skilled labor force where teams of workers take the lead in problem solving. The days are gone when youth can drop-out of school and find steady employment with enough pay to support a family. The demise of our railroads, closing of the mines, and reduction in factories all are a part of the changing economy of this country.

The strict discipline of the earlier part of the century won't work today either. Students have been encouraged to speak out, and in many cases latch-key kids have had to take over the parental role with younger siblings while their parents are working. Measures to re-create a strict external discipline code have resulted in more students getting expelled or suspended, and they in turn get into trouble, which helps account for increases in juvenile crime. What is sorely needed is a focused, persistent effort on the part of all adults to teach our youth problem solving skills and to become responsible for their own actions.

MYTH 3: Outcomes-based education is just another way to dumb down the curriculum.

People who use this argument simply don't understand outcomes-based theory. The theory is really quite simple. It is based on a belief that all students can learn and learn well, if given time. Those who don't subscribe to an outcomes-based approach believe in the scarcity model of economics that says that only a certain few can have something. Therefore, the belief is that only a few students can achieve an A, or B. Outcomes-based means that the expected skill and level at which the student is expected to learn that skill are well-defined prior to beginning teaching. Students, parents, and teachers clearly understand the expected outcome which takes all the mystery out of learning. Students and teachers become better focused on the skill, and those who need more time are provided with additional exercises, time, or adult intervention to achieve at that level. Anything less that the stated outcome is not acceptable. Therefore, all students achieve more and not less under this model. Enrichment activities are provided for those students who achieve the outcome early.

MYTH 4: Teaming experiences are not productive or helpful for gifted and talented kids.

One of the problems gifted individuals often encounter in the world of work is that they've not ever learned to work in teams. While they are "book" smart, they often have few people skills that are necessary for problem-solving in the real world. Often these individuals (our best and brightest) are unable to function in an arena other than the academic one, and therefore are not able to optimize their talents. These students can and should be our future leaders but unless they learn to work with a variety of other people, some with less intellect than they, we can predict they will not achieve success in today's modern world.

Corporations often say that they can teach people about their organization, the required technical skills, and even how to operate the machines, but they cannot teach them how to work together in teams. This is one area where our K-12 system is not meeting customer requirements.

MYTH 5: Not every student should be able to get an 'A.'

This again is an example of the scarcity theory of economics. Some people would argue that if student X can learn something in 10 days that takes student Y 15 days to learn, then only Student X can be said to deserve an 'A'. On the contrary, instead of measuring length of time to achieve something, isn't' it more important to measure actual learning? If both have learned, then what need is there to punish student Y by giving him a lower grade? We subscribe to doing away with grades since they automatically create winners and losers. Losers become to believe that they "can't" do things, and give up.

MYTH 6: Grades are an accurate measure of learning.

Think about your own experience in K-12. Did receiving an 'A' grade necessarily correlate with knowledge or was it more an indication that you were able to regurgitate back to the teacher information that you memorized, without truly understanding the concepts? A good measure of this is your ability to retell or reframe your understanding of that concept now. If you can, then you probably have a good understanding of the concept—if not, then ask yourself if you ever really understood it.

Grading systems vary from one teacher to another; from one school to another, and consequently are not true indicators of achievement and learning. Assessment based on quality factors, using operational definitions, provides the most accurate measure of learning.

MYTH 7:  Homework is essential to learning.

Many teachers give homework, and many school districts insist their teachers give homework. Often homework is repetition of the work done in class while other times homework is entirely new material.  If students truly understand the concept being taught during school, is there a need for homework?

Often parents are expected to "help" the child with his homework. For many, especially those who had difficulty in school, this creates anxiety and frustration. In many cases, doing homework becomes a source of tension between the child and parent(s).

The question we have about homework is this:  what is its purpose? What is the teacher's purpose and mission in the classroom? If the homework has relevance to what is being taught, is necessary, and if it relates to the real world, then there is a place for it. On the other hand, if homework is just repetition of what was covered in class, or busywork, the student will view it as irrelevant and/or punishment. In either case, if the goal is to create life-long learners, then school work must never be viewed as punishment or as irrelevant. Sometimes teachers lose sight of what it is like to be a child with almost every minute of their day structured with school, lessons, practice, chores, etc. Allowing time for relaxation and fun is an important feature of everyone's life and is an important thing for teachers to consider before assigning any homework.

## STUDENTS AS WORKERS

One aspect of the great paradigm shift for teachers is in the way students are viewed. Releasing oneself from the traditional view of students is critical to make the shift to quality. This is not to be taken lightly and must be carefully considered. In quality systems, students are viewed as both the primary customer and the worker within the system. In this chapter, we put the student-as-worker concept under the microscope. The diagram below helps draw the relationship of teacher as the classroom manager and the student as worker. That is, students are expected to perform the assignments or the work, within the processes leading to the system that the teacher has created.

**Teacher Works ON The System**

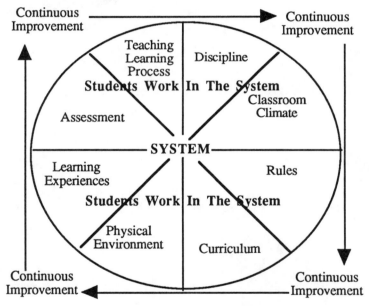

**Teacher Works ON The System**

Below we have flow charted an assignment in a traditional classroom.

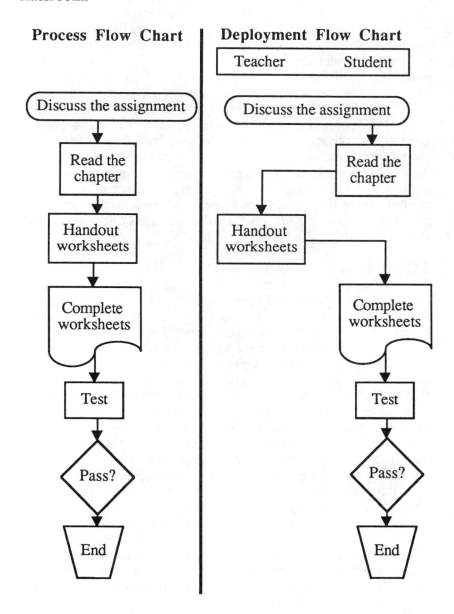

**Process Flow Chart**

Discuss the assignment

Read the chapter

Handout worksheets

Complete worksheets

Test

Pass?

End

**Deployment Flow Chart**

Teacher          Student

Discuss the assignment

Read the chapter

Handout worksheets

Complete worksheets

Test

Pass?

End

You can see from the flow charts that there is no room in the processes within this system for students to evaluate their activities or the way in which they are supposed to achieve the end product which, in this case, is to pass the test after having mastered the material. Consequently, if there is a mismatch between teaching and learning styles, a student in this class will be unable to function optimally. If there are too few materials, or if the materials are not adequate, students will be unable to achieve optimally. If the assignment does not have relevance to the student's world, or doesn't understand how learning this particular skill fits into his future, there is little incentive to conceptualize and assimilate the material. None of the above is an indictment of the teacher, but rather each represents system flaws that could be resolved with input from the workers. Deming and other quality experts believe that workers (down on the factory floor—i.e., those working within the system) are in the best position to make suggestions for improvement. It is not a stretch to view students as workers within the classroom system. Since they are the ones who day in and day out, must produce assignments within the rules that are controlled by the teacher.

## STEPS TO SYSTEM IMPROVEMENT
As previously discussed, begin the school year with an introduction to quality management theory. The conversation can begin with a historical overview of Dr. Deming and the other quality leaders, or that can take place later. This overview is necessary because students need to realize why you have chosen to do things differently. Everyone over 30 can understand the story about Japan and the products they produced as being JUNK. But what about students today? For the most part, they grew up in a world where Japanese products have been revered for their quality, reliability, and technology. Few students can recall when Japanese products were considered JUNK, so the brief history lesson about quality is important.

Along with that, we recommend a brief discussion about what has happened in our country with our major corporations. Some students, perhaps not the youngest, can relate very well to stories about the auto industry, television, video games, computer chips, etc. If you are unfamiliar with these stories, do some research. Children will be fascinated (depending on the way you tell the stories) and many can relate because their parents may work for one of those companies, or may work in a retail store that sells televisions, etc. You'll need to put the quality story into context for children and youth so that they can link the information to their own lives. Stories about Nintendo™, Domino's™ Pizza, Louisville Slugger™ bats, Etch-a-Sketch™, IBM™ and Apple™ Computer can help bring the quality story to life for students.

Follow this discussion with a general conversation about quality and what it means to do quality work. Then, move the students into a discussion about things that make it easier to learn and things that make it more difficult. You may get some excellent clues right away from the students as to what can be done to help make it better. Let the students know that you are serious about asking them for help. You might want to talk about an experience you had in school where no matter how hard you tried, you just couldn't understand something.

A personal example of this came when I (MLB) took high school chemistry. No matter how hard I tried to do the problems, I managed to get every one wrong. The mathematics part never made sense to me, and though my lab partner was a good student, she was unable to explain it adequately to me. It became clear to me that by not having learned the mathematics necessary to do the chemistry problems I would never be successful in chemistry. It also taught me that I never wanted to take another mathematics course because it would be impossibly difficult for me. The high school teacher never took the opportunity to talk to me about my difficulties, but simply graded every test and lab experiment and gave me C-, D's, and F's. I never took the opportunity to talk to the teacher about it either, perhaps out of fear of being considered *stupid*. I kept thinking that this would all end soon and was glad that I'd never have to take another science or math class. It never occurred to me to question whether or not my classmates understood, but instead we (the teacher and students) just continued along, never stopping to review the tests nor analyze incorrectly answered questions. One thing we did do is get through the curriculum. I'll never know how my classmates fared in that class, but I do know that for someone who had been given a chemistry set for Christmas one year and who loved the mystery of it all, that class squelched my interest in science in general.

Had my chemistry teacher viewed me as his customer, he would have realized that the opportunity for improvement was enormous. Clearly I didn't understand chemistry and in fact, became very frustrated and upset.

If my teacher had viewed me as a worker within that system, he could have tapped into a whole new source of information about his teaching techniques, the assignments, and the experiments. In effect, he lost the valuable resource that we refer to as research and development. Indeed, students are research and development experts, waiting like the proverbial diamond, to be discovered, cut, and polished.

Perhaps each of you can recall a time either in K-12 or higher education when things just weren't working for you in some class. It is hard to imagine one who hasn't been affected. The question is, if that teacher had taken the time to ask for your help would you have been willing to offer help? If so, do you think it would have helped make the class/course better for others besides yourself?

Sometimes teachers are afraid to ask students for help because they think the students will turn on them. Perhaps they are more afraid that they will *hear*, perhaps for the first time, that they are not a success. This must be tied to teachers' fear of evaluation. We have put teachers in the position of being the "expert" for so long, that it is frightening for them to think that they may not know all the answers.

Educators have long been known for their problem solving as evidenced in many traditional systems where problems are solved immediately by the principal or teacher. When scheduling problems arise, the administrative team hastily makes a decision to resolve them. Whatever the education related problem that has arisen, either the teacher or the administrator has apparently "solved" it. The problem is this: action without knowledge rarely makes the system better over time, and occasionally makes the situation worse! That has too often been the result of "problem solving" by educators.

**In a quality classroom, action is rarely if ever taken without first analyzing root causes of problems and embarking on a plan-do-study-act (PDSA) cycle for process improvement.**

Given this, what part does the student as worker play in the scheme of a quality classroom? The learning experiences in a quality classroom are characterized by student action, rather than passive receipt of processed information. Students are continually led into new work and unfamiliar territory. Once skills are "won," they must be reapplied to new problems in new ways.

In this configuration, students always operate at the edge of their competence. Therefore, it must be clear to them that a mistake is not a failure, but an attempt at innovation. They must realize that positive, constructive scrutiny of those mistakes by the rest of the class can only occur in an atmosphere free of fear where students never have to risk embarrassment.

Consider the situation in Mrs. Parker's sixth grade English class at Jonesville Middle School. Mrs. Parker has been using quality processes for over a year. She has tried to engage her fellow faculty members in moving towards continuous quality improvement but so far has been unsuccessful in gaining any allies. Two teachers have become very curious of late but are not convinced that this student empowerment stuff makes sense.

The first two weeks of school Mrs. Parker spent preparing her students to engage in quality. She started with a variety of trust-building exercises because she knew this was crucial to students working cooperatively without making cruel comments about each other. She believed in the importance of **building trust.**

Trust and respect remain the foundation upon which a Quality Classroom can be built. If the foundation is weak, progress will be sporadic and lead to frustration, and eventually the disenfranchised students will opt out.

---

**A Quality Classroom cannot be built
in an atmosphere of distrust.**

---

**Trust within the classroom means students can:**
• Take "learning" risks without fear of being shamed
• Express their opinions about the learning experience without fear of being punished, ridiculed, or ignored
• Be responsible for solving problems
• Focus on learning without a coercive atmosphere

**Trust within the classroom means teachers can:**
• Allow students to co-create the learning environment and learning experiences
• Release the "need" to control
• Focus on leadership
• Develop and use students' problem solving skills so more time can be spent learning
• Seek data from internal and external customers freely and use it as a basis for improvement

# TRUST BUILDING EXERCISES

There are a variety of trust activities you can engage students in. These range from a simple "fall back" into the arms of a classmate, to going on a "blind walk" to having the entire class (with teacher) go through a ropes course. A ropes course may not be readily available at school or in the community, but many of these activities can be done within the parameters of the classroom, gym, or outdoors. They can be adapted to fit the age of the students. As with any activity though, care must be taken to ensure the safety of all students.

## Example 1:  Fall Back

Have students get into pairs of about the same size and weight. Students who are going to do the "falling" will stand with their backs to their partners, one long step away. The "catcher" will extend his or her arms, and yell "Are you ready?" The one who will fall must respond loudly, "Ready!" The catcher then says: "Fall back NOW!" At which time, the faller stiffens her/his back and legs and with arms at their sides falls backward into the catcher's arms. Do not attempt this exercise without first stressing the seriousness of the exercise and let all students know the importance of keeping each other from getting hurt.

## Example 2.  Walk across the Swamp

Divide the students into teams. Cut out pieces of cardboard (rocks) of varying sizes and shapes, but be certain that each is only big enough for two feet (better to err slightly on the smaller size than the larger). Make enough "rocks" so that each team member has one. Mark out a distance of about 20 or 30 feet that represents the swamp and have the teams line up behind each other on one side of the swamp. The objective is to get everyone on the team across the swamp without anyone "falling in."

Prior to letting the students begin, embellish on the story of this particular alligator-filled swamp. Be certain to explain how hungry the alligators are, and that they are meat eaters so anyone who falls in will surely become eaten.

Each team must decide who the leader will be and what position each of the other team members will be in. Teams are given a minute or so to determine this. Then, give all the "rocks" to the last person in line. The team must decide the best way to get across the swamp.

If anyone falls off a rock, the team has to go back to the beginning and start over. It isn't necessary to make this a competition; however, most groups will automatically compete.

After everyone has successfully gotten across, have the team select someone other than the leader or the last person in line to be the recorder. Then, ask each team these questions:

- How did you determine your team's strategy for getting across?
- How important was the leader?
- How important was the last person in line?
- What was the role of the other team members?
- Was anyone more important or valuable to the team than the rest?
- Could you improve the way your team was moving across? Or did your team shift during the middle of the game?
- Is there a lesson to be learned from this exercise in terms of future teaming events?

There are many books that are helpful for trust and team building activities; for example, Karl Rohnke, *Bottomless Baggie* , Dubuque, Iowa: Kendall/Hunt Publishing Co, 1991.

Fear is an overwhelming issue for all students and the more fear invades the classroom, the less willing the students will be to work together. Building trust among students isn't as easy as it might seem. The older the student, the more negative experiences they may have had with classmates. You may have students with long-standing disagreements with classmates. Bias and prejudice are factors that must be overcome also. Students who have experienced put downs, name calling and the like are going to be understandably less willing to take risks than others.

Young children have fewer experiences upon which to judge others, and therefore are much easier to work with. However, by the fifth or sixth grade, building trust gets more difficult and high school students have definite opinions of who they trust. This is why it is crucial that we engage all students in teaming exercises as often as possible, and continue this method of problem solving throughout K-12. Students who can't or won't work together have a distinct disadvantage upon high school graduation.

We are not suggesting that every learning experience has to be a team effort, but that teaming become a routine part of schooling. There can and should be opportunities for students to engage in individual research as well, and the two experiences need not be at odds with each other.

## WHAT CAN BE DONE ABOUT STUDENTS WHO REFUSE TO PARTICIPATE?

As previously mentioned, you will undoubtedly find situations where some students simply refuse to work together. These may be students who present themselves as being "tough," but who refuse to engage in trust activities. These situations always present a dilemma to teachers.

First, understand that one reason they don't want to participate is that they are frightened. Second, they are frightened because of past experience or because of an imagined future. The point is they are unwilling to risk because they view the cost as too high.

Patience and understanding are your biggest allies. Some students can be teased into participating, but you'll need to know the kids and be careful when using that tactic. We recommend that you find ways to develop a rapport and see if they'll eventually share with you some of the reasons for the fear. Whatever you do, **never** embarrass or humiliate a student. It will be nearly impossible for you to establish a good rapport and engage him/her as part of the team or class because s/he simply won't trust you.

You can engage some of the more reluctant students more readily when you combine trust activities into teaming activities wherein kids have to solve puzzles as a group. The alligator in the swamp is one of those, but there are many others. These are also good ways to build rapport within a group. Set some guidelines for group discussion after the experience, and ask the students similar questions to those suggested for the alligator exercise.

The following are examples of team-building activities borrowed from Thompson Intermediate School in Houston, TX. Special thanks to Principal Vicki Thomas and Counselor, Patricia Sermas for sharing these.

| Activity | Purpose | Props | Length | Description |
|---|---|---|---|---|
| Team Beam Walk | Cooperation, Strategy, and Communication | Two 4"x 4"x 8' beams with holes drilled through the beam every 12' and 8 lengths of rope threaded through the holes. | 1 hour | Each team is allowed 45 minutes to develop strategy and accomplish the task. 8 team members step on the beams and hang on to the ropes. Each team must travel a preset course on the beams and must restart if they fall off. |
| Follow the Leader | Trust and Communication | Blindfolds for all team members except one | 1.5 hours | Students form a long line with hands on the shoulders of the person in front of them. All have blindfolds except the leader. The leader leads the team through obstacles and members must communicate with the person behind them. |

As in all learning experiences, allow time to reflect and debrief after every exercise. Students may not be used to having reflective time, or time to talk about the problems they encountered and how they would improve the process if there were time to repeat it. The debriefing sessions are as valuable as the actual activity. You are establishing a form for the class to take as you move through the school year. You'll want students to feel comfortable expressing their opinions in an effort to improve every single process. This is a key factor in engaging students as research and development experts. In essence, you are asking them to portray that role every time you debrief and engage in the Plan-Do-Study-Act cycle.

∧∧∧∧∧∧∧∧

The following is a checksheet tool to help the teacher to implement the **Quality Fusion** technique into their classroom.

Step 1: The mission, goals and academic integrity of your class are absolutely clear.
- √ Established a classroom mission statement.
- √ Developed personal goals for the class.
- √ Communicated mission and goals to parents/guardians.
- √ Aligned classroom mission and goals with those of the school district and the school.

Step 2: You are demonstrating leadership.
- √ Developed a definition of a total quality classroom.
- √ Walk-the-Talk about quality.
- √ Understand Deming's system of **Profound Knowledge**.
- √ Use a variety of teaching styles.
- √ Have a CQI program for self and for my students.

Step 3: All work is pertinent and flows from the students.
- √ Broke down barriers on day one by establishing a classroom mission statement with the students.
- √ Having students co-create learning experiences.
- √ Stressing the importance of teamwork in problem solving and decision making.
- √ Defined quality and what it means.
- √ Created interdisciplinary learning activities.

Step 4: The course content is connected to the surrounding community and the real world.
- √ Demonstrated the connectedness between work and the real world.
- √ Asked the students to analyze the learning assignments.
- √ Began TQM training for the students.
- √ Implemented student suggestions on how best to improve the learning system.

Step 5: The student is treated as a "worker," but s/he is also considered as a valuable team member of the "research and development" department.
- √ Gave the students an historical overview about the quality movement and discussed examples.
- √ Discussed the P-D-C-A cycle and root causes of problems.

## Chapter Six:  Peer teaching, small group work, and team work are emphasized.

In quality classrooms, students and the teacher view themselves as part of the larger group. Everyone has a sense of the need to work together and help each other. The concept of cheating doesn't exist since everyone is working towards gaining more knowledge and combining it with existing knowledge to create new knowledge. Students are led by their teacher and classmates to know where and how to access information which becomes more important than memorizing facts.

One must be careful not to imagine that some base knowledge is not important, because it is crucial and provides the foundation upon which all future knowledge is born. However, the way this material is presented and learned is different. For instance, dittos, if used at all, are kept to an absolute minimum. Rote memorization is seldom useful. This might cause some discomfort to those more traditional teachers who believe that certain things like: multiplication tables and spelling words; states and their capitals; president's names or certain historical dates must be memorized. Consider that all this information can be gleaned from using a dictionary, a calculator, a map, or a book. Doesn't it truly make more sense to have students learn to use the tools of learning that can open up the entire universe to them as they need it, rather than have them memorize some facts to store in their short-term memory to regurgitate on a test?

What changes in the quality classroom is the WHY question. Students and teachers must understand why they are being asked to learn something, and if it has no meaning in their life, they probably will resist learning it. Some students, those who are vested in pleasing adults, will go along with whatever the teacher asks, but even these students have trouble recalling facts that have not been placed in context or learned in the context of some assignment with meaning.

Many would argue that multiplication facts, along with adding, subtracting and dividing are crucial to the understanding of mathematics. True, we do need to understand the underlying logic, but to what extent must the short-term memorization proceed? It would seem that if teachers deem it important for children to learn their multiplication tables to 10, then there must be a fun way to do this. Repetitiveness makes learning drudgery.

## ENGAGE THE "WORKERS"
A key element of a quality classroom is engaging students to help make the learning fun! Teachers know the intended

outcomes, and students know what makes learning fun! Why not combine the expertise of all and seek help from students as to how best to learn something.

**Example:** Katy Sullivan's third grade class was ready to progress to multiplication tables. Katy introduced her children to the idea by bringing a magician to class. She had briefed the magician earlier on the lesson(s) she wanted students to gain from this experience. Her mission was to have them become so intrigued by the fact that he could take one or two items and turn them into 4 or 6 that the students would want to learn how to multiply. The magician used cards, brightly colored scarves, eggs, balls, and even rabbits and birds. The children were delighted and maintained their attention level throughout the show. Later that day, the students were asked to write a story, with illustrations, about the magic show and imagine themselves as the magician or his/her helper. She also asked them to recall how many brightly colored scarves, eggs, balls, and even rabbits and birds the magician had to start with and how many he ended with. She asked the students to speculate on how he did his tricks.

On the next day, Katy showed the students the math outcomes they would be expected to know, and asked them for suggestions about how they wanted to learn them. Students came up with a wide variety of suggestions. Some were: (1) counting peanuts within their shells or counting peas within their pods and graphing them to make a multiplication table; (2) using coins to multiply to come up with a fixed amount, *e.g.* how many dimes make a dollar? The group agreed that it would be fun to use everyone's suggestions and to create learning centers around the room. Eight teams of three or four students were formed and their task was to create a multiplication "game" for their classmates to use. The class agreed that in order to be successful, each game had to have clear directions, materials, and a chart that would be generated. Students would tell Ms. Sullivan what additional materials were needed to play the game and she promised to have them by the next day.

During the next day the students were busy preparing their games and experimenting with the directions. They played their own game and kept track of the time it took the team to finish. Each time, students kept a chart of how long it took from beginning to end to play. After several attempts, the students averaged the amount of time it took for them to complete the game, and this became the cycle time used for all teams. With the help of Ms. Sullivan they made the following table.

| Team | Attempt #1 | Attempt #2 | Attempt #3 | Average |
|------|-----------|-----------|-----------|---------|
| A | 48 min | 50 min | 45 min | 47.7 min |
| B | 38 min | 42 min | 40 min | 40.0 min |
| C | 46 min | 45 min | 40 min | 43.7 min |
| D | 59 min | 57 min | 50 min | 55.3 min |
| E | 39 min | 38 min | 35 min | 37.3 min |
| F | 46 min | 44 min | 45 min | 45.0 min |
| G | 45 min | 44 min | 42 min | 43.6 min |
| H | 49 min | 47 min | 44 min | 46.7 min |
| Total | 370 min | 367 min | 341 min | 44.9 min |

Teams added up their times and figured the average amount of time it took to play. Then, they calculated the class average and agreed upon 50 minutes for the cycle time as a start.

When they were finished, two groups (one student from each of the four other teams) formed and ran through a trial run of each of the four games. These students (the quality team) completed a questionnaire about each game and gave their responses to the team who created the game for improvement based on suggestions from the "Q" team. Students were thus able to get and give feedback without having anyone become upset. They were learning how to assess each other's work based on set criteria or quality factors.

Armed with the "Q" team suggestions for improvement, each team determined the feasibility of implementing the recommendations for change. They agreed to keep track of the changes made, and continue to give the questionnaire to all students who played their game to determine whether or not the improvements helped make the game more efficient by reducing cycle time, and added value (fun and complexity) to the game.

By the following day, everyone was ready. The students came in and set up their learning centers, and the class created a chart showing where teams would start and how everyone would move through the class so everyone had the opportunity to learn all the games. The class agreed to use one hour per day playing a game per day and taking time to complete the questionnaire. The team who constructed the game would then tabulate the questionnaires each day. Students also agreed to keep track of the time it took them to complete each game using a run chart. An example is shown below.

Name: <u>Bobby Martin</u>        Team # <u>1</u>

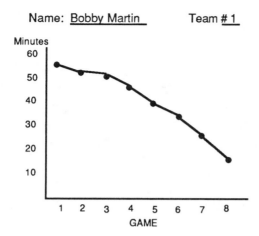

Ms. Sullivan knew what all the games were and how they related to multiplication tables. She became the facilitator for each team by supporting their ideas, getting the materials they needed, expanding their thinking about the game and the learning outcomes, and helping them with setting up their charts. She also knew where the gaps would be in learning multiplication from this method and counseled student teams to close the gaps.

Students noticed that by the end of the fourth day everyone was finished before the allotted fifty minutes. They agreed to go back and reduce the cycle time by recalculating the average amount of time it took students to finish the game. The agreed upon time was changed to forty minutes. After the sixth game, students were mastering each game much more quickly so the cycle time was again reduced, this time to twenty-three minutes. By keeping track of this on a large chart on the wall the students had a picture of their progress. This, too, became part of the fun.

Lastly, Katy also created some "games" for the students. These became the way students would be tested for mastery. The students viewed these as more games. This was all part of the fun. Some of the games were team games in which students could help each other. Other games were for pairs to work together, and last were the games for individuals. By the time this exercise was over, everyone knew the multiplication tables and had a good time. Katy was careful not to test everyone on all the tables, instead used a Bingo bin to select a random sample of tables, and this became part of the game. If everyone understands the concept, in this case, the underlying logic of multiplication, then there is no need to go through the entire times tables. It makes much more sense to randomly select 6-10 examples and have the students answer those.

Afterwards, Katy got out the calculators and told the students to quiz each other just for five minutes to see how many right answers they could come up with. One person on each team had the calculator and punched up the problem while the others gave the response.

Using this approach everyone had fun, learned the multiplication tables, and learned to use the multiplication function on the calculator.

From the above example, we can see how important team work is to a quality classroom, and how these kinds of activities while promoting faster learning are also fun! Classrooms where fun is combined with learning will achieve at a faster rate.

## NEVER A NEVER & NEVER AN ALWAYS

We **don't** suggest students always work in teams, however, because there is great benefit to learning to work independently as well. It is crucial that students also learn to follow a task through from start to finish. Some very, very bright students have so many creative thoughts running through their heads that sometimes they are unable to focus on anything long enough to complete a task. Learning to follow-through and accomplish the goal is vital to success in life. Therefore, we recommend teachers find a way to mix the learning experiences so that students spend part of each day working independently from a team or partner.

Independent work does not mean that you abandon the idea of peer teaching, having fun, or working on meaningful experiences. It does not mean that you revert to the use of dittos or answering questions at the end of a chapter. What we are talking about is an individual learning experience with varying degrees of complexity that has meaning to the student.

**Example**: Keith Axelrod is a 7 and 8th grade team teacher at Fort Walton Middle School. Keith has his students working on communication skills. Since this is a crucial skill for future success, he wants to have his students get as much practice as possible. He asks his students to complete a card indicating their hobbies, favorite foods, favorite books, favorite movie, favorite sport, biggest fears, what makes them happy, etc. Using this as a catalyst for a learning experience, he asks the students if they could communicate with one person they "look up to," perhaps a local hero or maybe a national figure, what would they like to say? They engage in the discussion and by the end of twenty minutes or so, each determined one person they'd like to write to. Names are placed on the board, beside the student's name.

Students then take about ten minutes to write "why" they'd like to communicate with the individual selected. Depending on the class, the results are discussed or kept private. This gives the students the opportunity to make decisions about what they want to share. Either way it doesn't detract from the learning experience.

Next, the students develop the conversation around ways to write an effective expressive letter. Have students expouse the "WOW" or quality factors. Those elements that are not mentioned by the students can easily be inserted by the teacher. Write all suggestions on the board.

Finally, the students give each other suggestions about the way(s) such a written piece of communication might be developed. For instance, students may need to do some research prior to writing. If so, what do they need to know in order to create a letter that communicates their ideas and generates the questions they would like answered. You may have to "prime the pump" at first, until everyone gets the idea, but it is much more powerful to allow students to come up with these suggestions.

For instance, you might have on the list that sentences must be complete and that there has to be an introduction, middle, and conclusion. These are listed on the board.

When all suggestions, including yours, are exhausted, explain to the students that they've created **operational definitions** (see appendix), or product specifications, for writing the best letter to their selected hero or national figure. Be certain to include an explanation of the importance of operational definitions. If you'd like, you can relate this to manufacturing, stating that these are the product specifications (the blueprints, if you will) that if met, result in a quality product or one that meets the identified "WOW" factors.

The above example is an individual learning experience, and one that you can integrate along with other team experiences throughout the day. Students will appreciate the variety, and productivity will increase.

## ASSESSMENT

However, individual learning experiences, can also be integrated with peer teaching and pairing. Part of this experience is teaching students to assess their work as well as the work of their peers. Assessing truly is an art, and one that requires facilitation and mentoring by the teacher. Children, especially at the middle and high school levels, often can be cruel with those they somehow view as "less" bright than they. This can become a difficult and tricky issue, and one that requires a great deal of sensitivity for teachers and students.

Peer assessment and/or self-assessment are skills that can be taught, and once implemented, can yield great rewards for students. However, you must realize that if the students have any fears of receiving a lower grade because of self-assessment it will be impossible for them to be honest in their assessment. Analysis of this makes perfect sense, since we generally do not willingly engage in things that we know will bring harm to us.

It is not difficult to imagine the sensitivity that must be used when broaching the subject of self-assessment and peer assessment. However, it is a key concept in a quality classroom due to the vast advantages that can spring forth from its use. For example, students who can assess their work demonstrate a tremendous ability to know how much more is required of them to complete the task. These students work on the concept of continuous improvement and are not concerned when others complete the task sooner. Furthermore, when students become comfortable with their peers assessing their work, they soon realize how important and valuable it is to gain feedback from another person. Too often, especially in writing assignments, the writer has difficulty viewing his work from another perspective. By using peer and self-assessment techniques, we can move students forward in creating much more refined works.

Sometimes peer assessment can split the class if some students decide to be particularly harsh when assessing classmates work. Realistically, we have to recognize that some students may have received ill treatment from their peers. That's why it is important to give whatever time it takes to teach students ways to assess others' work without making personal attacks on each other.

The next step is to provide everyone with some guidelines for assessing each other's work. The best way to keep peer assessment out of the personal realm is to remind students of the operational definitions and quality factors already agreed upon by the group. Use those as the rubric guide.

There really shouldn't be any questions (not many for certain) because the operational definitions must be measurable. For example: *The use of good paragraphs* is not an operational definition since "good paragraph" cannot be measured. How would one know necessarily what a good paragraph was except to mentally take a paragraph apart and analyze it. The result of your analysis does create operational definitions.

The class will be able to do this, but you may need to prompt them somewhat in the beginning. We suggest that after students complete the peer assessment rubric, they write some comments and suggestions for improvement. After, provide time for peers to reflect with their partner about the comments and rubric. This can be the most valuable part of the experience. Students learn excellent communication skills, and they also become mentors for their partner. It is this synergy of students working together to help each other make greater gains than they could have gotten independently that is so exciting for students and the teacher. Indeed, the reward of using this approach is not simply that individual students make greater gains, it is in seeing how students come to value each other in completely different ways. They begin to view each other as resources other than for social events.

To facilitate this process, it is a good idea to generate some samples and have students practice. Your samples can become more complex as they've had practice with the more obviously flawed one(s). After each practice run engage students in a conversation about how they've scored it and the comments made. Have them compare responses and provide samples until students become familiar with the format and begin to get consensus on scoring. Always remember to review the operational definitions and WOW factors prior to giving out the sample.

Our sense is that you could certainly do this with third graders and possibly even younger students. Certainly, it can become a routine part of every student's school experience from fourth grade through graduation.

Peer assessment has another almost immeasurable value too. That is, by assessing others' work your own improves. Just as research has shown that one of the best ways to learn something is to teach it, the same value comes from assessing others work. Though we know this to be true, few actually use this technique in the classroom. Many teachers have students correct the objective tests of others, but this is not what we're recommending.

The peer assessment method is so powerful that you'll wonder why you never tried it before. It is a natural outgrowth of the concept of continuous improvement, and based on the measurable operational definitions, gives students real guidelines for assessing without making personal attacks. This also teaches students the value of accepting constructive criticism gracefully.

In a real sense, the students are not criticizing, they are assessing each other's work for quality.

By the time the student is ready to turn the product of any learning experience into the teacher for assessment, there should be almost no doubt about whether it is quality. Indeed, the teacher is in the position of asking the student if s/he has met all the quality factors. If the answer is YES, then the product is accepted. If the answer is NO, then the student can ask the teacher for an assessment and recommendations for improvement. Students then go back and continue working until all quality factors are met. In a quality classroom, the only acceptable product is QUALITY!

## DRIVE OUT FEAR

Of course, you'll need to find a way to take the fear out of all this by reducing the dependency on grading. Students must be weaned away from passivity in their learning and become much more proactive. Passivity comes from fear! Educators have succeeded in training students not to evaluate their work, but to create products solely for the teacher and to become totally dependent on the teacher for information about their success or failure. If you're having trouble with this, do a reality check within your classroom. **These are the symptoms of fear:**

---

Students are:
- quiet, talking is reduced or secretive
- talking behind the backs of others
- spreading rumors
- absenteeism increases
- dropping out of the class
- hiding problems and mistakes increase
- unwilling to challenge classroom processes or each other.
- blaming others—teacher and/or classmates
- unwilling to participate

Questions and suggestions are seen as criticisms.

Students have an "US" versus "THEM" attitude

---

Furthermore, the effects of fear on the organization or class are:
- Lack of cooperation
- Unwillingness to go the extra mile

- Failure to succeed—mistakes are hidden
- Inability to solve problems
- Lack of creativity and innovation—new ideas are "blown out."
- Lack of self-esteem
- Lack of commitment, motivation, confidence.

Clearly, the result of a fear-driven class is devastating on the success of the whole, but also the achievement level of students. Teachers who operate in a fear-based culture experience the effects listed above and then wonder why students are unmotivated.

It is important to reduce fear as much as possible to optimize the learning experience. Some teachers fear that anarchy will ensue if they enlist the student's help in resolving classroom process problems. Nothing could be further from the truth, providing that students believe trust and respect reign within the classroom. Of course, without trust and respect, you'll never be able to come close to a quality classroom, so those issues must be addressed early.

The question of how to coexist within a system that forces you to give grades and have students become comfortable with self-assessment and peer assessment remains. There is really no good answer to that question, probably because as long as grades are involved there will always be a lingering element of fear. But some things can help.

For one thing, for each learning experience it is essential that a time line be established so that everyone can understand the logical cycle time for completion. Within that time line, make it clear to students that they are free to have peer evaluations at any time along the way, as often as they'd like. Encourage students to assess themselves along the way, too. Reduce the dependency on you, to the extent possible, by letting students know that you will be available for guidance and mentoring, but that it is important for them to engage their peers as well. Peer assessments help everyone since the assessor learns as much as the one being assessed. Therefore, assessments are a valuable part of the learning process.

## THE TEACHER'S ROLE
A major role of the teacher is to be aware of which students are "stuck" and need guidance. This means the teacher maintains an active role in facilitating and mentoring. Teachers within a quality classroom rarely have time to sit idly while their students are working. Certainly if a general trend becomes apparent, the

teacher will seize the opportunity to work with a group of students and/or the entire class in clarifying a point or providing further guidance. Perhaps it is a common, frequent grammatical error that students are making. The teacher might rightly assume that when this was taught, these students did not adequately learn it well enough to apply it to other situations. In such a case, the teacher would be wise to provide students with several examples of proper usage. There should be no shame or blame here, but quality teachers will take note, and at a later date do some investigating to determine where the breakdown in learning occurred. Although we will  not discuss this in detail , we recommend that when students repeatedly show deficiencies from previous classes that the teachers take any such information and recommend a cross-functional team of teachers to work together to improve the process at the point of breakdown in order to build quality into the student's education. Since this might become a sensitive point for some teachers, it is important to find a way to present the information without shaming or blaming your suppliers, *i.e.,* the previous teachers.

## PEER TUTORS.
Another example of students working with other students is peer tutoring. We really like the idea of having students help others. It provides a very strong, positive experience for all students, especially those who are having difficulty understanding. We've all heard about parents who object to having their child "tutored" by another, particularly one without top skills. Research has demonstrated, however, that teaching is the best way to learn. The reason is quite simple. In order to teach something you must have a deeper understanding of the subject, so the benefit to both teacher and student is enormous.

Another advantage of using peer tutors is that many times students respond better to their peers, or in one-on-one situations.  A rapport can be developed that will pay dividends well beyond one assignment. Once again, it is crucial that all students are trained in some basic principles of peer tutoring. Key among them is to ensure that no one uses coercion or other abusive tactics. Another is that the student being tutored must do the work and not the tutor. Sometimes students become impatient and want to do the work for their friend. In such cases, the child being tutored does not really make many learning gains.

You've probably already guessed that before engaging in any peer tutoring activities, you'll want to gather the class around and generate a discussion about how to optimize the effectiveness of the tutors. Ask students for suggestions about what is most helpful to them and be certain to include some things like: being friendly, calm, soft-spoken, etc. Make a list and keep it posted in the classroom. You'll probably also want the class to write these down as a constant reminder to them.

Another very effective technique is to have older students buddy up to tutor younger students. This works well on two fronts: (1) it makes the older student feel important and useful, and (2) it gives the younger student a support system beyond the class. Often a rapport develops that extends beyond the classroom into the lunchroom and beyond. Thus young students develop bonds with older students. This technique often makes everyone within the school feel that they share a common goal or purpose. This is truly a unifying force.

## CLASSROOM TEAMS

Teams within the classroom can take several forms. There are probably unlimited numbers and purposes of teams within the classroom. We will elaborate on several.

A **Quality Improvement Team** (QIT) functions to collect suggestions for improvement from other students, teachers, parents, and administration. This group might be selected randomly and changed every six or eight weeks. There are other ways to select this group, but in order to give everyone in the class an opportunity sometime throughout the year, and to select without bias, perhaps putting the names in a box and having students select the names is a better way to go. It's important not even to hint that only "certain" students will be selected. Invest everyone right away in the realization that this is their classroom and each person has an important role to play. As the names are selected, post them in a prominent place along with the period of time to be served. Next time, be certain not to include any names that were selected during the first round, and so forth until everyone has had a turn.

The importance of this team is to maintain the suggestion box, and/or to collect suggestions from students or teams throughout the school year. These are read with the teacher, and a determination is made how to proceed. Encourage students to make suggestions for improvement and post the names of students whose suggestions are implemented..

The team can select a leader who reads to the class any suggested improvement recommendations. Students are then polled to prioritize which suggested improvements they want to implement.

A **Quality Leadership Team** (QLT) provides over-all leadership to the class. Students are randomly selected from the entire class. The team probably functions best with only three members. They, too, should rotate monthly or at least periodically so everyone in the class has the opportunity to participate. This team takes care of collecting money, checking attendance, and tardiness. They collect data and use quality improvement tools to post the information so everyone can see where improvement takes place and where efforts for improvement still need to be looked at. The QLT works in tandem with the quality improvement team, and often bring ideas forth based on the data they've collected.

**EXAMPLE:** Sue Forester's eleventh grade social studies class has several projects going on that require meticulous attention, plus the school district also has strict policies on attendance and tardiness, so someone has to maintain careful records. The quality leadership team consists of Jose, Barbara, and Kelly. Their functions are to:

- Take attendance and monitor tardiness
- Collect money for field trips
- Maintain log of volunteer hours each student completed
- Maintain the calendar of events, with target dates for project completion and field trip expenses
- Meet with teacher to organize the field trip, including the itinerary and contacts with officials.

The team members work together to determine who will take responsibility for specific duties, what type of data needs to be collected, what form it will take, where it will be posted, and when and how they will report to the class. This class has determined that these three individuals will maintain their responsibility throughout the marking period since some of the activities, such as the field trip, will occur at the 7th week of school.

Once QLT members were selected, they led the class in a discussion about the possibility of going on a fall field trip. One of the first things the class had to determine was the criteria for selecting a site. They agreed that an optimal social studies field trip would 1) have a direct relationship to the course of study—government, 2) have interest for everyone, 3) be close enough to go and come in one school day, and 4) have potential for future resources and/or mentors. With these criteria stated on the board, the class engaged in a **nominal group process** (see appendix) for selecting a field trip. This brainstorming technique allows everyone the opportunity to participate in an organized, time-efficient fashion. The question students addressed was: *WHERE WILL WE GO ON OUR FALL FIELD TRIP?*

Each student was given a series of short forms. Each student was given five minutes to complete Form A, and to list three to five possible field trip opportunities that met the criteria. Kelly then asked each student to list his/her suggestions for Barbara to write on a flip chart. Below is the list generated that was generated.

### FORM A

| Item # | Field Trip Suggestion |
|--------|----------------------|
| 1      |                      |
| 2      |                      |
| 3      |                      |
| 4      |                      |
| 5      |                      |

The class compilation of suggestions was as shown in the following chart.

### CHART 1

| ITEM # | FIELD TRIP SUGGESTIONS | Initial Value | Final Value | Final Rank |
|--------|------------------------|---------------|-------------|------------|
| 1 | City Hall | | | |
| 2 | History Museum | | | |
| 3 | State Capitol | | | |
| 4 | Newspaper office | | | |
| 5 | Federal Court | | | |
| 6 | County Courthouse | | | |
| 7 | Governor's Office and Home | | | |

When all suggestions were listed, the students prioritized their top five sites. The importance of doing this was to give them an opportunity to think about all the suggestions, not simply their own. The ranking process (#5 = the most important and #1= the least important) provided a better way to select a field trip opportunity than merely a hand vote. In this way, even if a student's first site was not selected, their second one might be. After doing an initial prioritization, the class discussed the results and did a final prioritization.

When the final values were tabulated, it was clear to everyone where they'd be going on their field trip. This entire process took about 45 minutes to complete, but by so doing a consensus was reached and students were empowered to make their own decision based upon criteria they had selected. Below is the list that was generated.

| ITEM # | FIELD TRIP SUGGESTIONS | Initial Value | Final Value | Final Rank |
|--------|------------------------|---------------|-------------|------------|
| 1 | City Hall | 90 | 69 | 5 |
| 2 | History Museum | 30 | 8 | 7 |
| 3 | State Capitol | 150 | 205 | 1 |
| 4 | Newspaper office | 100 | 40 | 6 |
| 5 | Federal Court | 70 | 95 | 3 |
| 6 | County Courthouse | 73 | 96 | 2 |
| 7 | Governor's Office and Home | 72 | 72 | 4 |

The class agreed that if the QLT could not establish a date to go to the state capitol they would give them permission to pursue a trip to the County Courthouse and if that didn't work out, to the Federal Court.

**FINALLY**
After the students recommended going to the state capitol for their field trip, the next step could have been to have them complete a **Force Field Analysis** tool which would have helped the class or the QLT to identify the perceived driving and restraining forces towards effecting the recommendation. The QLT could have taken these results and completed a **Systematic Diagram** as a planning tool to determine the specific action steps that would be necessary to accomplish the steps. These tools are described in the appendix.

ΛΛΛΛΛΛΛΛ

The following is a checksheet tool to help the teacher to implement the **Quality Fusion** technique into their classroom.

Step 1:    The mission, goals and academic integrity of your class are absolutely clear.
√    Established a classroom mission statement.
√    Developed personal goals for the class.
√    Communicated mission and goals to parents/guardians.
√    Aligned classroom mission and goals with those of the school district and the school.

Step 2:    You are demonstrating leadership.
√    Developed a definition of a total quality classroom.
√    Walk-the-Talk about quality.
√    Understand Deming's system of **Profound Knowledge**.
√    Use a variety of teaching styles.
√    Have a CQI program for self and for my students.

Step 3:    All work is pertinent and flows from the students.
√    Broke down barriers on day one by establishing a classroom mission statement with the students.
√    Having students co-create learning experiences.
√    Stressing the importance of teamwork in problem solving and decision making.
√    Defined quality and what it means.
√    Created interdisciplinary learning activities.

Step 4:    The course content is connected to the surrounding community and the real world.
√    Demonstrated the connectedness between work and the real world.
√    Asked the students to analyze the learning assignments.
√    Began TQM training for the students.
√    Implemented student suggestions on how best to improve the learning system.

Step 5:    The student is treated as a "worker," but s/he is also considered as a valuable team member of the "research and development" department.
√    Gave the students an historical overview about the quality movement and discussed examples.
√    Discussed the P-D-C-A cycle and root causes of problems.
√    Took action to establish an atmosphere of trust.

Step 6:   Peer teaching, small group work, and team work are emphasized.
√   Engaged the students in activities that emphasized teaming and making learning fun.
√   Engaged students to work independently away from the team, but encouraged them to report the results to their peers.
√   Provided guidelines and opportunities for students to assess each others' work.
√   Emphasized the systems approach and regularly asked the student of how we could reduce fear.
√   Provided students with the opportunity for peer tutoring.
√   Elaborated upon the types of quality teams.
√   Introduced the students to additional TQI tools and techniques.

# Chapter Seven: Students should have aesthetic experiences.

Superintendents, principals, and teachers alike have criticized the Secretary's Commission on Achieving Necessary Skills (SCANS) report from the U.S. Department of Labor for not including any creative or aesthetic experiences. Usually, the criticism is followed by a comment such as: "I'm not going to let business tell me how to educate children." One must be cautious about imposing this kind of criticism on business for the following reasons. First, the purpose of the report was simply to report to educators, corporate leaders, and government what skills will be required of the work force of the 21st century in order for the United States to remain competitive in a global economy. Second, the Department of Labor, which commissioned the report, never intended to tell schools these were the only desired skills or competencies, but rather the requisite work-related skills.

Any comment about not letting business tell educators what they should teach, and/or the skills students need to succeed in the future simply conveys ignorance about who the customers of education are. There are few ultimate customers of education and one of them happens to be business. They employ the students who come out of our educational systems and therefore have a major stake in the knowledge, skills, and abilities the students acquire. Indeed, the fact that educators have lost touch with employers is perhaps one of the causes of the decline in our educational system. So, if you haven't been communicating with local business and industry, this may be the time to do some outreach and start networking.

## WHY CREATIVITY?

It is possible that students can continue to crank out products for learning experiences that do not involve any creativity on their part, but it is impossible to imagine that anyone would take great joy or pride in doing so. Part of what drives human beings is the desire to create new things— new knowledge as well as new ways of doing something. Thus, creativity can be built into every learning experience simply by asking students how they want to learn. Left to their own devices (with some guidance from teachers) students will become more creative, take more learning risks, and value the experience more.

Imagination is what has made America great and what has kept us economically ahead of other countries. Imagination is the soul of learning. It is what future scientists, inventors, dancers, musicians, and yes, even corporate executives begin with. The very notion of questioning what is, and then asking "what if" leads to our greatest breakthrough inventions, technology, the arts, and even athletics. Everything great starts with an idea; a thought seed. If it can be imagined, it can happen! The axiom is simple, yet very profound.

Part of what makes learning fun is being able to use your imagination and ponder such questions as: what if the earth were square...or what would the world be like without any guns...or what will travel be like in the year 2020? These and similar questions force our brains to reach outside our current paradigms and build our current knowledge to create new knowledge. Speculation is one of the first steps to discovery.

Children who have regular opportunities to practice using their imaginations continue to use these skills and eventually become better communicators and more critical thinkers. These skills must be nurtured and allowed to grow, never stifled.

Adults often try to squelch the use of imagination in children perhaps because they (adults) have been so squelched that they've not used their imaginations for many years. Most adults seem much more comfortable in a world of facts than in a world of "what ifs." We often observe parents telling their small children to "be quiet," or become abrupt with them after the children ask the fourth "What is that and how does it work?" question. We believe that this is because parents (and perhaps teachers) don't know the answers, therefore, they become impatient and uncomfortable because they don't know. Wouldn't it be fun to let go of those fears and simply be able to go into a child's world of curiosity? Not knowing should never be an excuse for not wanting to know. So if students are curious and you don't know the answer, suggest that you discover it together. This kind of spontaneous learning might be what turns that child on to learning for life.

Perhaps more important for teachers is the research done by Elizabeth Kerr-Rike, the foremost authority on brain research and literacy in children. She makes a strong case for symbolic dramatic play beginning at about age 18 months or at the onset of language development. This is critical since research has shown that children who are deprived of the opportunity to engage in dramatic play (with the assistance of an adult) are left with few literacy skills. Children with these deficiencies never catch up when teachers use traditional methods. On the other hand, when these children are given the opportunity to engage in symbolic guided dramatic play, reading, writing and speaking skills do increase. Rike has successfully worked with toddlers, young children, adolescents, and adults and found this theory to be true under many difficult conditions. All elementary and middle school teachers, and English teachers or those who work with students with disabilities would profit from reading Rike's work *Guiding Dramatic Play* (1992). There are many simple, yet fun exercises you can do with students of all ages that will help them expand their thinking and improve their skills. Role playing is an excellent exercise and can be used in any class K-12.

## AESTHETICS IN EDUCATION

An educated person displays a keen interest in a wide variety of topics and has an appreciation for art, music, theater, and nature. Traditional schools don't do a very good job of nurturing students holistically, yet there is much more to life than the cognitive activities of school. Quality classrooms are able to engage students in a broad range of activities and demonstrate how they interface with each other.

The systems approach to learning emphasizes that nothing exists in a little box, separate from everything else, but that everything is a part of a larger whole. We must provide many opportunities for students to understand the connectedness of their world, and the universe to what we are teaching. This presupposes that we have spent time exploring the world beyond our subject matter as well.

Elementary art, for example, can be taught using the masters as examples, but also bringing in form, color, focus, and all the other elements of art. We've seen schools where even the youngest students are studying Picasso, Degas, Monet and the like. The students respond beautifully to this approach.

What if, however, we took this approach further, and it became part of a learning pod. Would it be possible to create a learning experience that encompassed one or more of these great artists with music of the period, history, psychology, and great authors of the period; and then study the like from a contemporary perspective? What lessons could be learned from doing that? For example, did Picasso, Degas, or Monet influence any modern artists? And then, let students run with this and either independently or in teams create their own art and/or music and have them do a personal history. They could even interview each other and discover some things about experiences that have influenced their use of color, style and form. Have students do some research on contemporary music and the influence of history and culture on it. As a result, have a showing with the students' creations and either through video or live action, show them performing original musical works. We have just touched on the surface, but you can see how this kind of learning experience brings together the old, the new, and the newly created. It can easily incorporate many, many curricular outcomes while totally engaging students. What might once have been viewed as a "drag" by students who had to sit through art history classes, can turn into an exciting experience and may forever alter the students' appreciation for the arts.

Reflect for a moment on the life most of your students live. A disproportionate number live in concrete jungles. Some inner city children have never been out of the city and seen a farm, let alone the mountains, a natural lake, mountain streams, or the woods. Imagine living a life without any natural beauty. Imagine not being able to get out of the city and breathe clean air, feel the exhilaration of witnessing a spectacular sunset or the awesome sight of the Rocky Mountains. Imagine never having seen the ocean with its pulsating ebb and flow. Imagine never having witnessed the spiritual beauty of the Redwood forest or some of our spectacular national parks. Imagine never being able to see the beauty of the Grand Canyon, the lush green Appalachian Trail, the stark beauty of the desert, the intriguing swamps of Louisiana and Florida or the vast expanse of the Great Lakes. Too many of our youth have never experienced any of these things. A life lived without nature may well be a life without living.

There is something very restful, healing, and unique about each of the sights listed above. How can we bring these experiences to our students who live in isolated places or in inner cities with no transportation to get out? Field trips can provide a catalyst for learning that sometimes can become a life-changing experience for students. And soon, virtual reality will be available for those unable to experience it firsthand. Like everything else, though, one must give great thought to optimizing each experience, otherwise it may be perceived as a chance to escape the drudgery of school and nothing else.

Picture this scenario. Whatever your grade level or subject matter, take a few minutes to envision that your students are engaged in 'X' learning pod. Write down all the possibilities for that learning pod. Stretch your imagination to extend that learning pod into nature. It could be physics, mathematics, science, English, Social Studies, art, physical education, etc. Whatever, get out of your box-like thinking and bring your imagination to bear on how you can extend your subject matter into the realm of nature. Think about air, wind, and fire. Think about plants or the planets; rocks - mountains - volcanoes and earthquakes; the sun - space - stars.

There are field trips like going to the woods or hiking in the mountains, but there are also experiences that can recreate these, like museums of natural history, viewing a Cinemax movie or even some home videos. You can go to arboretums and aquariums, too. Whatever you decide to do, it is important to DO IT! Get the students out so they can see a part of nature that heretofore has escaped them. Use the opportunity to have students create an original poem or some other writing. Have them imagine how a great author or songwriter must have felt when s/he stood in that very spot. Allow them time to engage in the beauty of the world because far too many of our students live with the constant threat of violence and never have the opportunity to experience peace and tranquillity.

The last thing you'd want to do is plan a trip that means students will have to rush from one thing to the next because there isn't enough time. Plan small and think big because truly witnessing something always takes more time than imagined. It is always a good idea to have the students follow up after they get back to school, with some thoughts or ideas that they want to share about the experience. This kind of debriefing is important to students and can provide valuable feedback to you for another day.

One thing that always puzzled me when I (MLB) was in school was the annual trip to the zoo. It seemed so out of context. We never spent any time talking about the animals we might see, studying their habits or places they naturally lived. We never even talked about it except to get excited about this "end of the year" trip. I suspect that kind of thing still happens in schools around the country. Couldn't this be as meaningful a learning experience as any that happened throughout the school year? Does the end of school each spring mean that we take a vacation from learning? It seems to me that this was always viewed as a special occasion and a time to have fun without regard to learning. Upon reflection, doesn't that seem antithetical to what we hope will be every student's experience with school? Why not make every day an adventure that is fun and where real learning takes place? If every day is precious and there is no time to waste, then why do educators willingly "waste" the last day of the school year? Think about it, and imagine ways that you, with the help of your students, can breathe life and excitement into every day of the school year so that at the end of the year students are clamoring for more.

Lastly, it is our contention that students and teachers today live with far too many stresses and not many opportunities to relieve them so they can be free to learn, let alone experience joy in learning. Therefore, we suggest the use of baroque music and reflection time for students to relax and practice deep breathing at the start of every day, and immediately after lunch. Baroque music has 60 beats per minute, approximately the time of the human heart at rest. It allows people to get into a relaxed state so they can be free to learn. This is an accelerated learning technique that is most helpful used sporadically throughout the day. Deep breathing is practiced to get more oxygen to the brain. Research has shown that people today live with too little oxygen and too much carbon monoxide in their blood streams. This is largely due to the numbers of emissions in the air and the fact that most of us don't get any aerobic exercise that stimulates deep breathing. Have the students stand and take five deep breaths each morning—breathing in through the nose to a count of five or six and out hard through the mouth for the same count. Arms can be lifted along with the deep breathing as well, but is not necessary. This brings a greater flow of oxygen to their brains and put them in a more alert state. Imagine starting the day with a little baroque music while students are quietly reading or writing at their desks followed by some deep breathing. It is just a nice way to start the day!

∧∧∧∧∧∧∧∧

The following is a checksheet tool to help the teacher to implement the **Quality Fusion** technique into their classroom.

Step 1:   The mission, goals and academic integrity of your class are absolutely clear.
√   Established a classroom mission statement.
√   Developed personal goals for the class.
√   Communicated mission and goals to parents/guardians.
√   Aligned classroom mission and goals with those of the school district and the school.

Step 2:   You are demonstrating leadership.
√   Developed a definition of a total quality classroom.
√   Walk-the-Talk about quality.
√   Understand Deming's system of **Profound Knowledge**.
√   Use a variety of teaching styles.
√   Have a CQI program for self and for my students.

Step 3:   All work is pertinent and flows from the students.
√   Broke down barriers on day one by establishing a classroom mission statement with the students.
√   Having students co-create learning experiences.
√   Stressing the importance of teamwork in problem solving and decision making.
√   Defined quality and what it means.
√   Created interdisciplinary learning activities.

Step 4:   The course content is connected to the surrounding community and the real world.
√   Demonstrated the connectedness between work and the real world.
√   Asked the students to analyze the learning assignments.
√   Began TQM training for the students.
√   Implemented student suggestions on how best to improve the learning system.

Step 5:   The student is treated as a "worker," but s/he is also considered as a valuable team member of the "research and development" department.
√   Gave the students an historical overview about the quality movement and discussed examples.
√   Discussed the P-D-C-A cycle and root causes of problems.
√   Took action to establish an atmosphere of trust.

Step 6:    Peer teaching, small group work, and team work are
emphasized.
√   Engaged the students in activities that emphasized
teaming and making learning fun.
√   Engaged students to work independently away
from the team, but encouraged them to report the
results to their peers.
√   Provided guidelines and opportunities for students
to assess each others' work.
√   Emphasized the systems approach and regularly
asked the student of how we could reduce fear.
√   Provided students with the opportunity for peer
tutoring.
√   Elaborated upon the types of quality teams.
√   Introduced the students to additional TQI tools and
techniques.
Step 7:    Students should have aesthetic experiences.
√   Encouraged students to use their imagination daily.
√   Discussed the importance of art, music, nature,
relaxation techniques, mediation, and exercise.

# Chapter Eight: Classroom processes should include reflection.

Seldom within the educational setting do either teachers or students have time to reflect on their work or their goals or their accomplishments. We seem to focus on the "doing" of things rather than "why" we are doing them. Often teachers will say they have no time to think; no think to pause and reflect on the teaching/learning process or about the progress the class or individuals are making. Yet without adequate reflection time, things seem to go on and on and never get any better.

We must give serious thought to the necessity for reflection. In Deming's Plan—Do—Study—Act (PDSA) cycle, the planning phase is crucial—see Figure 9.1. It is the phase that provides the underpinnings for every process, and includes reflection of cause and effect as well as study of current processes for "best practice." **Without adequate reflection and planning it is simply not possible to build quality into the processes that make up the activity of the classroom.**

*Figure 8.1  P-D-S-A Cycle*

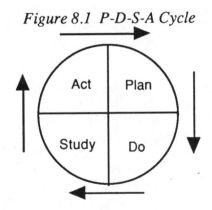

Consider the case of a second grade teacher who wants to institute quality management principles in her classroom. She has 29 students, all bright and active children who are eager learners but with little self-discipline. She starts school at 8:00 AM and finishes at 3:30 PM. At the end of the school day, Mrs. Little has six sets of ditto sheets, math papers and spelling tests to correct, lesson plans to make, and materials to collect and put together for a new unit she is starting. Once Mrs. Little leaves school she has to take her seven-year-old to piano lessons, her nine-year-old to soccer practice and then rush home to fix dinner. By the time she helps her children with their homework and tucks them into bed, it is after 8:30 PM. She is tired and still has not gotten to the work she brought home. Mrs. Little stays up until 11:00 PM doing her work and then retires. The next day, she arrives at school after dropping her own children off and busily runs off her ditto sheets for the day.

She arrives at the classroom about five minutes before the children, who race in, filled with things to tell her and their friends. Mrs. Little keeps the children busy moving from one curricular area to another, has recess duty, reprimands several students for misbehavior and sends them to the office, and the afternoon continues in the same fashion as the morning. This pattern (or a similar one) is repeated most days.

At no time during the day has Mrs. Little had time to reflect on anything that is happening. She has the scope and sequence for Math, Science, Language Arts, and Physical Education to keep up with, which gives her a map for creating unit and lesson plans.

What Mrs. Little doesn't realize is there is a better way to manage her time. She is not aware of how continuous quality improvement principles and processes can help relieve her of many burdens she now carries alone.

Imagine Mr. Jones, the eleventh grade math teacher who has six classes per day: two general math, two algebra, one calculus, and one computer science. His classes average 32 students each, with the algebra classes at 35 and the calculus class at 28. This is Mr. Jones' first year at National High School, though he has taught for about 15 years. Mr. Jones believes in daily homework, so every night he goes home with 192 papers to grade. Sometimes he doesn't take them home but has the other students grade them. He gives pop quizzes and weekly tests. Mr. Jones also coaches football and baseball. He feels he has to do this to supplement his teaching contract, but the price is pretty high since Mr. Jones doesn't get home from school until 6:45 PM each school night, and Friday nights he either has a game or scouting responsibilities. Mr. Jones has no time to reflect about classes or the teams, though if pushed he would admit to spending more time planning football plays than working on lesson plans. Mr. Jones' thinking is that because he has taught mathematics for so many years, he has learned the best ways to go about getting the material across to the students. He isn't particularly aware or concerned.

If either Mrs. Little or Mr. Jones had time to reflect, each would probably agree that some processes were not working optimally, and that with help from students, parents, and/or colleagues the learning environment as well as learning experiences could be dramatically improved.

## INSTANT FEEDBACK
In a quality classroom, both Mrs. Little and Mr. Jones would engage the students to help them reflect on various classroom processes each day. This might be called fast feedback, or debriefing, or simply reflection time. The essence of this is that teachers cannot possible carry the burden for the classroom alone. Shared responsibility and shared decision making is one of the tenets of quality. For example, the fast feedback form for Mrs. Little's class might look like this:

Table 8.1: Fast Feedback 2nd Grade

| Activity | Too Fast — OK — Too Slow | | | | |
|---|---|---|---|---|---|
| Math | 5 | 4 | 3 | 2 | 1 |
| Writing | 5 | 4 | 3 | 2 | 1 |
| Reading | 5 | 4 | 3 | 2 | 1 |

Almost instantly Mrs. Little will recognize who needs help and which student(s) would benefit from some peer assistance as well as hers. If she added a large circle at the right side of the chart and asked the children to draw a picture of their face today, they could indicate a happy or sad face which would also give her valuable feedback.

Next day Mrs. Little could reorganize the class into groups with at least one student who was excelling at the particular activity and one who was having some difficulty. In this way, students could help each other and Mrs. Little could be of greater help to the entire class by moving between groups.

She might also ask the students for more general information about what they need to make the activities more interesting or to help them learn. Maybe some students work best with manipulatives; some may be better with paper and pencil while others may do better on a computer. Mrs. Little would do well to accommodate the students by reorganizing them and reassessing her assignments.

Teachers of mathematics might borrow a lesson from the Japanese. In their elementary schools, one concept (one problem) is presented each day and it is always a real world problem. Students work in teams to resolve the problem. The teacher prepares the problem and provides each team with a copy, then writes the problem on the board. Then, she reads the problem to the entire class. Students first attempt to solve the problem on their own, writing down the steps in their logic journal. Next, the team discusses the problem and members compare their notes. For second graders this will be rudimentary, but if students get into the habit of writing their thinking down, they more readily learn the logic errors they've made and can self-correct many of them.

The teacher's role is to present the problem and then allow students time to reflect on the answer. Towards the end of the time, the teacher brings the class together for a discussion of the problem by asking teams what answer they came up with. She never indicates right or wrong, but moves from one team to the next until all have given their answer. The teacher writes each response on the board.

Next, she calls on the team who has gotten the problem wrong to look at their logic journals and tell the group how they arrived at the answer. Throughout the process, no one shouts out the answer, but the teacher carefully guides them through the process. Generally, as students discuss the logic of their answers they quickly pick up where they made a mistake and will say something like, "Oh, I see that can't possibly be correct." The teacher encourages the team to go back, review their logic journals and see what they come up with. All the time, the teacher must resist giving the correct answer or allowing others to shout out the answer. If necessary, s/he may have one or more teams work together, perhaps one which got the correct answer paired with another that did not. Using this method, assuming that all the students fully understand the concept that the problem was meant to get across, there is no need for homework. If you feel compelled to give homework, then two or three similar word problems would be sufficient to reinforce the learning that took place but not enough that the student would view homework as punishment.

Mr. Jones could employ the same method as the Japanese do in his mathematics classes. In fact, all math problems should be application problems with real world models or examples. Imagine starting the day with a mathematical puzzle that is in 3-D form that teams of students could work on, maintain logic journals, and by the end of the period solve the problem. Scope and sequence of curriculum doesn't dictate the numbers of problems that students must do in order to understand something. On the contrary, doesn't it make more sense to learn well and understand the logic of one or two problems per day than attempting to do 15 or 20 and then have a like number for homework?

A fast feedback form for Mr. Jones might look like:

Table 8.2: Fast Feedback Form For High School

Circle the number that best represents your thoughts on today's work.

1 = Strongly Agree;  2 = Agree;
3 = Somewhat Disagree  4 = Disagree

1. I understand the logic of today's problem.
   1   2   3   4
2. I could apply this logic to another situation.
   1   2   3   4
3. This class is moving at a good pace for me.
   1   2   3   4

Signature (optional):

_____

Both these teachers would do well to allow their students to give them continuous feedback much like that suggested above. Unless we know (specifically and systematically) what difficulties the students encounter, how can we possibly know how to create a better learning environment or learning experience? (The examples above are not meant to be the only feedback questions that are valid or useful.) The teacher probably would want to experiment with these and with practice discover how to ask questions that provide the best information in a short amount of time.

We recommend that students be given the option of signing their names so that the teacher can provide them with the help needed. If a third or more of the students report that the class is moving too slow or too fast, the teacher would be wise to find a way to accommodate them. The optimum use of time is to have most of the students (with just a few reporting too fast or too slow) reporting that they agree, or number 2. After the students get accustomed to fast feedback, you can random sample students rather than the entire class.

Never underestimate the power of students' help. They reflect on classes often outside of school and/or during class when you may surmise they are daydreaming. They are the ones working in the system and, therefore, as Deming says, are in the best position to offer assistance about ways to build quality into the system or process.

## STUDENT REFLECTION

Another valuable resource for students is reflection. Rarely do we provide opportunities for students to participate in any reflection about their work or the work of their team or classmates. By not doing so, in essence educators perpetuate the short term recall with little attention paid to the larger questions that arise with learning experiences that require students to do research and create new knowledge. Whenever one is engaged in creating new knowledge or testing a new theory, reflection is a critical step.

One school in Colorado has its day organized thus: in the morning, students stay at school studying academic subjects in a traditional atmosphere; in the early afternoon, students go out into the community to study or participate in some volunteer effort; later in the afternoon, students get together at the school in small groups and engage in Socratic discussion and reflect on the connections between their experiences in the community that day and the morning's lessons. This provides students with instant connections, allows them to reassess and reflect on the meaning of their morning work, and broadens their knowledge base by connecting book learning with the real world.

Students who engage in regular reflective time also seem to gain insights into their own lives and behaviors in the context of the larger world. This leads to goal setting and valuable lifelong skills. Young students at Kate Sullivan Elementary School in Tallahassee, Florida, engage in weekly goal setting. The model they use can be implemented or adapted to fit the student's age. This self-assessment requires each child to reflect on her/his behavior for the week and to set personal goals. The results from this type of activity have kept the students more focused, thus allowing them to learn more each week. Parents like the idea of having their children write personal goals and engage in some reflection and self-assessment, too. In fact, some students report they have their families engage in goal setting. See Table 8.3.

Table 8.3:  Kate Sullivan Personal Goal Sheet

| Name:                                        Week of: |
|---|
| **Crocodile Quality:    Getting it Together Personal Goal Sheet**<br>We at Kate Sullivan realize all of us have areas of our lives which can be improved upon. During the course of our lives we all set goals and try to accomplish them. We feel this is a skill which needs to be taught, so our students will learn to reach out to achieve more. "Only our best is good enough." |
| I will: |
| Look at how I'm doing!<br>   Day 1       yes   no<br>   Day 2       yes   no<br>   Day 3       yes   no<br>   Day 4       yes   no<br>   Day 5       yes   no<br>How do you feel about your progress? |
| Behavior:   Excellent          Good          Fair          Poor |
| Work Study:<br>Quality work completed     Incomplete      Not attempted |
| I have seen my child's Personal Goal, Citizenship, and Work Study Sheet this week.<br><br>Parent Signature:_____<br><br>My child has read each day:<br>Yes_____     No_____<br><br>Comments: |

The self-assessment sheet that follows is for elementary or middle school students to reflect on their citizenship as well as work and study habits. See Table 8.4. Notice the portion that has to do with quality improvement and how they have contributed to making the class better.

Table 8.4: Sample Self-Assessment Sheet for Elementary and Middle School Students.

| Name: | | | Week of: | | |
|---|---|---|---|---|---|
| **Respect for Self and Others** | **Mon** | **Tues** | **Wed** | **Thur** | **Fri** |
| I listen while someone else is speaking. | | | | | |
| I come quietly into the room. | | | | | |
| I wait my turn to speak. | | | | | |
| I cooperate and contribute to my team's work, | | | | | |
| I use self-control and good manners. | | | | | |
| I respond promptly to directions. | | | | | |
| I help others when they ask me to. | | | | | |
| I do not disturb others with my voice or actions. | | | | | |
| **Work and Study Habits** | | | | | |
| I am ready to begin work. | | | | | |
| I do my best work and am proud of my work. | | | | | |
| I finish my work on time. | | | | | |
| **Quality Improvement** | | | | | |
| I made at least one suggestion to improve our class this week. | | | YES | NO | |
| I improved my work this week. | | | YES | NO | |

High school students can engage in **Force Field Analysis** and other continuous improvement tools that cause them to reflect on behavior and habits leading to success or failure. An example of a force field analysis completed by a high school student is Table 8.5. Notice that we have not included anything related to quality improvement of the class. This example is for continuous self improvement. You might want to include regular times for your students to complete a force field analysis on their efforts to improve the overall quality of the class. Or, this could become part of a total class effort led by the quality leadership team, and students could engage in cause/effect diagrams also.

Table 8.5:  Completed Force Field Analysis for High School Student.

| FORCE FIELD ANALYSIS | |
| --- | --- |
| Name:  Rick | Week of: November 9-13 |
| Class:   Algebra 2 | Period:   6th |
| Goal:  To finish my homework each night. | |
| Driving Forces | Restraining Forces |
| 1.  Stay eligible for football team<br>2.  Drive the car to school<br>3.  Get a college scholarship<br>4.  Keep parents off my back | 1.  Talk to girlfriend on phone<br>2.  Too tired after football practice<br>3.  Don't always understand the homework problems<br>4.  Not interested—don't always see a need for it |
| ACTION PLAN:<br>1. Set timer—limit phone calls to 30 minutes once per night<br>2. Speak to teacher and ask for clarification of problems<br>3. Eat a snack for more energy after football practice<br>4. Do Algebra 2 homework from 7-7:45 PM each night before calling girlfriend | |

The method or continuous quality improvement tool you select is not nearly as important as taking the time to include reflection as a routine part of the quality classroom. Students and teachers both can benefit from this activity. We suggest that students fill a notebook with the story of their continuous quality improvement journey. Such a notebook can be filled with pages of force field analyses, cause/effect diagrams and/or the suggested formats listed above. This can be become part of their portfolio and is evidence to them as well as their parents and teachers that they've grown in their reflective ability and improved their performance as a result.

ΛΛΛΛΛΛΛΛ

The following is a checksheet tool to help the teacher to implement the **Quality Fusion** technique into their classroom.

Step 1:   The mission, goals and academic integrity of your class are absolutely clear.
√   Established a classroom mission statement.
√   Developed personal goals for the class.
√   Communicated mission and goals to parents/guardians.
√   Aligned classroom mission and goals with those of the school district and the school.

Step 2:   You are demonstrating leadership.
√   Developed a definition of a total quality classroom.
√   Walk-the-Talk about quality.
√   Understand Deming's system of **Profound Knowledge**.
√   Use a variety of teaching styles.
√   Have a CQI program for self and for my students.

Step 3:   All work is pertinent and flows from the students.
√   Broke down barriers on day one by establishing a classroom mission statement with the students.
√   Having students co-create learning experiences.
√   Stressing the importance of teamwork in problem solving and decision making.
√   Defined quality and what it means.
√   Created interdisciplinary learning activities.

Step 4:   The course content is connected to the surrounding community and the real world.
√   Demonstrated the connectedness between work and the real world.
√   Asked the students to analyze the learning assignments.
√   Began TQM training for the students.
√   Implemented student suggestions on how best to improve the learning system.

Step 5:   The student is treated as a "worker," but s/he is also considered as a valuable team member of the "research and development" department.
√   Gave the students an historical overview about the quality movement and discussed examples.
√   Discussed the P-D-C-A cycle and root causes of problems.
√   Took action to establish an atmosphere of trust.

Step 6: Peer teaching, small group work, and team work are emphasized.
- √ Engaged the students in activities that emphasized teaming and making learning fun.
- √ Engaged students to work independently away from the team, but encouraged them to report the results to their peers.
- √ Provided guidelines and opportunities for students to assess each others' work.
- √ Emphasized the systems approach and regularly asked the student of how we could reduce fear.
- √ Provided students with the opportunity for peer tutoring.
- √ Elaborated upon the types of quality teams.
- √ Introduced the students to additional TQI tools and techniques.

Step 7: Students should have aesthetic experiences.
- √ Encouraged students to use their imagination daily.
- √ Discussed the importance of art, music, nature, relaxation techniques, mediation, and exercise.

Step 8: Classroom processes should include reflection.
- √ Developed instant feedback form with students in order to measure classroom processes.
- √ Distributed instant feedback forms in order to examine classroom processes.
- √ Reflected on my mission, goals, and classroom processes.
- √ Set time aside for students to reflect on the relevance of course work to real world issues and encouraged them to discuss their perceptions.
- √ Developed self-assessment and goal setting instruments with students.

## Chapter Nine: The teaching/learning system should undergo constant evaluation.

It is very important that the teaching/learning process continuously be assessed. This can be accomplished daily and/or weekly through a variety of methods. It is critical to the continuous quality improvement of the class, and its importance must not be overlooked. In fact, without it, the classroom is not likely to improve as quickly, if at all. Unfortunately, some teachers are frightened by the possibility of having their work under such close scrutiny. They have become used to doing all the planning, creating, and teaching with only the scrutiny of the principal (or peer review team) several times per year if their name falls into the evaluation cycle for that year. This has suited many teachers just right except when the reviewer makes some suggestions for improvement, and then too many become defensive and view the review as punishment rather than an opportunity for positive growth.

Just like students, teachers become upset when they feel they've been rated and are not at the top. Teachers have difficulty understanding how they can give up the A-F grading scale when that seems fair to them (because they are not the ones being rated), yet they cannot translate their feelings about evaluation to the students. What an interesting dichotomy—one that deserves more time than this work allows. However, we hope to make the paradigm shift away from a once or twice each year external evaluation system to the hope and encouragement that can be found in regular, routine assessment from students and the teacher him/herself.

Deming points out quite rightly that ratings and yearly evaluations for raises or merit pay are destructive to the organization as they decrease morale and sense of worth. Individuals who are made to feel as if they are contributing less without any help from the system to improve their performance are likely to have lower self-esteem and produce less.

Teachers need to understand how destructive their attitudes about assessment of self and students are. The first premise that we must agree on is that no one is perfect. If you agree with that, then you can probably also agree that improvement is much faster when the environment is free of fear and fosters growth and continuous feedback.

Fear is really at the heart of the problem and needs a closer look. Some administrators want/need everyone to like them. These are the people who don't like the process of having to do classroom visitations for the purpose of evaluating the teacher and become uncomfortable with the idea that they may say something to hurt the teacher's feelings. Such an administrator may rate every teacher the same—either excellent in all categories, or above average in all categories. It is doubtful that an administrator with this type personality would rate all teachers "average." The teachers naturally talk amongst themselves at lunch or recess, after the principal leaves. If it appears that everyone gets the same rating then all is well, though the principal may be subjected to some criticism once the teachers leave the building and get home. They will invariably make comments somewhat like this, "I don't understand how Joe could have gotten the same rating as I got, when everyone knows all he does is have students do the same thing every week."

Administrators like those described above are not helpful. In their zeal to make everyone appear to have the same competencies, they do not help their teachers, and isn't that the purpose of the evaluation? In traditional schools, the principal is the educational leader of the school. Good leaders allow people to take risks, to make mistakes and then learn from them, and to encourage those who are struggling by helping provide what they need to improve.

On the other hand, when a dedicated principal goes into the classroom and takes notes and fills out a check sheet it makes many teachers nervous. Some even become hostile that s/he dare to make any judgments based on one or two observations. In essence we have created a monster when it comes to assessing teacher performance. It has, in many school districts, become a hotly contested negotiating point, and has resulted in less than desired results no matter what format the assessment takes.

In a few schools, peers evaluate each other. This makes teachers nervous because they wonder who made the select few "God," and leads to isolation for those chosen to be the evaluators. Of course, one cannot generalize these responses to include the universe, but suffice it to say the negative aspects of teacher evaluation far outweigh the good that might come from a engaging in continuous assessment.

An important part of the idea of assessment is that everyone can improve and no one is ever "there." Indeed, "there" in a quality classroom continues to move forward, making stretch goals the norm for everyone including teachers and students.

## TEACHER ASSESSMENT

In terms of teacher assessment, we recommend two things. First, teachers engage in a yearly self-assessment based on the

Malcolm Baldrige Award Criteria using data to support improvement claims and trends on student achievement. This process, extremely different from current assessments or evaluations, is described by Byrnes et. al. in *The Quality Teacher* (1992) and is elaborated upon in great detail by Byrnes' new book *Weave Quality Into Your Schools: A Case for Hoshin Planning and Teacher Self-Assessment* (1994). It examines eight categories to measure the quality of the classroom system, namely:

1. Leadership
2. Classroom Environment
3. Information and Analysis
4. Strategic Quality Planning
5. Human Resource Utilization
6. Quality Assurance of Products and Services
7. Quality Results
8. Customer Satisfaction

This takes the assessment process out of the subjective (anecdotes are not sufficient to describe trends, achievement, and improvement) and into the objective. Once the self-assessment instrument is completed, the teacher is asked to prepare an action plan based on the school district's identified priority goals. Upon meeting with the principal or Quality Council, each teacher is then offered the help s/he needs to make the desired improvements.

Second, teachers are curious about the TQM concept that students, as "workers" within the system, are in the best position to help improve it and build quality into each process in the beginning. Teachers must come to recognize that they cannot get along without regular feedback from their students. Once you try this, and can let go of any sense of defensiveness or personal attack, you will discover the merits of allowing students to help.

We suggest that you examine your fears in relation to having students help assess the teaching/learning process. Perhaps you fear that if given a chance, anarchy will ensue. To this, we ask that you recall a time when you were having a difficult time in a given class. Perhaps you were bored. Perhaps the subject matter was confusing. Maybe the teacher was moving too quickly or too slowly and the assignments were meaningless. Whatever the situation, the question is, if that teacher had asked you for input could/would you have been willing to help? The answer is probably, YES! Why then, do you fear anarchy when you take the risk and ask students? They will be only too happy to help. Besides a willingness to help, the students will feel empowered and have more ownership of the class thus relieving you of many (if not most) discipline problems.

A word of caution: if you ask students for help in assessing the teaching/learning process then you have to be ready for whatever they say and listen without judgment. The minute you become defensive or try to explain, they will realize that you aren't really serious. If that happens you will have some problems with the students because you'll have broken the trust bond between you and it will take a long time to repair. Sometimes when we "create" something, our sense of ownership is so great that any criticism or suggestion is taken negatively. You can think about this in a more detached way if you can remember your constancy of purpose. The purpose of any teacher should be to optimize the students' learning. School isn't about teaching, it is about learning! Teachers cannot do this alone, nor should they, but sometimes fears override the decision to go to those who can be the most help.

We strongly urge you to reach out to your students. Explain to them what you're doing and the necessity you see in doing it. Unless every one of your students is currently operating at 100% efficiency and engaged in stretch goals every day, all day, there is room for improvement. Let go of those fears. It isn't easy to do especially if you've been teaching for a long time and maybe you've won the outstanding teacher award for your school or district. Perhaps you're afraid that someone will find out that you're not as good as you thought you were, or as others thought you were. These are genuine fears that are shared by many, many teachers.

Not too long ago I (MLB) encountered an experience that brought this to light, but it pertained to a school district and its decision to listen to some students about their satisfaction rate with the high school. We gathered a group of students representing grades 9-12 and included a cross-section of student groups. Some of them were honors students and others barely passing; others were considered discipline problems, while others were considered student body leaders. The administration promised the group that they would not be punished for whatever they revealed and that some action would be taken on whatever problems they revealed. The amount of fear within the district became evident the minute the students entered the room. We had previously determined that the only administrator present would be someone from the central administration (Curriculum Director) who would be as non-threatening to the students as possible. My role was a community representative who would facilitate the discussion.

At first the students were reluctant to talk, but once they were reassured again and again, gradually they began to say what was on their minds. The administrator was shocked at some of the complaints, and perhaps more shocked to discover that all students had some, even those considered "good" students. By the end of the session, there were approximately twenty fairly serious complaints ranging from the way the buses were scheduled for students enrolled in the vocational-technical option to the history teacher(s) who read newspapers in class rather than teach. Many of the problems were system problems and only a few had to do with personalities.

The administration did look into all twenty of their complaints. However, since they were not engaged in quality improvement processes, the administration did not prioritize the problems and get together a quality improvement council to study them. Instead, they took a more traditional approach, decided what the causes were, and acted solely on their own intuition. The results were less than satisfying. While the students left the meeting feeling better because they got the issues off their chests, they later became somewhat bitter because nothing really happened to make it any better.

The moral to this story is that if you are going to ask students for their input, then do it without judgment and without becoming defensive, and always follow by asking their help in making it better. Students will be eager to help make the classroom processes better if they can see proof that changes have been made based on their input. They will also become angry and bitter and refuse to cooperate if they believe their suggestions are falling on deaf ears.

## DEBRIEFING
Debriefing can take many forms. It is always important to do some type of debriefing after every learning experience, especially if your goal is continuous improvement. The example found in the table on page 64 can be modified to include any and all materials and resources used in the learning experience. It takes just a minute or two but can yield very powerful and invaluable information for teachers. Student members of the quality leadership team can assist with the tabulation efforts. That process might take them 10 minutes for a class of 30 students. As they become more familiar with the debriefing sheet, the time to tabulate the responses will become less, too. It certainly is more powerful to have students do as much of this as possible, but if it is too frightening for you, then you can tabulate it yourself. Either way, in a very short time you've

gotten feedback that you can use to alter the resources, materials, and lecture you used.

Be prepared to consider what, if anything, you'll do if one-fourth or one-third of all students say your lectures were no help at all? We recommend you drop whatever sense of ownership you feel about those carefully prepared lectures and let go of them, or at a minimum modify them and continue to ask for feedback on their usefulness. Sometimes we feel too much of ourselves is wrapped up in what we do, and for teachers often that is lecture. Remember the purpose: optimize the students' learning. If the lectures are not helpful, then let them go and be relieved that your students have felt they could be honest with you. It only hurts the first time, believe us.

Other debriefing efforts can be in the form of fast feedback which is used daily to assess how students felt they progressed that day in completing the learning experience. Fast feedback approaches depend on the age of the students. Very young children will need a simpler form to follow, but either way you'll want to structure your questions to solicit responses that will prove the most helpful for the following day. Some teachers prefer to use a very open-ended approach, others like the Likert Scale or a Yes/No response. Perhaps for students from third grade on, a combination is best since often the Yes/No response doesn't provide enough information. Questions using the Likert Scale can be especially enlightening if they are worded correctly; otherwise you may not get the kind of information you need.

Whenever you use fast feedback, start by asking yourself what you need to know in order to improve the teaching/learning process for all the students. You don't *need* to know the names of all respondents, but it certainly would help you provide some assistance to students who indicate they need help. If anonymity is important to the students then it would be wise to comply with their wishes. We recommend that you leave signature optional and stress that if they are having difficulty then you can best help if you know what their specific needs are.

Like most things having to do with quality, honest answers are predicated on trust. It takes a tremendous amount of trust for students to feel totally free to respond honestly rather than with what they think will please the teacher. Too often in education, teachers withhold love and respect from students who are honest with them. As Calvin from *Calvin & Hobbs* says, "It isn't fair to kill the messenger." When you ask for feedback, be willing to listen and remember the **purpose** for asking: **to improve the teaching/learning system**. The most effective teachers are those who seek and use suggestions from students since it enhances trust, pride, cooperation, and teamwork.

## STUDENT DEBRIEFING

As with teachers, students need to debrief as well. The format should be determined based on the type of learning experience the students just completed. Debriefing may start as an individual or team effort and then progress to the class as a whole. It can be formal, as in having students complete a questionnaire, or informal by having discussion follow some sort of format. In either case, results should be recorded and analyzed for making decisions about future projects, learning experiences, team selection, materials, etc.

With informal debriefings, we recommend a student be selected (providing leadership opportunities to all students) to lead the discussion based on a format such as the following:

Table 9.2:  Typical interview questions that a student quality improvement representative might ask of the class.

---

- The thing I liked best about this learning experience was:

- The thing that I didn't like was:

- The best thing about my group was:

- The thing I'd like to change about my group was:

- These kinds of learning experiences are:

- The thing(s) I learned from this is/are:

---

Have a student write all responses on the board. Students can then engage in creation of a **Pareto Chart** to determine the most critical problem(s). This information can be used to set parameters for the next learning experience. For example, in response to the question *The thing I didn't like about this learning experience was...* , Mrs. MacElroy's fifth grade class gave the following responses:

| Number of Responses | Issue |
|---|---|
| 11 | working in the media center |
| 3 | the media teacher was crabby |
| 9 | not enough access to computers |
| 6 | books were outdated |
| 1 | not enough time to do research |

Figure 9.1: Pareto Chart from Student Debriefing Exercise

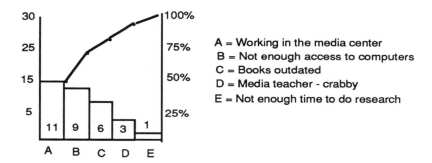

A = Working in the media center
B = Not enough access to computers
C = Books outdated
D = Media teacher - crabby
E = Not enough time to do research

You can easily see that 14 of 30 students (nearly 50%) indicated some problems with the media center directly. Three students felt that the media specialist was crabby, but eleven other students indicated they did not like working in the media center. At this point, there is not enough information to clearly understand the problems students were having with the media center. There is ample evidence that points to getting more information about the cause of their problems with the media center. Figure 9.2 shows a **Cause & Effect** diagram that the students completed in response to: Don't like working in the media center.

Figure 9.2 Cause & Effect Diagram

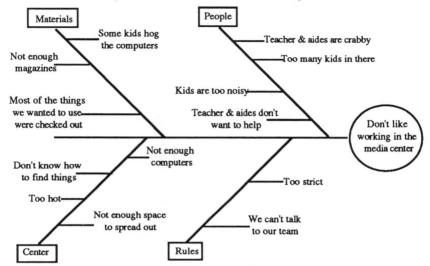

With this information you now know precisely what the problems are revolving around the use of the media center. The class can help create an action plan for improving the situation, but with some of the issues you'll want to engage the media specialist and his/her aides.

If these are the things that are keeping the students from optimizing their achievement and learning, then they need to be addressed immediately. But this is just one type of evaluation.

## PORTFOLIO AND SELF-ASSESSMENT

As your classroom moves more toward quality, you will want to teach the students to perform regular self-assessment. This is usually something new for the students and you'll need to teach your students some ways to do it. One of the first things you'll want to do is post the quality factors and operational definitions on the classroom wall and also be certain each student has a copy for each learning experience. These provide the guideposts for students as they determine whether or not they've achieved quality. Everything that is done in the classroom should be under the guise of the quality factors and operational definitions.

**Example:** Let's look at a learning experience the students in Mr. Short's wood shop class are engaged in. The students are creating wheelchair ramps for ten people living within the school district boundaries without wheelchair access to their homes. This project was developed from a community survey done within the churches during the summer. A local lumber yard donated all the lumber, nails, and other materials required to do the job.

Mr. Short asked three wheelchair bound individuals to come to class and brainstorm with his students the WOW or quality factors of a wheelchair ramp. They came up with this list:

√ Sturdy, able to withstand five hundred pounds
√ Low angle up to house
√ Fit squarely to front door threshold

Then they created operational definitions for the ramps by answering the question: If you were going to tell someone how to build the best wheelchair ramp, how would you tell them to do it? With Mr. Short, the students agreed upon these:

- Vertical grade must not exceed 10% up to house
- Surface should be smooth, not rough
- Boards must fit together tightly, with no gaps
- The foundation braces must be laid in concrete
- Four by fours must be used for the foundation braces
- Arm railings must extend no higher than 24 inches above the ramp
- The horizontal surface must be even
- The foundation must be glued, then secured with 4.5 inch nuts and bolts
- Surface boards must be nailed with no bent nails or nails sticking out the sides
- Structure must meet specifications on the plan
- Arm railings must have vertical braces every 2 feet
- Arm railings must have a top rail and a rail at 12 inches
- Arm railings must be glued, then nailed together with no bent nails.
- Arm railings must be constructed of 2 x 2 inch boards, sanded so there will be no splinters

Armed with these operational definitions, students working alone or in teams can readily check to see if they are on the course. The final product will be assessed only for quality factors, but construction must include all the above items. Mr. Short took the operational definitions and quality factors and put them together on a Learning Experience Sheet and gave one to each student. See Table 9.3.

Table 9.3: Learning Experience Sheet for Wheelchair Ramp
Project

| Operational Definition | Yes | No | Date |
|---|---|---|---|
| • Vertical grade must not exceed 10% up to house. | | | |
| • Surface should be smooth, not rough. | | | |
| • Boards must fit together tightly, with no gaps. | | | |
| • The foundation braces must be laid in concrete. | | | |
| • Four by fours must be used for the foundation braces. | | | |
| • Arm railings must extend no higher than 24 inches above the ramp. | | | |
| • The horizontal surface must be even. | | | |
| • The foundation must be glued, then secured with 4.5 inch nuts and bolts. | | | |
| • Surface boards must be nailed with no bent nails or nails sticking out the sides. | | | |
| • Structure must meet specifications on the plan. | | | |
| • Arm railings must have vertical braces every 2 feet. | | | |
| • Arm railings must have a top rail and a rail at 12 inches. | | | |
| • Arm railings must be glued, then nailed together with no bent nails. | | | |
| • Arm railings must be constructed of 2 x 2 inch boards, sanded so there will be no splinters. | | | |

## ADDITIONAL WAYS TO ASSESS EFFECTIVENESS

There are many other ways to use surveys to assess the
effectiveness of the teaching/learning process and/or the overall
classroom climate. These include: 1) student climate surveys; 2)
parent surveys; 3) colleague surveys, also known as internal
customer surveys; 4) post-secondary institutional surveys; 5)
graduate surveys; and 6) employer surveys.

Each survey has a purpose and can provide valuable
information if done in a systematic, regular fashion. In part, the
type of survey you would send out depends on the age level of

your students, but everyone should do regular student, parent, and internal surveys. The colleague survey, for instance, can provide valuable information to you from the teachers who receive students who have completed your grade or course. They can assess whether or not the students have the requisite skills to be successful in their class. They can also provide information about the student's problem solving skills and teaming ability. Once you gain feedback from internal customers then you can identify continuous improvement projects and participate in a cross-functional team to create an action plan.

Parent surveys are very important, too, since parents can respond to questions about their child's academic achievement and also how happy the child is in your class. If you give parents the opportunity to assist through a survey, they will have the impression that you are working hard and do care about their child. We can almost guarantee that parents who feel their child's teacher cares will become much more willing to help either with situations as they arise with the child or perhaps even in the classroom.

For too long, educators have ignored parents unless their child was in trouble. Creating a quality classroom requires the combined efforts of all customers and suppliers working together with the teacher/leader to optimize the learning experiences for *all* students. Parents, like the students, will want to know how their responses were implemented into the classroom. Survey results should be returned to parents, along with a report to parents indicating any changes due to their responses. Survey results can also be posted in the classroom for all to see. Charting or graphing the responses gives everyone a simple, clear understanding of what the survey results showed. If you create a newsletter for parents, then include the survey results and any changes.

∧∧∧∧∧∧∧∧

The following is a checksheet tool to help the teacher to implement the **Quality Fusion** technique into their classroom.

Step 1:   The mission, goals and academic integrity of your class are absolutely clear.

√   Established a classroom mission statement.
√   Developed personal goals for the class.
√   Communicated mission and goals to parents/guardians.
√   Aligned classroom mission and goals with those of the school district and the school.

Step 2:   You are demonstrating leadership.

√   Developed a definition of a total quality classroom.
√   Walk-the-Talk about quality.
√   Understand Deming's system of **Profound Knowledge**.
√   Use a variety of teaching styles.
√   Have a CQI program for self and for my students.

Step 3:   All work is pertinent and flows from the students.

√   Broke down barriers on day one by establishing a classroom mission statement with the students.
√   Having students co-create learning experiences.
√   Stressing the importance of teamwork in problem solving and decision making.
√   Defined quality and what it means.
√   Created interdisciplinary learning activities.

Step 4:   The course content is connected to the surrounding community and the real world.

√   Demonstrated the connectedness between work and the real world.
√   Asked the students to analyze the learning assignments.
√   Began TQM training for the students.
√   Implemented student suggestions on how best to improve the learning system.

Step 5:   The student is treated as a "worker," but s/he is also considered as a valuable team member of the "research and development" department.

√   Gave the students an historical overview about the quality movement and discussed examples.
√   Discussed the P-D-C-A cycle and root causes of problems.
√   Took action to establish an atmosphere of trust.

Step 6:    Peer teaching, small group work, and team work are emphasized.
   √  Engaged the students in activities that emphasized teaming and making learning fun.
   √  Engaged students to work independently away from the team, but encouraged them to report the results to their peers.
   √  Provided guidelines and opportunities for students to assess each others' work.
   √  Emphasized the systems approach and regularly asked the student of how we could reduce fear.
   √  Provided students with the opportunity for peer tutoring.
   √  Elaborated upon the types of quality teams.
   √  Introduced the students to additional TQI tools and techniques.

Step 7:    Students should have aesthetic experiences.
   √  Encouraged students to use their imagination daily.
   √  Discussed the importance of art, music, nature, relaxation techniques, mediation, and exercise.

Step 8:    Classroom processes should include reflection.
   √  Developed instant feedback form with students in order to measure classroom processes.
   √  Distributed instant feedback forms in order to examine classroom processes.
   √  Reflected on my mission, goals, and classroom processes.
   √  Set time aside for students to reflect on the relevance of course work to real world issues and encouraged them to discuss their perceptions.
   √  Developed self-assessment and goal setting instruments with students.

Step 9:    The teaching/learning system should undergo constant evaluation.
   √  Used modified Malcolm Baldrige Quality Award Criteria to judge the effectiveness of my classroom processes.
   √  Refined my professional work plan and based it on the mission and goals of my district and school.
   √  Discussed my professional work plan with my principal.
   √  Constantly interviewed and surveyed my students as to the effectiveness of the teaching/learning system.

√   Taught students additional TQI tools, including the use of portfolios for self-assessment.

## Chapter 10: New activities should constantly evolve from the old.

In quality classrooms there is never an absolute end to learning; rather, learning experiences simply evolve one from another and the flow of knowledge continues to build with new concepts being introduced in wave like fashion. In the traditional model of learning, one concept is introduced with lessons directly related to it, homework is assigned, then students take a test to determine their rate of learning. Whether or not the concept was learned, students continue on to the next and the next. The ramifications of this approach to learning are that many, many students don't understand basic concepts and then are forever behind their classmates who do. There are no provisions to ensure all students gain the necessary knowledge to move on. Hence, there are failures and in some cases, students are being held back.

We propose a very different approach to learning. In this model (and others proposed by Myron Tribus, David Langford, and Susan Leddick), students start with the outcomes they are expected to achieve during any semester or year. This list of outcomes is determined by adults, not by students, and is based on child development; basic skills essential for living; the hierarchy of skills within a discipline; as well as district, state, and national standards. Hopefully, in the not too distant future, we will also take into consideration international standards since so few of our students can successfully compete with students graduates of Japanese, German, Australian, or Canadian schools.

The outcomes must be continuously reviewed and upgraded as students learn more and achieve more using the quality learning approach. This means that even though the outcomes may be listed for fifth grade, they must be fluid enough so that students who go beyond the fifth grade are not penalized or put into a "holding" pattern, but can continue to move forward. David Langford, the educational pioneer who first taught quality principles in his computer applications class, tells a phenomenal story of his curriculum. He had carefully prepared the curriculum and taught it for several years, believing that it optimized the students' ability to use computers and that it moved at the fastest pace possible. Within two years of using quality principles he realized that what he had previously taught in four years, was now possible to complete in three years. Within one or two more years the students were learning everything in two years that previously had been covered in four years. Is it possible that we are holding the students back with our archaic methods and traditional thinking about learning? The answer is definitely YES!

Robert Gavin, while CEO of Motorola, recently suggested to a group of educators that they start thinking about how they can pack fifty percent more into each class they teach. He said that this was the kind of thinking that Motorola had to do in order to be competitive and stay in business. Furthermore, this continues to be the challenge of business—to do more in less time with less money and to continue to improve the product to satisfy customers while anticipating their future needs.

Many educators do not feel the sense of urgency of business because of the belief that public education will always remain a mainstay in America. The tragedy of this kind of thinking is that there is no real understanding of how the work of K-12 education (as a system) interacts with business or the systems that comprise our communities. It seems that educators would benefit from summer internships in TQM operated businesses wherein they would shadow the employees from the corporate leader to those on the factory floor. The principle of continuous improvement is a way of life in companies that expect to stay in business. For those who ignore the customer, their suppliers, data, and their competition, success (if there is any) will be fleeting and those companies will soon be out of business. It is a fact that we *must* change the way we do business in education: **we can no longer sit back and pretend that we are doing a good job or that our students are competitive in the global economy**. Most students in the United States today are not getting the education we promised them in the Bill of Rights, and only a handful are fully prepared to meet the challenges of the 21st century.

## ACCEPTING THE STUDENT AS CUSTOMER AND WORKER

If we can no longer sit back and pretend that we are doing a good job or that our students are competitive in the global economy, what can be done? First, accept the idea that students are both your primary customer and also workers within the system. As such, they are in the best position (as previously stated) to help make suggestions for improving the system to build in quality. Second, recognize that as customers, everything that is done in the classroom must be student focused and nothing should interfere with that constancy of purpose: to optimize the learning experiences for all students. Third, give yourself a reality check. After determining your mission and goals, review everything that is done within the classroom—including rules and discipline methods, assignments, teaching methods, classroom arrangements, materials, and resources—to ensure that each is focused on the student and there are no deterrents or road blocks in the path. If there are, then get rid of them NOW! The sooner you recognize those things that are not focused on achieving your constancy of purpose, the sooner the classroom will become a place where all students can achieve.

If you aren't sure about what is getting in the way, write down precisely what you do each day, paying special attention to how you treat all the students, and at the end of the day reflect on each of those. Have you provided the optimal learning environment so that all students can learn? Don't confuse safety issues with strict, top down boss management that is based on coercive tactics or intimidation. The latter have nothing to do with student safety. Students, if given the opportunity, will gladly help you determine rules (if they are necessary) to provide a safe classroom experience.

Another word of caution, if you are frightened of the students (as many educators are these days), the students will sense your fear and take advantage of that. Fear based environments never result in optimizing student achievement. Unfortunately, teachers, new and experienced, often imagine that they must begin the school year with a very tough stance in order to quickly establish authority. However, the long range consequences of this are devastating to the overall success of the class. This approach does nothing to drive out fear and establish a friendly climate where everyone feels a part of some larger group, but it does pit teacher against student and student against student. Teachers who successfully meet the needs of their students for the 21st century, who use quality improvement principles in the classroom, do not need to start the school year that way. They realize the necessity to begin differently in order to have a different end result. Build quality into the classroom from the first moment of the fall and then continue to seek help from students to make your classroom a place without fear where learning is serious but also joyful and where a great deal of pride comes from achieving more than anyone ever imagined.

## EXPANDING THE VISION
Teachers, students and parents have all been brainwashed into believing that only a certain amount of material can be learned within the nine school months. Indeed, textbook companies and authors of curriculum materials have made a fortune selling products based upon this belief. The problem with this limiting

belief is that students learn even less because teachers can't imagine how to get through the book anyway. In fact, this is exactly what has been happening in classrooms across the nation for generations.

Some educators would have us believe that society sends us defective kids, and without those kids and all their problems, teachers would have time to teach more and students would achieve more. That is an interesting argument, but one that doesn't hold up under scrutiny. It is akin to the argument that if more money were put into the educational system then teachers could do a better job and students would learn more. Neither of these makes any real sense, but are and have been convenient excuses that many use and too many others believe.

It is true that too many students come to school with burdens that are the result of living in poverty, with violence, and without proper parental guidance. It is also true that educators are not going to make a major difference in those issues without the help and support of society in general. Many educators believe these problems are so overwhelming to the students that the school can't make a difference. This is a faulty belief! Studies show that for many children and youth, the difference between failure and success is the caring relationship with one adult, and often that adult is a teacher. We can do something about the lives of these children, but we must learn how to. The fact that so many come with problems does not relieve teachers of the burden to create a positive learning environment free of fear so that each student can optimize his learning potential.

The money issue is also false. We are not suggesting that more money would not be nice to have in education, but we do believe that more money, without changing the system, will not have any positive effect on the outcomes. The truth is that about 85 percent of all school budgets is for salaries of professional and support staff. The remaining 15 percent is for everything else. If more money were available, teachers would no doubt demand higher salaries, and still about 15 percent would be left for everything else. The sad fact is that while teacher salaries have increased dramatically in the past ten years, student achievement rates have not significantly been raised. Can we agree that putting more money into teacher salaries is not the answer to a better educational system? Can we also agree that as the educational system shows improvement (through the application of quality principles and processes) there will be cost savings from reducing waste and taxpayers will become enthusiastic education supporters?

By the same token, the purpose of school is not a place to house teachers or to employ teachers, but to optimize the learning experiences of students. Schools are about learning— not teaching! Yes, you can learn without having a teacher, but that is not what we are subscribing to. We use that statement simply to make the point, that learning and teaching are two different and separate events. Just as someone can teach yet no one learn—the same can be said for the reverse; someone can learn yet no one has taught. Remember this, it will be helpful to you in creating a quality classroom.

So, without excuses for the way things are, we must focus on the vision of the future. Create your vision of the optimal learning environment. What does it look like, sound like? What kinds of activities are going on? How are students organized? Create this vision not just from your limited past, but break out of the mold that you've always been in and imagine your utopia in an educational setting. To do this, it will be necessary to eliminate all your biases about people, the community, the school district, the world. Eliminate them and open yourself to the possibilities of having *all* your students achieve way beyond your wildest imagination. Include in your vision of excellence, those students who have been difficult for you, those with disabilities, and those who are different. This is a learning environment that is totally without fear and where students help each other, where the teacher is the leader, mentor, and facilitator and learner right along with the students. Remove from your vision all the limiting thoughts you thought were reality. They are just your reality, and will disappear as you create a learning environment based on quality learning principles.

Realize that your limiting thoughts are your fears and not reality. Fears are difficult, but not impossible to release. Don't expect yourself to do this immediately, but allow yourself the freedom to imagine the possibilities, and then as you introduce quality principles into the classroom you'll find yourself releasing your limiting thoughts one at a time. Try to recall what it was like for you to be a student, and how similar the learning experience today is to those days when you were the student. Perhaps you were a good student. If so, recall whether or not you thought your teacher stretched your learning capabilities. Maybe you were an average or poor student. What kept you from extending your capabilities beyond what you were doing? Fear keeps people down, whether it be the fear of failure or even the fear of success. The fear of people discovering that you are really frightened or not what you appear can also be debilitating.

Imagine a classroom devoid of fear and you can begin to feel the excitement and energy immediately.

## WHAT ABOUT LESSON PLANS

How can you change the vision from the traditional to the new—towards continuous quality learning? These two examples are possibilities for you to consider. They are not intended to be perfect, but we hope that you can take them as possibilities and then imagine going beyond our limited thinking and create your own. One word of caution: we recommend highly that students be allowed to co-create these learning experiences. Teachers can and should start the process by creating the first one or two experiences, but beyond that students can play a major role in determining their own learning experiences.

With students as co-creators of learning experiences, teachers need spend almost no time doing lesson plans. The plans are created together as the year progresses, which does not mean that anarchy will ensue, or that no one is focused. On the contrary, the outcomes or results that are required by the district that meet state and/or national standards are carefully charted and given to all students and their parents. Everyone knows what is expected, but why do we have to be rigid in determining how these outcomes will be achieved? If students are allowed to help in creating the learning experiences, they will be motivated to accomplish them. In the traditional view, teachers are responsible for planning and creating everything that happens in the classroom. The problem is that either only those students who are eager to please or who are blessed with some internal discipline that keeps them focused buy into the assignments. As a consequence, many students do little or nothing and therefore learn nothing while a handful are engaged.

We suggest that even those students one typically thinks of as being fully engaged are only about half engaged and that we have absolutely no idea how far they could advance if given the opportunity to co-create their own learning experiences. The majority who seem unmotivated or disinterested in school will never do any better than they currently do unless something dramatic changes in the system to make a learning environment that works for them. Do not sell these students short. They are NOT unmotivated to learn!

One of the most frequent complaints students have about school is that everything is repeated, taught exactly the same way over and over again. They complain that nothing is ever new or fun! This is more nearly true in social studies and science than in either math or language arts, though we've known school districts where the language arts curriculum repeats itself over and over again with only slightly different readings. Another complaint is the lack of known relevance of the curriculum to the real world. If students don't know how something can benefit them, they most likely will not fully invest in learning it. They might do the "work," but few will retain it other than in their short term memory, and if asked the following year to build on previously learned concepts, they will have no recollection of learning it at all. This is frustrating for teachers who have worked so hard only to discover that their students go to the next class where the next teacher complains that the students weren't taught the necessary prerequisites for success in their class.

Imagine taking an entirely different approach to the teaching/learning process. Imagine asking the students how they want to learn the desired outcomes and for input into how much time they need to learn. Imagine creating a tree diagram together that shows specific tasks and the order each should be done, along with a time table and an indication of who's responsible. This is the way to engage students and relieve yourself of the burden of daily lesson plans. Of course, with very young children (probably up to second or third grade) you'll have to guide this process more but allow the students as much freedom as possible, and through this they will grow in their capabilities.

Examine the district's outcomes for each of the areas of language arts, science, social science, mathematics, and the arts. You may believe that one or more is inappropriate or too difficult for students to grasp. We believe that you can take any subject matter and reduce it to simple forms that even the very youngest child can understand.

You can assist all students to learn even the most complex concepts, provided you find ways to create an experience that they perceive as fun, interesting, and intriguing, and always related to their world. That is the key to creating learning experiences that are meaningful and stretch the limits of previous knowledge.

Let's imagine this is the first learning experience of the fall. You've determined that fifth graders are keenly interested in learning more about themselves (which they are) and how they fit into the world. You know all the outcomes that are listed for the year and you are eager to get the students moving. The first learning experience you create has enough imagination and creative space for the students as they desire and which you and the class can agree on. Students select a partner for this activity

and you introduce them to the idea of working with someone
else so later you can put them into teams.

Selecting partners can be tricky. By the time you get to this
activity we trust that you'll have engaged the students in trust
activities, discussed and established the "rule(s)" of the
classroom, introduced them to quality, and provided some
training.

It's also a good idea to have engaged in the True Colors™
program so that students know what their primary color is and
who would be a good partner. True Colors™ isn't very difficult
to understand and is a great deal of fun for students and adults.
Based on the Meyers-Briggs personality test, it is a simple way
for students and the teacher to identify learning styles and
behavior patterns. Our recommendation is that after all these
prerequisites, you allow students to select their own partners, at
least for this first learning experience.

When creating the learning experience, do it with the end in
mind. What would you like the students to know, demonstrate
and create at the end of this experience?  Point out the outcomes
that are included in this experience and have the students put a
circle around each one. Discuss the ways they will demonstrate
they've achieved each of these outcomes and have the students
put a little check mark in the appropriate column for each
outcome. Now, they know your expectations.

Let's assume you've decided that the students start with their
heritage and learn about their family history. This experience can
then be expanded. Students can create a family tree and learn
about their ancestry. Out of this process can come interviews
with parents or guardians, grandparents, aunts, uncles, and
other relatives. Students can do audio tape interviews or
videotape them. They can write the family history, and trace
their family back several generations to discover their country of
origin. By studying eye and hair color, students can learn
genetics. Each student can have a large poster on the wall and
build upon it with each new piece of information they discover.
Family customs can become a part of this experience too.
Students can bring in recipes (with samples for everyone) of
traditional food their family eats for holidays and other
celebrations. The culture of all students can be shared either
through a demonstration (such as a traditional dance), by having
students read books from authors representing their culture,
showing a video or film, having a guest from that culture come
to class. The possibilities are endless.

Children who are adopted and know little about their birth
parent(s) can concentrate on their adoptive family. If they are of

a different race from the adoptive family they can talk to their family about their ethnic origin and study that along with a study of the adoptive family's origins. In this way, they can appreciate the blending of both cultures while learning more about their own heritage.

For children living in poverty this is an excellent project too. It can give them renewed pride in their family and ethnic heritage. It is very important to be sensitive to issues that many children face today. You will want to discuss the importance of respecting and appreciating all different kinds of people and how interesting our nation is because we are so diverse.

Each child might be asked to share something with the class about his/her country of origin. That can culminate in a heritage festival where all parents are invited and indeed, where parents may be asked to bring an ethnic dish that the entire group can share. Another idea for the heritage festival is to have parents and/or grandparents come and tell a story of what it was like when they were children. Tape record the story and later have the students draw a picture or write a poem relating to the story. These can be bound, along with the audio tape and given to that child to take home or they can have a permanent place in the classroom. If they are kept in the classroom, encourage children of differing ethnic backgrounds to read and listen and you'll be developing an appreciation for diversity among your students.

As this experience is being worked through, have the students maintain a record of which outcomes they've accomplished. They are asked to fill in the space that indicates they've mastered each outcome, but only after they are able to demonstrate this. Thus, for some of the outcomes perhaps you've agreed that students must demonstrate competence. To do this, you either schedule a day or two for these activities or they can demonstrate it to you independently of the class. I highly recommend that demonstrations be done in front of the class, and as the school year progresses expand the audience to include other classes, parents, families, and the community.

The teacher facilitates the learning and acts as the mentor. You'll be very busy assisting students as they grapple with this information, and you'll want to work closely with the media specialist to help students find the information they need. You may organize a field trip to the local library or city/county clerk of records office to find information about their families. The teacher is responsible for expanding the vision for all students, through asking questions and suggesting other possibilities. Though you don't have any lesson plans to hang on to, you'll want to keep a journal of the activities students engage in, and how they assist in achieving the learning outcomes. Keep good track of all materials used, places visited, videos, and other resources as you'll need this information for the debriefing activity.

Each day you'll want students to give you a minute of their time for fast feedback. This is the way you'll keep updated on how each student is progressing, where their frustrations are, and how you can help. If you don't have the opportunity to get to each student each day, the fast feedback will give you very valuable information.

Of course, you've set a time limit for this activity, and students have created a **Tree Diagram** for themselves or a **Flow Chart** with key process points fixed so you can assess how they are doing.

## NEW ACTIVITIES FROM THE OLD

When the first learning experience is over, you should debrief your students so you can get a clear picture of what worked for them and what didn't. Have students review the outcomes for the semester or year and see how they can build upon the previously learned ones. Then brainstorm with students how they want to build onto this experience. Allow everyone time to share their ideas and move towards building consensus. The product they end up with may be very different, but the learning experience can be the same for all.

Imagine your students building upon this first learning experience by wanting to do something to make their neighborhood better. They might research opportunities for helping within the neighborhood, or there may be some pressing concern that interests them. Build a consensus among students as to what direction they would like the learning experience to take and write the purpose (mission) on the board. Next, ask students what they'd consider quality factors or WOW factors to be. This will be the basis for evaluation or the expectations upon which the project will be assessed. Next, ask students if they were to describe the "best" way to accomplish the project, what would they say. In other words, you will want students to define their expectations. If they don't come up with all the pertinent ones, then you, as a partner in the class, can add yours.

Prior to asking students to commence, review the expected yearly outcomes and see which one(s) will be accomplished by completing the learning experience. Have students again go through and circle those that apply, and place a small check mark at the level at which the class agrees each outcome must be achieved.

With students create a flow chart of the process that will be used for this learning experience. Students will then have a picture of how the learning experience will unfold and what the process check points will be. You can add a time line and identify the person responsible on any flow chart simply by creating a deployment flow chart and adding dates.

With this method students have information that gives them a clear picture of expectations, responsibilities, check points, and results. Everyone knows what is expected, and everyone knows what criteria will be used to assess the final product. This takes away excuses, but more importantly allows students the freedom to work without fear of a breakdown in the process. Enthusiasm will run high when the learning environment and learning experiences are established collaboratively, with students identifying their products.

## THE FINAL PRODUCT
We've been schooled to believe that an assignment means that everyone does the same thing. In quality classrooms there is plenty of room for creativity and invention. Many students may be creating new and different products from the others', though the learning experience is the same for' all. Remember the importance of the constancy of purpose and think about how to optimize the learning experience for all students. Some students may view the product visually, others will want to write, while still others will want to use a different approach. With time, all students can expand their approach to learning by experiencing it in many forms.

An example of this might be that your students are working on applied technology projects. One team may have constructed a robot that can be used to perform simple functions such as picking up things in one place and moving them to another place. Another team has decided to invent a means of assisting muscular dystrophy patients out of bed. Still another team has created a short, animated film using computers. The last team decided to build a model roller coaster. The end product of each team is very different, but each meets the goal of the learning experience.

Through a process of teaching students how to create learning experiences that are fun and real world oriented, and then applying quality improvement tools for planning and studying the results, students can and do become fully engaged in their own learning. These students are enthusiastic and energetic learners, eager to stretch the limits of their knowledge and hence their world.

If all adults erased from our minds the limiting beliefs we have about what, how, why, and how much students can learn, we would be simply amazed at what they can do. The power of curiosity is phenomenal, and by using quality process techniques, students can learn to unleash their curiosity to accomplish great feats.

At the end of each school year students will be eager to continue. No longer will the last two weeks of school be wasted collecting textbooks, cleaning lockers, etc. In classrooms where quality improvement is a way of life, students eagerly work to the last day of school.

ΔΔΔΔΔΔΔΔ

The following is a checksheet tool to help the teacher to implement the **Quality Fusion** technique into their classroom.

Step 1:  The mission, goals and academic integrity of your class are absolutely clear.
√  Established a classroom mission statement.
√  Developed personal goals for the class.
√  Communicated mission and goals to parents/guardians.
√  Aligned classroom mission and goals with those of the school district and the school.

Step 2:  You are demonstrating leadership.
√  Developed a definition of a total quality classroom.
√  Walk-the-Talk about quality.
√  Understand Deming's system of **Profound Knowledge**.
√  Use a variety of teaching styles.
√  Have a CQI program for self and for my students.

Step 3:  All work is pertinent and flows from the students.
√  Broke down barriers on day one by establishing a classroom mission statement with the students.
√  Having students co-create learning experiences.
√  Stressing the importance of teamwork in problem solving and decision making.
√  Defined quality and what it means.
√  Created interdisciplinary learning activities.

Step 4:  The course content is connected to the surrounding community and the real world.
√  Demonstrated the connectedness between work and the real world.
√  Asked the students to analyze the learning assignments.
√  Began TQM training for the students.
√  Implemented student suggestions on how best to improve the learning system.

Step 5:  The student is treated as a "worker," but s/he is also considered as a valuable team member of the "research and development" department.
√  Gave the students an historical overview about the quality movement and discussed examples.
√  Discussed the P-D-C-A cycle and root causes of problems.
√  Took action to establish an atmosphere of trust.

Step 6:    Peer teaching, small group work, and team work are emphasized.
    √ Engaged the students in activities that emphasized teaming and making learning fun.
    √ Engaged students to work independently away from the team, but encouraged them to report the results to their peers.
    √ Provided guidelines and opportunities for students to assess each others' work.
    √ Emphasized the systems approach and regularly asked the student of how we could reduce fear.
    √ Provided students with the opportunity for peer tutoring.
    √ Elaborated upon the types of quality teams.
    √ Introduced the students to additional TQI tools and techniques.

Step 7:    Students should have aesthetic experiences.
    √ Encouraged students to use their imagination daily.
    √ Discussed the importance of art, music, nature, relaxation techniques, mediation, and exercise.

Step 8:    Classroom processes should include reflection.
    √ Developed instant feedback form with students in order to measure classroom processes.
    √ Distributed instant feedback forms in order to examine classroom processes.
    √ Reflected on my mission, goals, and classroom processes.
    √ Set time aside for students to reflect on the relevance of course work to real world issues and encouraged them to discuss their perceptions.
    √ Developed self-assessment and goal setting instruments with students.

Step 9:    The teaching/learning system should undergo constant evaluation.
    √ Used modified Malcolm Baldrige Quality Award Criteria to judge the effectiveness of my classroom processes.
    √ Refined my professional work plan and based it on the mission and goals of my district and school.
    √ Discussed my professional work plan with my principal.
    √ Constantly interviewed and surveyed my students as to the effectiveness of the teaching/learning system.

√  Taught students additional TQI tools, including the use of portfolios for self-assessment.

Step 10: New activities should constantly evolve from the old.

√  Presented the outcomes that the students are expected to achieve during the semester/year.

√  Reaffirmed that all classroom processes are student-focused.

√  Constantly revising my vision of the optimal learning environment.

√  Co-created learning experiences with the students.

√  Integrated many of the learning experiences and demonstrated how they relate to the real world.

√  Facilitated new activities that arose from the old.

## Chapter 11: There must be an audience beyond the teacher.

In the past, educators have created assignments that students "do for them." That is to say, the teacher creates the assignments based on the scope and sequence of the curriculum, and students complete the assignments and turn them in to the teacher who grades and returns them to the student. The cycle goes from teacher to student to teacher to student.

In this model, the student performs work for the teacher and solely for the teacher. Seldom is there any intrinsic reward or pride in workmanship. It is fantasy to imagine that students complete their work in traditional classrooms for anyone but the teacher. Although occasionally, a student will be motivated by wanting to please parents or some other adult figure. Rarely, do students learn and complete complex tasks because they see the inherent virtue in doing it, or because they know this is but one step along a long road towards some far-off career goal. No, most students go through the motions of completing assignments because someone has "assigned" or given them something *to do*. It is a wonder that as many students complete their work as there are, especially when considering how irrelevant so many assignments are.

In the above model, the teacher is the final customer. In other words, the teacher has to be "satisfied" if the student is to be rewarded with a grade. The classroom becomes "teacher-centered," rather than "student-centered."

Perhaps we would be better off thinking about learning experiences rather than assignments. The word assignment assumes that an external force has directed us to do something or carry out a task. This is exactly what we need to consider changing. In quality classrooms, students are responsible for co-creating their learning experiences. By engaging in this exercise, students create experiences that have meaning to them, and therefore view them as a labor of love rather than as punishment (at worst) or as going through the motions of learning.

173

By studying the psychology portion of Deming's theory of profound knowledge, we are able to understand that what motivates human behavior is not producing for others, but producing or creating something for ourselves. When students have break-through learning, they experience an exhilaration that extends far beyond the satisfaction of performing a task because they have been told to do so. It is interesting that we educators have studied so much psychology and learning theory, yet so often we really don't understand what motivates people. There are quite simply no external rewards that can compel students to learn using high levels of critical thinking skills. You may argue that prisoners do things because they are told to do them, or that small children do things because they are told to do them but this argument does not hold up under scrutiny.

Let's examine the case of prisoners first. It is a well documented fact that what keeps prisoners of war mentally healthy is their ability to sabotage the enemy's efforts at coercion and their ability to fantasize about life on the outside. It is also true that while individuals incarcerated in our prisons may obey the commands from the guards, they have little or no interest in doing a good job and are seldom given jobs that would/could result in pride in workmanship.

Pride in workmanship comes from performing feats and solving "puzzles" that are a stretch beyond our current limitations. It comes from the good feelings about being able to do something for oneself. Consider the case of the two year old who is asked to help Mommie by carrying a big box of diapers from one room to the next. The box may be nearly as big as the child, and must seem overwhelmingly difficult. But, the Mommie has high expectations, presents the puzzle to the child and gives the child, encouragement and support along the way. Even as they walk into the other room, Mommie might say something like: "Wow, you are so strong and what a big boy/girl you are. Look how helpful you are to Mommie." These are encouraging words which help build self-esteem and give the child a real sense of pride in him/herself to have accomplished a great feat. On the other hand, if the mother were to ask the small child to pick up a 30 pound weight and carry it into the next room, the child would feel frustrated at not being able to budge the weight. Eventually, s/he might begin to cry thinking s/he had let Mommie down. In short, the experience would not be positive.

As children grow and explore their world, their curiosity becomes the driving force for most of their activity. It is this curiosity about the world that our school system has stifled over the generations, and now is causing us to reconsider ways to optimize the learning experiences for all students. Humans are naturally curious beings, and in schools where experiences for exploration are encouraged, the students become better problem solvers and engage in higher level thinking skills. In schools where rote memorization and learning by regurgitating facts is a way of life, less critical thinking, less creativity, and less curiosity are achieved. These students may have learned to memorize and remember long enough to give back answers on a test, but they've learned nothing about how to collect many sources of information to generate a hypothesis or create new knowledge from previously learned material. In the latter case, students "learn" because someone directs them. In the former case, natural curiosity and invention make learning a joy, and the resulting product is a source of great pride to the student, her/his parents, and others.

**Example:     Integrating a Middle School Curriculum**
As an example, consider this scenario with some middle school students. The previous spring the teachers got together and agreed that they would work together with students to eliminate all busywork and combine assignments when possible. Students and teachers together could co-create the experiences. Since this was new for the teachers, (also for the students), they were somewhat concerned about how this would happen, but were determined to forge ahead. Since students and teachers were already organized into teams (called families), it provided an organizational pattern that could work.

In the fall, Family A gathered together and asked the students for suggestions about what interested them and explained that the plan was to build educational experiences around their interests. With some guidance the students were able to list a wide range of topics including AIDS, the environment, violence, and music. Next, the teachers led the group in a discussion of "how do you want to learn about these things." This naturally led to "what will the product of our education be...or how will we demonstrate that we've learned."

One group decided they wanted to produce a school musical about the environment. It would include doing research on the environment; writing the story, and then the script; writing the music and lyrics; designing the set; constructing the set; painting the set; designing and making the advance posters and banners; designing and printing the program; designing and making the costumes and props; learning the music and playing and/or singing; acting and directing; and printing and selling tickets.

From this list of tasks or steps to achieve the goal, the students and their teachers listed all the curricular activities that were involved. A partial list includes:

- Mathematics
  - > Geometry—set design and construction
  - > Addition, subtraction, division, multiplication—tickets, programs, costumes, props, etc.
- English
  - > Research
  - > Writing and composition
  - > Instructions
  - > Speech
- Social Studies-Research
  - > History
  - > Current Events
  - > Geography
  - > Sociology
- Science
  - > Biology
  - > Ecology
  - > Chemistry
- Music
  - > Music composition
  - > Read music
  - > Instrumental
  - > Vocal
  - > Harmony
  - > Rhythm
- Art
  - > Graphic design
  - > Form
  - > Style
  - > Different Media
  - > Printing - silk screen and offset
- Shop
  - > Carpentry
  - > Electrical
- Business—Sales
- Computer Applications
  - > Word Processing
  - > Spreadsheet
  - > Desk Top Publishing

- Technical
    > Editing
    > Camera Work
    > Audio
    > Lighting
    > Electricity
- Costume
    > Design
    > Sewing
    > Pattern Making
    > Tailoring

The students and teachers became very excited about the possibilities of performing this production for the community and other schools around the area. Next, they looked at the outcomes required for seventh and eight graders at their school. Together the students and teachers agreed that throughout the year, this is what they would focus on and the production would be the culminating activity for the year. They agreed that each student and teacher would keep a daily journal of their activity and record their feelings about it and the project.

The next thing they did was establish quality committees to oversee the project. One committee was the Quality Leadership Team, which consisted of four students, two teachers and two parents. The principal was an ex-officio member who attended all the meetings and whose primary responsibility was to serve as a liaison to the central administration and the community. This group met monthly in the evening to go over quality improvement team reports and help maintain the focus for the year. The team was carefully selected at a meeting with parents, students, and teachers. The Quality Leadership Team's mission was well defined.

The quality improvement committees consisted of one teacher and six students. The purpose of these committees was to facilitate continuous process improvement throughout the year, and to survey students, parents, teachers, administrators, and the community for their satisfaction levels periodically during the year. These committees also had the responsibility for collecting suggestions and engaging the family in a Plan-Do-Study-Act (PDSA) cycle for improvement. As situations (opportunities for improvement) arose, these committees led the process improvement plan. Student membership on the quality improvement committees changed every six weeks—they were staggered to maintain the benefit of student experience to provide leadership opportunities for more students.

Family A used quality planning and process improvement tools to lead them towards their goal. First in smaller groups, then by coming together and combining their ideas, the family determined what the quality factors (WOW factors) would be for this environmental play. When consensus was reached, these were written in large letters and placed in every classroom. Next, came the operational definitions for each component. These were discussed and agreed upon within each discipline then brought back to the group as a whole for fine tuning and final agreement. The planning process, though difficult, provided the foundation for achieving the goal. If they had not adequately planned, the work could never have been accomplished.

As the students progressed through the school year, they along with the teacher, determined which of the outcomes would be satisfied by completing a certain chunk of the larger task. As students and teachers worked, more and more results (outcomes) were accomplished. In many cases, such as mathematics, the student's work far exceeded the expected outcomes. Teachers were careful to flow chart each process with their students and agree upon critical points in the process that required an evaluation by the teacher. Students were also taught ways to critique their own and each other's work. Learning styles were accommodated since this project allowed students some flexibility to determine the way in which they wanted to contribute. Everyone was actively involved and received valuable hands-on, applied learning.

In the Spring, the students performed their production. Every student was involved in some aspect of the performance, either on stage, in the orchestra, choir, or on the technical crew. They created a survey for the audience that asked questions about increased knowledge of the environment due to this play and also a general satisfaction with the overall performance and production. It was a major production and students, parents, teachers, administration, school board and the community took great pride in the work of these students and teachers. The production was videotaped and copies were sold to raise money for the following year. The "Family" had previously agreed to spend 25-30 percent of the revenues on a year-end celebration for a job well-done. Best of all, there were no motivation problems during the year. Students were very empowered to take leadership roles and had great pride in their work.

On a smaller scale, English, Social Studies, Science and Mathematics teachers can work together and provide common learning experiences that allow students to prepare one significant piece of research that can be assessed by teachers of each discipline for style and content. Students can take pride in work that has meaning to them, that stretches the limits of their capabilities, and that meets high quality factors.

If you maintain low expectations, the resulting work will be less than you anticipated, and neither you nor the students will take pride in accomplishing it. Joy in learning comes from knowing that you have accomplished a difficult task and that it has meaning in your life. Low expectations simply result in lower morale and a sense of worthlessness. No one likes people to waste their time, and this is as true for students as it is for adults. Be creative. Better yet, allow the students the opportunity to help create their own learning experiences so each can have meaning beyond the classroom and so the product of that experience can extend to the home, community, state, region, or nation.

## STUDENTS' HOPES AND DREAMS

One of the key problems of at-risk youth is their sense of hopelessness and the feeling that there will be "no" tomorrow. These feelings come from a life of poverty and sorrow, a life of chaos and crisis. Remember that many of these students come from neighborhoods where violence is common, and many of them have witnessed murders of friends, neighbors, or family members. Even though race and gender are also at-risk factors, the significance of these pales in importance when compared with poverty. Unfortunately the numbers of children living in poverty is growing yearly in our nation. What can or should teachers do for these children?

First, we must gain an understanding of what each child wants to "do" when s/he grows up. If you know this, then you can help children create a dream. We call it a dream machine. It is crucial to one's sense of hope for the future. Let's say that Charlie wants to be a policeman when he grows up. Charlie is five years old, lives in one of the government projects with his Mom, Grandma, and three older siblings in one of our nation's inner cities. His family lives on welfare.

As a teacher, as soon as you discover that Charlie wants to be a policeman, explore that with him. Find out what he knows about what policemen do. Then, find some books that relate to policemen and see if you can get a hat, badge or jacket for the dress-up corner. Talk to your local police department to see who might have the beat in Charlie's neighborhood and invite that individual to come to class. Have Charlie introduce him. You might also ask the police officer if s/he will take Charlie under his/her wing. This is the perfect mentoring relationship. It may not be a part of an official mentoring program within your district, but will it help Charlie? Yes! Will it help Charlie keep his dream alive? Yes!

Use your imagination to offer Charlie more learning experiences that relate directly to his dream. Engage him in drawing, creating a collage, painting, or other art forms that can be an outward manifestation of keeping his dream alive. Relate the school work directly to whatever his interests are. In fact, in the early grades (or in non-graded primary schools) this is crucial. Expand your notions of what children have to do to achieve the outcomes dictated by your district or state. In other words, explore the possibility that not everyone has to "do" the same thing, or create the same picture, or write the same story. Learning experiences for small children that engage them in opportunities to connect school with their world will go a long way towards decreasing discipline problems and increasing motivation.

Parents love to watch their children. As often as possible have the students create learning products or demonstrate their knowledge for parents and the community. One word of caution: **NEVER** allow the production or demonstration to be just for the purpose of entertaining parents. Attach everything to learning outcomes or results. With students as co-creators, arrange learning experiences that are meaningful and that can demonstrate extension of knowledge so that whatever the class is demonstrating in the spring represents a major leap forward in knowledge, skills, and abilities from what was demonstrated in the fall and winter. When students perform their work or demonstrate their work to others, they grow in communication skills and self-esteem. These are major elements in ensuring future success, and with practice comes growth.

At all levels of education, we want to invite others into the building and classroom regularly. Allow students to share with visitors what they are working on. They should be able to explain how any learning experience relates to the required outcomes, and if they are going to go beyond the required outcomes to attain much higher levels of learning, that, too, should be noted. Empower students to speak to visitors since they assume a lead role in the learning experience. This expands students' abilities to communicate with adults as well as enables them to demonstrate pride in workmanship. The focus of any classroom must remain on the students, since they are the reason for schools.

Portfolios also provide a means of demonstrating growth in knowledge and capabilities. Students determine what belongs in their portfolios based on the Quality factors agreed upon by the class and their own sense of "best" work. Since students are selecting their best work for the portfolio, it follows that they are in the best position to relate this information to parents and other visitors.

Other ways to demonstrate student growth is by producing videos of them in action. Parents and students truly enjoy seeing the results of their progress. A videotape also provides valuable feedback to the student(s). Teams of students can critique their own teamwork and their results. Individual students can do a self-assessment of their progress and be taught to look for the quality factors. Teams and individuals can even be taught to critique each other's work and thereby provide valuable feedback. In the end, the results of any videotaped experience can extend far beyond the particular learning experience that has just been completed.

Some schools are videotaping students to use as "evidence" of misbehavior within the classroom or building. Maybe this can be an effective quality tool if used in conjunction with cause/effect diagrams, relations diagrams, or force field analysis. We would resist the idea of using the video camera simply for establishing blame and as an punitive measure, however, if used as a beginning for a personal continuous improvement project, it may have great merit. Otherwise, it becomes an arm of "Big Brother" driving fear and intimidation into the building, which is not helpful in improving the learning experience of students. The aim in a quality school and classroom is that all students will be responsible for their own behavior. This is accomplished by teaching them a problem solving model, allowing them to co-create learning experiences meaningful to them, and allowing them pride in workmanship.

## VOLUNTEER OR SERVICE LEARNING

While it is important for students to experience pride in creating educational products that extend beyond the classroom, it is also important for students to give back to their community and thus gain a sense of oneness with their community. Some school districts have implemented a volunteer project as a requirement for graduation. We believe that service work or volunteerism can and probably should become a part of everyone's educational experiences each year beginning in kindergarten.

The experiences that students co-create can easily include volunteerism. Also, intergenerational volunteer experiences can help provide a connection to other adults that is often missing in the lives of many youth.

## ENTREPRENEURSHIP

Mt. Edgecumbe High School in Sitka, Alaska has a student-run salmon business that uses quality management principles. In fact, they export salmon to Japan. This is an excellent example of how a school can apply learning to real world situations, and where students can immediately see their successes and/or failures. What is happening in Mt. Edgecumbe can certainly be emulated in other schools around the country.

Students at Old Orchard Beach High School in Old Orchard Beach, Maine operate a picture-frame shop which teaches students how to run a small business from the framing skills to sales and billing.

ΛΛΛΛΛΛΛΛ

The following is a checksheet tool to help the teacher to implement the **Quality Fusion** technique into their classroom.

Step 1:  The mission, goals and academic integrity of your class are absolutely clear.
√  Established a classroom mission statement.
√  Developed personal goals for the class.
√  Communicated mission and goals to parents/guardians.
√  Aligned classroom mission and goals with those of the school district and the school.

Step 2:  You are demonstrating leadership.
√  Developed a definition of a total quality classroom.
√  Walk-the-Talk about quality.
√  Understand Deming's system of **Profound Knowledge**.
√  Use a variety of teaching styles.
√  Have a CQI program for self and for my students.

Step 3:  All work is pertinent and flows from the students.
√  Broke down barriers on day one by establishing a classroom mission statement with the students.
√  Having students co-create learning experiences.
√  Stressing the importance of teamwork in problem solving and decision making.
√  Defined quality and what it means.
√  Created interdisciplinary learning activities.

Step 4:  The course content is connected to the surrounding community and the real world.
√  Demonstrated the connectedness between work and the real world.
√  Asked the students to analyze the learning assignments.
√  Began TQM training for the students.
√  Implemented student suggestions on how best to improve the learning system.

Step 5:  The student is treated as a "worker," but s/he is also considered as a valuable team member of the "research and development" department.
√  Gave the students an historical overview about the quality movement and discussed examples.
√  Discussed the P-D-C-A cycle and root causes of problems.
√  Took action to establish an atmosphere of trust.

Step 6:    Peer teaching, small group work, and team work are emphasized.
√    Engaged the students in activities that emphasized teaming and making learning fun.
√    Engaged students to work independently away from the team, but encouraged them to report the results to their peers.
√    Provided guidelines and opportunities for students to assess each others' work.
√    Emphasized the systems approach and regularly asked the student of how we could reduce fear.
√    Provided students with the opportunity for peer tutoring.
√    Elaborated upon the types of quality teams.
√    Introduced the students to additional TQI tools and techniques.

Step 7:    Students should have aesthetic experiences.
√    Encouraged students to use their imagination daily.
√    Discussed the importance of art, music, nature, relaxation techniques, mediation, and exercise.

Step 8:    Classroom processes should include reflection.
√    Developed instant feedback form with students in order to measure classroom processes.
√    Distributed instant feedback forms in order to examine classroom processes.
√    Reflected on my mission, goals, and classroom processes.
√    Set time aside for students to reflect on the relevance of course work to real world issues and encouraged them to discuss their perceptions.
√    Developed self-assessment and goal setting instruments with students.

Step 9:    The teaching/learning system should undergo constant evaluation.
√    Used modified Malcolm Baldrige Quality Award Criteria to judge the effectiveness of my classroom processes.
√    Refined my professional work plan and based it on the mission and goals of my district and school.
√    Discussed my professional work plan with my principal.
√    Constantly interviewed and surveyed my students as to the effectiveness of the teaching/learning system.

√   Taught students additional TQI tools, including the use of portfolios for self-assessment.

Step 10: New activities should constantly evolve from the old.

√   Presented the outcomes that the students are expected to achieve during the semester/year.

√   Reaffirmed that all classroom processes are student-focused.

√   Constantly revising my vision of the optimal learning environment.

√   Co-created learning experiences with the students.

√   Integrated many of the learning experiences and demonstrated how they relate to the real world.

√   Facilitated new activities that arose from the old.

Step 11: There must be an audience beyond the teacher.

√   Encouraged students to "dream" about what they want to do in the future.

√   Allowed students to invite others into the classroom and to share with them what they are working on.

√   Encouraged students to share their portfolios with parents and other visitors.

√   Extended learning experiences into the community.

# Summary

The benefits of using total quality management processes in combination with Foxfire principles are enormous. The synergy creates an experience that engages all students to become active, co-partners in their education. For generations, we (educators) have created a climate that encouraged students to become passive learners. With the examples in this book, we've attempted to demonstrate successful ways teachers can impact the lives of their students by exciting them about learning, empowering them to become actively engaged in continuous improvement, and encouraging them to work in partnership with teacher and fellow students to improve the classroom processes.

The responsibility for improving the classroom, and all its processes, rests with the teacher. Leadership must precede action and improvement, therefore, we hope that we've been successful in providing some guidelines upon which to act.

Prior to beginning, be certain that you've a thorough understanding the theory of total quality improvement. This is a necessity, otherwise, you're apt to select those elements that most nearly complement your current paradigms and disregard those that seem in conflict. Study the theory through the eyes of the late Dr. W. Edwards Deming, Dr. J.M. Juran, and other quality experts. Include in your studies, works by Dr. William Glasser, particularly *The Quality School,* since he addresses, so aptly the issue of student responsibility.

Once you begin implementing quality improvement processes in the classroom it is necessary to continue learning and reading about quality. What may seem so simple at first, becomes rather complex when one tries to implement it. Armed with a thorough understanding, you'll be in a better position to discuss continuous quality improvement with colleagues, administrators, parents, students and the general public.

If your school district has not adapted the principles of quality, there will be an even more important need for you to be an articulate spokesperson for the new ways you'll be working within your classroom. Only by your own continuous improvement journey, and study will you feel adequately prepared to meet whatever challenges may come your way. We cannot emphasize the need to embark on a program of continuous education and improvement yourself.

Our goal has been to draw connections for the reader to ways to meld continuous quality improvement into an educational system that succeeds in expanding the learning experiences for all students. We have spoken repeatedly of the concept of continuous improvement and hope that you've been able to grasp that every classroom process and every learning experience is a potential continuous improvement project.

Throughout the school year, engage students in leadership roles for improvement. Have them collect data for system change, and also for personal change. Combine debriefing exercises with regular customer satisfaction surveys. These will provide you with valuable information. Be certain to inform students and others of the feedback you're getting and encourage their participation by providing suggestions for improvement. Each of these activities will lend great value to your improvement efforts.

The time has come for educators one and all to realize that things can and must be improved for the sake of students, communities, and the nation. No one can afford to rest on current levels of success—continuous improvement must become a way of life—every day and in every way. As educators, we have an obligation to be role models for this philosophy and mentor students to become problem solvers.

Great schools and great classrooms share these elements:

- Trust
- Pride
- Quality
- Fun

Begin today to create the quality classroom that you imagined earlier in this book, and don't be distracted by those who say "it cannot be done." More and more teachers across the nation are joining the move to continuous quality learning. They have ceased blaming students, parents, administration, government or others for the problems that beset them and realize that it is the system that is keeping everyone (including themselves) from being successful.

Our advice is to confront whatever fears you may have about empowering students and letting go of control and move forward in spit of them! Continue to push the limits of your comfort zone and you'll experience feelings of renewal that will encourage you to continue.

Remember, this approach is not a silver bullet! It is not a quick fix! However, by following these suggestions, you will witness gradual improvements that can be sustained over time while making additional improvements. Don't be discouraged because you think improvement is coming too slowly, or if mistakes are made along the way. Our experience is that students, provided there is a trusted, safe, and respectful environment will want to help. The name of the Total Quality Game is continuous improvement. This means that problems are viewed as opportunities for improvement. Patience, persistence, and belief will carry the day.

Good luck!  You can make a difference!

# References

Barker, Joel . *Future Edge: Discovering the New Paradigms of Success*. NY: Wm. Morrow & Co., Inc., 1992.

Byrnes, Margaret A., Cornesky, Robert A., and Byrnes, Lawrence W. *The Quality Teacher: Implementing Total Quality Management in the Classroom*. FL: Cornesky & Associates, Inc. 1992.

Covey, Stephen R. *The Seven Habits of Highly Effective People*. NY: Simon & Schuster, 1989.

Crosby, Philip B. *Quality Without Tears: The Art of Hassle-Free Management*. NY: McGraw-Hill Book Co., 1984.

Deming, W. Edwards. *Out of the Crisis*. Cambridge, MA: Productivity Press or Washington, DC: The George Washington University, MIT-CAES, 1982.

Glasser, William. *The Quality School* . NY: Harper & Row. 1990.

Glasser, William.*The Quality School Teacher*. NY: HarperCollins Publishers, Inc. 1993.

Kerr-Rike, Elizabeth. *Guiding Dramatic Play*. TN: 3 R't's Press, Second Edition, 1980.

Wigginton, Eliot. *Sometimes a Shining Moment: The Foxfire Experience*. NY: Doubleday, 1985.

# APPENDIX

# AFFINITY DIAGRAM

The **Affinity Diagram** was invented by Kawakita Jiro and is used as a planning tool. Unlike the Scenario Builder which roughly quantifies the outcomes resulting from a change in a system, the affinity diagram is more of a creative procedure that tries to organize the issues concerning a process or a problem without quantification.

An **Affinity Diagram** is especially useful in elucidating a problem or issue that is difficult to understand, or a problem or issue that appears to be enormous and in disarray. One benefit of using the **Affinity Diagram** at the very beginning of a TQI process is that it helps build consensus among the task force members studying the problem.

An **Affinity Diagram** is rarely used alone. However, when used with the **Scenario Builder**, and/or with a **Relations Diagram**, and/or with the **Nominal Group Process**, it can help an action team and/or task force to identify the major root causes of a problem or issue. When the major root causes of a problem or issue are identified, the group can direct its efforts more efficiently.

## Procedure
### 1. Statement of the Problem
Under the direction of a team leader the members of the team should arrive at a statement of the problem or issue being addressed. For example: The Mr. Jones' tenth grade social studies classes wanted to include a community service project as part of the curriculum. The students wanted to volunteer to improve their community in some capacity. A task force of students and Mr. Jones, along with two parents agreed to work on the problem. The question they asked was: What are the obstacles to including a community service project requirement in Mr. Jones' tenth grade social studies classes?

### 2. Recording the Perceptions
Working alone, each person writes his/her comment on sticky note paper or on an index card after announcing his/her idea to the group. The purpose of announcing the perception is to permit others to piggy back any related ideas. Only a single idea should be entered on one note paper/index card. This proceeds until all of the people have exhausted their perceptions. Remember, as in any brainstorming session, there is no verbal exchange between the members. All of the notes are placed on the wall or in the center of a large conference table. Let's assume

the following perceptions were generated and posted.

```
┌─────────────────┐
│  The school     │
│  board won't    │
│  permit it.     │
└─────────────────┘

┌─────────────────┐
│  Students lack  │
│  transportation │
└─────────────────┘

┌─────────────────┐
│  Class periods  │
│  are too short. │
└─────────────────┘

┌───────────────────┐
│  The principal won't │
│  support it.      │
└───────────────────┘

┌───────────────────┐
│  The superintendent │
│  won't support it.  │
└───────────────────┘

┌───────────────────┐
│  There is no need. │
└───────────────────┘

┌─────────────────┐
│  Other teachers │
│  won't support  │
│  the idea and   │
│  cooperate in   │
│  flexible       │
│  scheduling.    │
└─────────────────┘

┌────────────────────────┐
│  The liability of having │
│  students out of the building │
│  is too great.         │
└────────────────────────┘

┌────────────────────────────┐
│  The community doesn't want │
│  students out of school     │
│  unsupervised (too difficult │
│  to supervise).             │
└────────────────────────────┘

┌────────────────────────┐
│  Community service isn't │
│  perceived to be a school │
│  function.             │
└────────────────────────┘

┌──────────────────────────┐
│  Parents don't want students │
│  out of school.          │
└──────────────────────────┘

┌──────────────────────────┐
│  Students lack commitment. │
└──────────────────────────┘
```

3.  Group Similar and/or Related Perceptions

The members of the group place similar cards (or sticky notes) into related groups. These are said to have an "affinity" for each other. It is important that the members of the task force do this is silence. The note pads (or cards) can be moved any number of times. It is not uncommon to have ten related groups, although one may have a few as three.

The grouping that resulted from the aforementioned example are shown below.

## GROUP 1

The school board will not permit it.

The Superintendent won't permit it.

The Principal won't support it.

Community service is not perceived a function of the schools.

The liability of having students out of the building is too great.

## GROUP 2

There is no need.

Students aren't interested.

Students lack transportation.

Students lack commitment.

## GROUP 3

| Parents don't want students out of school. |

## GROUP 4

| Impossible to supervise. |

| Parents don't want students out of school. |

| Other teachers won't support the idea and cooperate in flexible scheduling. |

| Class periods are too short. |

## 4. Assign a Name to Each Group with a Header Designation

The team leader should read all of the cards in each group and the members should agree to a name that can be assigned to each of the groups. The team leader then writes a header card for each group.  If there is a miscellaneous group, the task force should exam each perception and, if possible, place each note or card into one of the groups. If not, it is acceptable to have a group named "miscellaneous."  In the above example, the four header groups are shown below.

## GROUP 1: THE ADMINISTRATION

| The school board will not permit it. |

| The Superintendent won't permit it. |

| The Principal won't support it. |

| Community service is not perceived a function of the schools. |

| The liability of having students out of the building is too great. |

## GROUP 2: THE STUDENTS

| There is no need. |
| --- |

| Students aren't interested. |
| --- |

| Students lack transportation. |
| --- |

| Students lack commitment. |
| --- |

## GROUP 3:  THE PARENTS

| Parents don't want students out of school. |
| --- |

## GROUP 4:  THE TEACHERS

| Impossible to supervise. |
| --- |

| Parents don't want students out of school. |
| --- |

| Other teachers won't support the idea and cooperate in flexible scheduling. |
| --- |

| Class periods are too short. |
| --- |

5.  Draw the Affinity Diagram

The task force members should tape the cards/sticky notes in each group either onto a board or a large flip chart. With the header cards at the top the leader should draw borders around each group. In the figure below the completed **Affinity Diagram** is shown for the above example.

6.  Discuss Each Group

The task force members should discuss each of the groups and how they relate to the problem. This will result in a better understanding of the issues and/or processes making up the problem.

In order to arrive at deeper understandings of each of the

root causes, the task force may want to use a **Relations Diagram** for each of the groups. Depending upon the problem or issue, the **Scenario Builder, Systematic Diagram,** and **Cause & Effect Diagram** may be of value.

**AFFINITY DIAGRAM**
**OBSTACLES TO ESTABLISHING A COMMUNITY SERVICE PROJECT REQUIREMENT**

**The Administration**

| | |
|---|---|
| School Board will not permit it. | Liability is too great |
| Superintendent Won't permit it. | Community service is not perceived as a function of the schools |
| Principal won't support it. | |

**The Students**

| | |
|---|---|
| There is no need. | Student's aren't interested. |
| Students lack commitment. | Students lack transportation |

**The Parents**

Parents don't want students out of school.

**The Teachers**

Impossible to supervise

Class periods are too short

Parent's don't want students out of school.

Other teachers won't support the idea and cooperate in flexible scheduling.

# CAUSE AND EFFECT DIAGRAM

The **Cause and Effect Diagram** was developed by Kaoru Ishikawa in 1943. It is also referred to as a "fishbone" diagram since it looks like a fish skeleton, or an Ishikawa diagram after its inventor.

A **Cause and Effect Diagram** (CED) is extremely useful for getting input regarding the root causes of a specific problem. It can be used in brain storming sessions within a task force or committee or action team; or as a method to get input from an entire class, school, or district since the CED can be posted at various sites.

The CED is rarely used alone. However, when used with a **Relations Diagram**, an **Affinity Diagram**, and/or a **Nominal Group Process**, it can help an action team and/or a task force to look at the root causes of a problem in many different ways.

## Procedure
1. Statement of the Problem
   A specific, identified problem contributing to a non-quality result is identified. It is placed on the far right hand side of an overhead, paper, flip chart or butchers paper.

2. Recording the Perceptions
   After the backbone and the box with the either the identified problem or the effect is drawn, add the primary causal category boxes (people, equipment, materials and procedures [some also add "environment"]) and draw arrows to the backbone. This is the beginning of the CED. Some institutions have reusable 3' x 2' boards with the skeleton and primary causal categories painted on permanently. They have Highland ™ note pads attached so that written remarks could be added by those participating in the analysis.

201

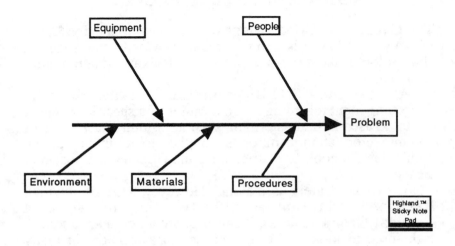

The **Causes** and **Sub Causes** are written on the sticky note pads and are placed in one of the primary causal categories.

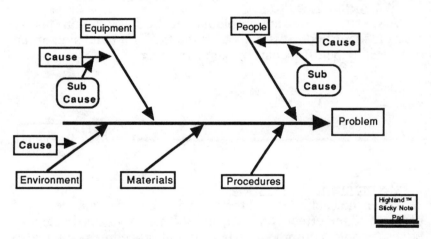

In some instances additional levels can and should be added to **Sub Causes**.

3. Complete the Cause and Effect Diagram
    Shown below is the CED showing the perceptions of Mr. Lake's students as to why they are doing poorly in Chemistry.

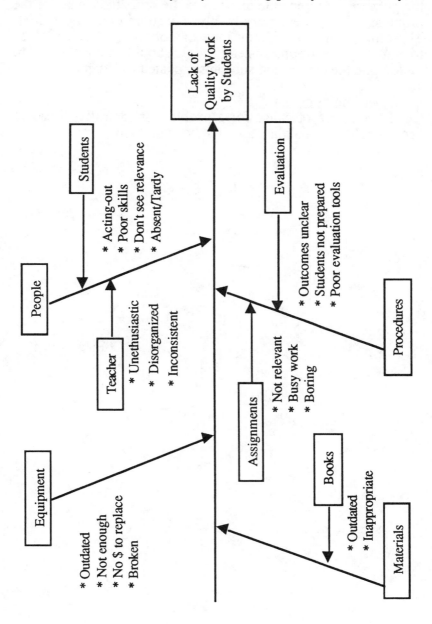

4.  Record and Discuss the Results

The results are recorded and discussed in order to determine the root causes of the undesired effect or problem.  Remember the purpose is to generate ideas as to the probable causes of the problem and to get everyone involved in submitting suggestions. Therefore, criticism of any idea or comment should not be tolerated by the group.  Instead people should be encouraged to build upon the causes and sub causes posted by others.

5.  Other Suggestions

If a major root cause for a problem is identified it could become a likely candidate for a fishbone problem.

# CONTROL CHARTS

**Control Charts** are used to test the stability of a system. They measure the number or proportion of nonconforming items. They all have a common centerline which represents a process average and lines that display upper and lower control limits that provide information on the variation. They are used to identify either "common" or "special" causes of variation and to prevent over- or under-control of the processes within a system.

The charts are drawn by gathering samples, called subgroups, from a process, product, or service characteristic. Control limits are based on the variation that occurs within the subgroups. The centerline of the chart is taken to be the estimated mean of the sampling distribution while the upper control limit (UCL) is the mean plus 3 times the estimated standard error and the lower control limit (LCL) is the estimated mean minus 3 times the estimated standard error.

We will describe two control charts in detail, namely the np-chart and the p-chart. Both charts are **attribute** (characteristic) charts in that the characteristic under study gives an yes/no, good/bad, pass/fail, or present/absent answer. Two additional charts, the c-chart and the u-chart, will also be described briefly. They are used when the characteristic under study is too complex for a simple answer.

The np-chart is used to plot the **number** of nonconformances and the subgroup size is constant. The p-chart is used plot the **proportion** of nonconformances and the subgroup size is either **constant** or **variable**.

## np-Chart

A np-chart, an attributes control chart, is used when the stability of a system is to be measured. The attributes control chart is used when the characteristic under study has a definite yes/no answer, the subgroups are of equal size, the sampling time is consistent, and the data is plotted in the order it was taken.

1.  Select the Data to be Analyzed

We have assumed that the Task Force or the individual studying a system has collected the attribute (counts) data. In the case study below the number of incomplete homework assignments in Miss Wright's basic math classes for six weeks (30 days) were examined. Miss Wright had a total of 60 students in her math classes and she gave a homework problem after every class period. The homework problem was to be returned at the beginning of the following class period.

2. Record the Data
   Record the data in the order which it was collected.

| k<br>Day # | Day | n<br># Students<br>Sample Size | np<br>Homework<br>Assignments<br>Not Completed |
|---|---|---|---|
| 1 | M | 60 | 3 |
| 2 | T | 60 | 6 |
| 3 | W | 60 | 14 |
| 4 | H | 60 | 12 |
| 5 | F | 60 | 15 |
| 6 | M | 60 | 2 |
| 7 | T | 60 | 6 |
| 8 | W | 60 | 14 |
| 9 | H | 60 | 17 |
| 10 | F | 60 | 16 |
| 11 | M | 60 | 1 |
| 12 | T | 60 | 8 |
| 13 | W | 60 | 11 |
| 14 | H | 60 | 18 |
| 15 | F | 60 | 20 |
| 16 | M | 60 | 5 |
| 17 | T | 60 | 6 |
| 18 | W | 60 | 25 |
| 19 | H | 60 | 12 |
| 20 | F | 60 | 26 |
| 21 | M | 60 | 6 |
| 22 | T | 60 | 21 |
| 23 | W | 60 | 18 |
| 24 | H | 60 | 17 |
| 25 | F | 60 | 17 |
| 26 | M | 60 | 11 |
| 27 | T | 60 | 26 |
| 28 | W | 60 | 27 |
| 29 | H | 60 | 29 |
| 30 | F | 60 | 33 |
| Totals | | 1,800 | 442 |

3. <u>Do the Calculations</u>

The **Average,** the **Upper Control Limit** (UCL) , and the **Lower Control Limit** (LCL) have to be calculated in order to determine the stability of the "system." Note, however, that a minimum of 25 to 30 subgroups are required to calculate the control limits.

3.1    **The average** = total number / number of subgroups

$$= \Sigma np \div k$$
$$= 3 + 6 + 14 + 12 + ... + 33 \div 30$$
$$= 442 \div 30$$
$$= 14.73$$

This number (14.73) should be recorded with the space labeled "Avg" in the control chart.

3.2    **The Upper Control Limit** (UCL) is calculated using the formula:

$$UCL = Average + 3\sqrt{Average\,(1 - Average \div n)}$$

$$= 14.73 + 3\sqrt{14.73\,(1 - 14.73 \div 60)}$$

$$= 14.73 + 3\sqrt{14.73\,(1 - 0.2455)}$$

$$= 14.73 + 3\sqrt{14.73 \times 0.7545}$$

$$= 14.73 + 3\sqrt{11.1138}$$

$$= 14.73 + 3\,(3.333)$$

$$= 14.73 + 10.00$$

$$UCL = 24.73$$

This number (24.73) should be recorded with the space labeled "UCL" in the control chart.

3.3    **The Lower Control Limit** (LCL) is calculated using the formula:

$$LCL = Average - 3 \sqrt{Average (1 - Average \div n)}$$

$$= \quad 14.73 - 3 \sqrt{14.73 ( 1 - 14.73 \div 60)}$$

$$= \quad 14.73 - 3 \sqrt{14.73 ( 0.7545)}$$

$$= \quad 14.73 - 3 \sqrt{11.1138}$$

$$= \quad 14.73 - 3 (3.333)$$

$$= \quad 14.73 - 10.00$$

$$LCL \quad = \quad 4.73$$

This number (4.73) should be recorded with the space labeled "LCL" in the control chart.

## 4.  Draw the Chart

The first thing one has to do is to scale the chart.  Begin by determining the largest number in your data and compare this with the UCL number.  In our example the largest number is 33 and the UCL number is 24.73.

A rule of thumb is to count the lines on your chart paper and multiply it by 0.66.  The chart paper in our example is shown below.  It has 30 lines, therefore, 30 x 0.66 = 19.8, or ≈ 20.

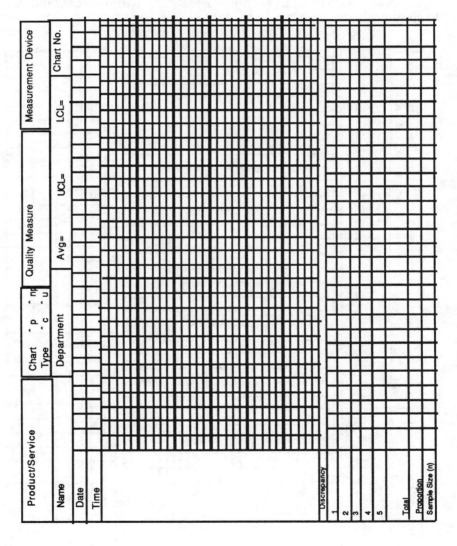

Divide the largest number in your example by 20 to obtain your increment value: $33 \div 20 = 1.65$.  Always rounding the figure upwards, every line in this case will represent 2.

The lines are usually numbered from the bottom up.  The bottom line is 0 and every line will represent two incomplete homework assignments.  (In other cases it may be necessary to label the lines with other multiples such as 5, 10, 25 etc.)  The attributes control chart completely labeled with our example is shown below.

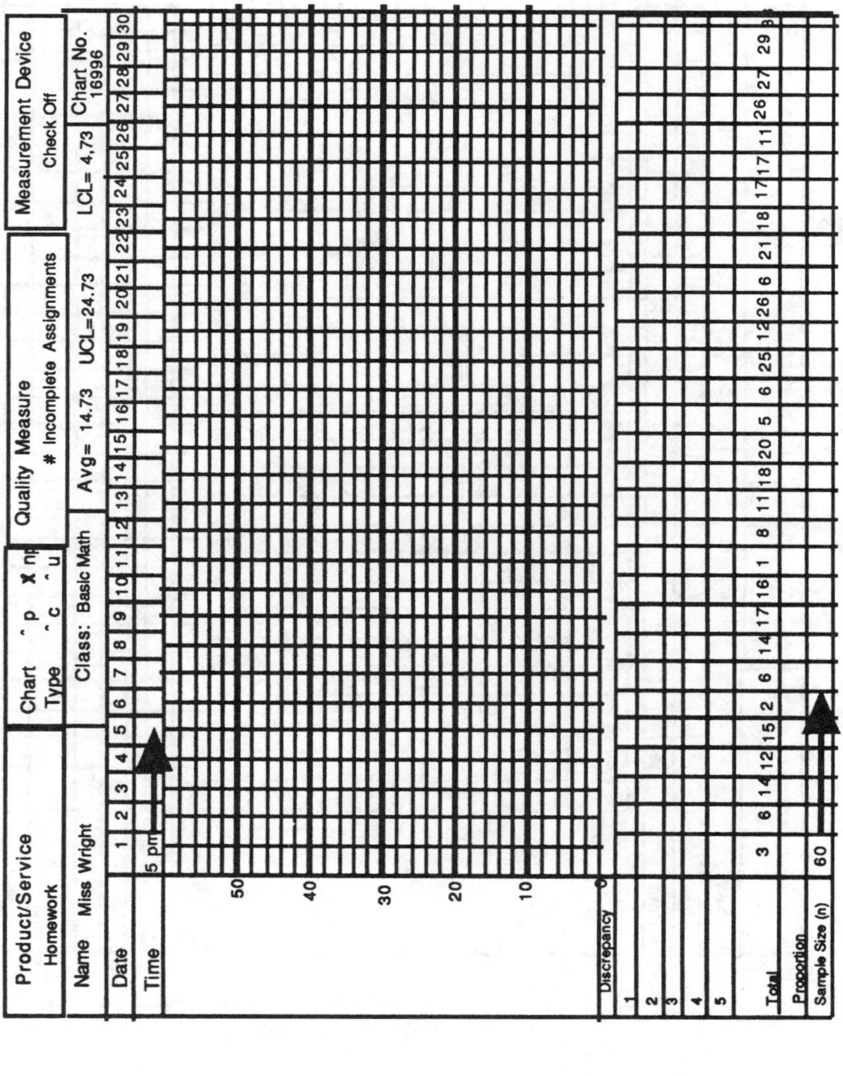

Now draw the center line and the control limits  then plot the values and connect the points. The completed chart is shown below:

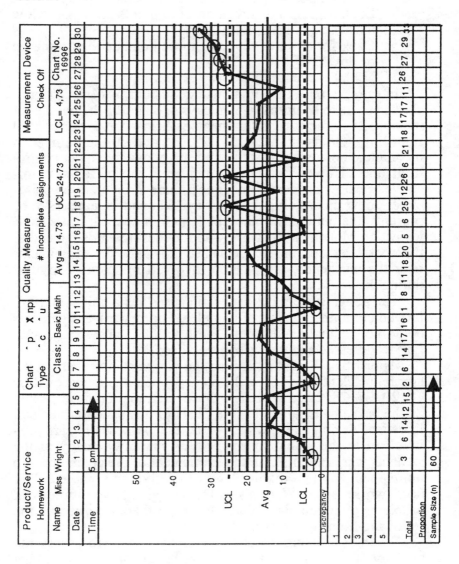

5. Analyze the Chart

All control charts are analyzed using basic rules:

> Look for points above or below the control limits.
> Look for a run of seven or more points above or below the average (center line).
> Look for a run of seven or more points either going up or down.
> Look for cyclical patterns.

In our example the "homework" system in Miss Wright's class appears to be unstable. On days 1, 6 and 11 the number of incomplete homework assignments is below the lower control limit line. On days 18, 20, 27, 28, 29, and 30 the number of incomplete homework assignments are above the upper control limit line. However, there are neither a run of seven points above or below the center line, nor is there a run of seven points either going up or going down. A cyclical pattern appears to be present: the number of incomplete assignments appears to be lowest on Monday and Tuesday and highest towards the end of the week. Perhaps, the students have time to do the assignments over the weekends, but get too involved in school activities during the week.

The above system has "special causes" as a defect and improvement in the number of completed homework assignments could not be undertaken until these special causes were analyzed, addressed and the system stabilized.

After Miss Wright examined the circumstances behind the apparent lack of completing the home work assignments on days 18, 20, 27, 28, 29, and 30, she discovered that on days 18 and 20 the basketball team made the finals for the state tournament; likewise, during the days 27—30, the basketball team was involved in the actual tournament. Apparently, many of the students were caught up in the excitement of the championship tournament and that might be why they did not complete their homework. Miss Wright's solution: give five homework problems after Monday's class and have them returned by the following Monday. It worked!

When first using np-charts you may want to assess the stability of a system and then analyze the factors that contribute to variations. However, after improvements are generated and the system under study is determined to be stable, you may want to begin to collect data in a different way and to stratify your data by day of the week, time, location and redo the np-charts. Of course recalculations of new control limits will eventually be needed but this should be delayed until enough data are gathered to make the new chart statistically valid.

## p-Chart

A p-Chart is used when one wants to plot the **proportion** of nonconformances and the subgroup size is either **constant** or **variable**. Like the np-chart, the p-chart is an attribute control chart that studies a characteristic that has an either/or, pass/fail/, yes/no answer. For example:
> A teacher may want to plot the proportion of students failing his/her class over the term.
> A teacher may want to plot the proportion of students not completing homework assignments over the semester.
> A principal may want to plot the proportion of graduating seniors who have a SAT score above 1000 over a period of time.

The p-chart, like any control chart, helps determine "special" and/or "common" cause variations in a system so that proper action can be taken for improvement without exerting over- or under-control. It is used by task forces to help determine the stability of a system and to monitor the improvement of the system after action is taken.

1. Select the Data to be Analyzed

In the case study below we will examine the proportion of students that failed "Introduction to Accounting" per term over a 7.5 year period. Since number of students who took the course varied over the seven year period, the sample size is variable. As a result the p-chart had to be used.

## 2. Record the Data

| k # | Term-Yr | n Subgroup Size | np Number of Failures | np + n Proportion |
|---|---|---|---|---|
| 1 | 1-84 | 100 | 15 | 0.150 |
| 2 | 2-84 | 100 | 6 | 0.060 |
| 3 | 3-84 | 100 | 11 | 0.110 |
| 4 | 4-84 | 100 | 4 | 0.040 |
| 5 | 1-85 | 94 | 9 | 0.096 |
| 6 | 2-85 | 94 | 7 | 0.074 |
| 7 | 3-85 | 94 | 4 | 0.043 |
| 8 | 4-85 | 94 | 8 | 0.085 |
| 9 | 1-86 | 91 | 3 | 0.033 |
| 10 | 2-86 | 91 | 2 | 0.022 |
| 11 | 3-86 | 91 | 1 | 0.011 |
| 12 | 4-86 | 91 | 10 | 0.109 |
| 13 | 1-87 | 91 | 7 | 0.077 |
| 14 | 2-87 | 91 | 25 | 0.275 |
| 15 | 3-87 | 91 | 5 | 0.055 |
| 16 | 4-87 | 79 | 3 | 0.038 |
| 17 | 1-88 | 79 | 8 | 0.101 |
| 18 | 2-88 | 79 | 4 | 0.051 |
| 19 | 3-88 | 79 | 2 | 0.025 |
| 20 | 4-88 | 79 | 5 | 0.063 |
| 21 | 1-89 | 79 | 5 | 0.063 |
| 22 | 2-89 | 72 | 7 | 0.097 |
| 23 | 3-89 | 72 | 9 | 0.125 |
| 24 | 4-89 | 72 | 1 | 0.014 |
| 25 | 1-90 | 72 | 3 | 0.042 |
| 26 | 2-90 | 72 | 12 | 0.167 |
| 27 | 3-90 | 72 | 9 | 0.125 |
| 28 | 4-90 | 72 | 3 | 0.042 |
| 29 | 1-91 | 72 | 6 | 0.083 |
| 30 | 2-91 | 72 | 9 | 0.125 |
| | Totals | 2,535 | 203 | 0.0801 |

3. Do the Calculations
   3.1    The **Proportion** for each subgroup has to be calculated. As shown in the table above, this is accomplished by dividing total number (np) by the subgroup size (n). In our first entry above 15 (number of failures during the first term of 1984) is divided by the 100 (sample size). Carry the calculations out to three places.

   3.2    The **Average Proportion** is calculated by taking the total number in the sample size row (2,535) and dividing it by the total number in the subgroup row (203).

   Average Proportion  $(\overline{p})$   =   total number /
                                             number of subgroups
                       =   $\Sigma np \div \Sigma n$
                       =   203 ÷ 2,535
                       =   0.0801
   This number (.0801) should be recorded with the space labeled "Avg" in the control chart.

   3.3    The **Average Subgroup Size** $(\overline{n})$ is calculated by dividing the total number of the subgroup size (2,535) by the number of the subgroups taken (k).

   Average Subgroup Size  $(\overline{n})$   =   $\Sigma n \div k$
                         =   2,535 ÷ 30
                         =   84.5

   3.4    Make certain that none of the subgroup size varies more than ± 25% of Average Subgroup Size (84.5). This is done by multiplying 84.5 by 1.25 for the number greater than 25%; and 84.5 by 0.75 for the number less than 25%.
          >25%  =   84.5   x   1.25   =   105.6
          <25%  =   84.5   x   0.75   =    63.4
   Since none of our sample sizes (n) were higher than 105.6 or less than 63.4, separate calculations for the control limits do not have to be done. If, however, you have subgroup sizes 25% above or below 84.5, you will have to calculate separate UCL's and LCL's on **EACH** of the points by substituting the appropriate number (n) in the formula shown below. These

points with their separate UCL and LCL are plotted on the same graph. (Refer to the example in the u-chart at the end of this section.)

3.5    Do the calculations for the **Control Limits**.

$$UCL = \overline{p} + 3 \sqrt{\frac{\overline{p}(1-\overline{p})}{n}}$$

$$= 0.0801 + 3\sqrt{0.0801\ (1 - 0.0801) \div 84.5}$$

$$= 0.0801 + 3\sqrt{0.0801\ (0.9199) \div 84.5}$$

$$= 0.0801 + 3\sqrt{0.0737 \div 84.5}$$

$$= 0.0801 + 3\ (0.02953)$$

$$UCL = 0.1687$$

Now calculate the lower control limit:

$$LCL = \overline{p} - 3 \sqrt{\frac{\overline{p}(1-\overline{p})}{n}}$$

$$= 0.0801 - 0.0886$$

$$LCL = 0$$

## 4. Draw the Chart

The scaling and plotting are done in exactly the same manner as in the np chart.  The largest proportion of failures in our example is 0.275 and 66% of the number of lines in our graph is 20, therefore, each line has to be 0.275 ÷ 20 = 0.014, and since adjusting is always done upwards, each line represents 0.020.

The completed chart is shown below.

Product/Service   Intro to Accounting

Chart Type: X̄ p ·np ·c ·u

Quality Measure: # Failing

Measurement Device: Final Grade

Chart No. SS

Name  Mr. Breck     Department Sec. Sci.

Avg = .0801     UCL = 0.1687     LCL = 0

Scale: 0.30   0.20   0.10

UCL, p̄, LCL

Discrepancy

Total

Proportion

Sample Size (n)

5. Analyze the Chart

All control charts are analyzed using basic rules:

> Look for points above or below the control limits.
> Look for a run of seven or more points above or below the average (center line).
> Look for a run of seven or more points either going up or down.
> Look for cyclical patterns.

In our example the system appears to be unstable since one of the points lay outside the UCL, *i.e.* the second term of 1987. During that time the number of failures was above the upper control limit line. However, there are no run of seven points above or below the center line, nor is there a run of seven points either going up or going down, nor are there any cyclical patterns.

The above system appears to have "special cause" as a defect and implementing TQI processes to improve the number of students who would pass could not be undertaken until these special causes were analyzed, addressed and the system was stabilized.

After the teacher examined what occurred during that time, he informed us that the local textile plant announced massive layoffs and that it would be phasing out its operations in that area over the next several years. As a result, many students were more concerned about having to relocate and losing their friends than their final grades. A check of the high school records indicated that an unusually high rate of failing grades were given in the entire school that particular term. When this special cause is removed the system could be considered to be stable and the Mr. Breck may begin to add changes in order to increase the passing rate. Remember, however, that new control limits have to be calculated when changes are made on the system.

## OTHER CONTROL CHARTS

There are two other control charts that should be described, both of which can be useful in the academic setting. They are the **c-chart** and the **u-chart**. Like the np-chart and the p-chart, the c-chart and the u-chart are used to test the stability of the system and both are attribute control charts.

The c-chart and the u-chart measure the number of nonconforming items. The c-chart is used when the number of nonconformities are measured and the subgroup size is the constant, while the u-chart is used when the number of nonconformities are measured and the subgroup size is either constant or variable.

Since the preparation of the c-chart and the u-chart are very similar to the np-chart and the p-chart described previously, we will present briefly when they may be appropriately used as well as the formulae.

## c-Chart

A c-chart is used when the stability of a system is to be measured. It is an attribute control chart that is useful when the characteristic under study is too complex for either a simple yes/no, or a positive/negative answer. In other words, the data may have a number of discrepancies per subgroup. An example might include the type of errors while composing a letter in a word-processing class. The errors might include: 1) format, 2) grammar, 3) punctuation, 4) spacing, 5) date, and 6) spelling. (If you wanted to calculate the number of mistakes in composing a letter regardless of the type, you would use the np-chart; if you desired to calculate the proportion of nonconformances regardless of the type of mistake, you would use the p-chart.)

As with the other control charts, one should 1) Select the Data to be Analyzed, 2) Record the Data, 3) Do the Calculations, 4) Draw the Chart, and 5) Analyze the Chart.

1.  Select the Data to be Analyzed

Before using any control chart, it is essential that the operational definition of the nonconforming characteristics be carefully identified in order to insure consistency in the collection process. In our example, a teacher and the students identified four major problems in the five sections of the word-processing classes, namely: 1) format, 2) grammar, 3) punctuation, and 4) spacing. These were perceived to be the major problems of the students not being able to produce an error free letter the first time. They decided to randomly sample two letters at the end of the five classes for one week (*i.e.* 5 straight days).

## 2. Record the Data

The data are recorded as shown in the table and in the completed c-Chart below.

The date, class period, type and number of mistake, and the total number of mistakes in Mrs. Herbst's word-processing classes.

Type of Mistake

| Date | Class Period | Format | Grammar | Punctua-tion | Spacing | Total |
|------|------|------|------|------|------|------|
| Jan. 7 | 1 | 2 | 0 | 1 | 1 | 4 |
|  | 2 | 2 | 3 | 2 | 1 | 8 |
|  | 3 | 1 | 1 | 2 | 2 | 6 |
|  | 4 | 1 | 0 | 1 | 0 | 2 |
|  | 5 | 0 | 0 | 0 | 0 | 0 |
| Jan. 8 | 1 | 3 | 1 | 2 | 0 | 6 |
|  | 2 | 1 | 0 | 0 | 1 | 2 |
|  | 3 | 3 | 3 | 0 | 2 | 8 |
|  | 4 | 0 | 0 | 0 | 0 | 0 |
|  | 5 | 1 | 1 | 1 | 1 | 4 |
| Jan. 9 | 1 | 2 | 1 | 1 | 0 | 4 |
|  | 2 | 2 | 1 | 2 | 1 | 6 |
|  | 3 | 0 | 0 | 0 | 0 | 0 |
|  | 4 | 1 | 1 | 1 | 1 | 4 |
|  | 5 | 3 | 2 | 2 | 1 | 8 |
| Jan. 10 | 1 | 0 | 0 | 0 | 0 | 0 |
|  | 2 | 3 | 1 | 1 | 1 | 6 |
|  | 3 | 1 | 1 | 1 | 1 | 4 |
|  | 4 | 3 | 3 | 2 | 0 | 8 |
|  | 5 | 0 | 0 | 0 | 2 | 2 |
| Jan. 11 | 1 | 3 | 1 | 1 | 1 | 6 |
|  | 2 | 0 | 0 | 0 | 0 | 0 |
|  | 3 | 2 | 0 | 0 | 0 | 2 |
|  | 4 | 2 | 1 | 0 | 1 | 4 |
|  | 5 | 0 | 1 | 1 | 0 | 2 |
|  | Totals | 36 | 22 | 21 | 17 | 96 |

3. <u>Do the Calculations</u>
    3.1    The **Average Number** is calculated according to the formula:

$$\overline{c} = \text{total number} \div \text{number of subgroups}$$
$$= C1 + C2 + C3 + ... + Ck \div k$$
$$= 4 + 8 + 6 + ... + 2 \div 25$$
$$= 96 \div 25$$
$$= 3.8$$

This number is placed in the placed marked "Avg."

3.2    The **Control Limits** are calculated according to the formulae:

$$\text{UCLc} = \overline{c} + 3\sqrt{\overline{c}}$$
$$= 3.8 + 3\sqrt{3.8}$$
$$= 3.8 + 5.8$$
$$\text{UCLc} = 9.6$$

$$\text{LCLc} = \overline{c} - 3\sqrt{\overline{c}}$$
$$= 3.8 - 3\sqrt{3.8}$$
$$= 3.8 - 5.8$$
$$= -2$$
$$\text{LCLc} \approx 0$$

## 4. Draw the Chart

Do the scaling as described previously. In this case the largest c number is 8 and the UCLc is 9.6, therefore, take the 9.6 value and multiply it by 0.66 of the number of lines on your graph. In our case the number of lines is 30 and 0.66 of 30 is ≈ 20. Each line, in our case, has an incremental value of 9.6 ÷ 20 = 0.48. Adjusting upward we have an incremental value of 0.5. The completed c-control chart is shown below.

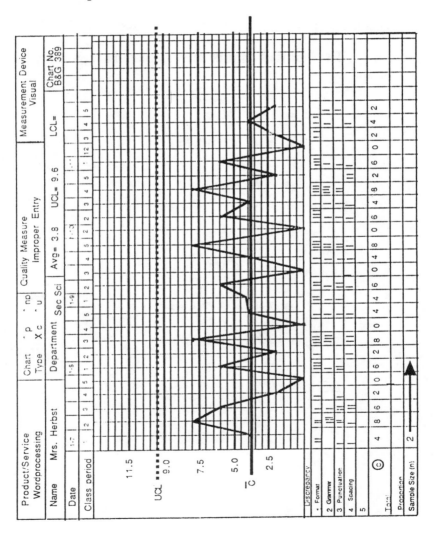

## 5. Analyze the Chart

The above chart does not demonstrate any special cause variation, therefore, the variability in the system appears to be due to common causes which can be reduced by improving the processes within the system. Both the teacher and the students in all five classes were happy to hear that they did not have to consider any special causes and that they could now begin to work as a team to improve the learning experiences for all!

## u-Chart

A u-chart is used when the stability of a system is to be measured. It is an attribute control chart that is useful when the characteristic under study is too complex for either a simple yes/no, or positive/negative answer. In other words, the data may have a number of discrepancies per subgroup. An example might include laboratory reports that are incorrectly completed because of errors in filling out one of many entries. (If one desired to calculate the number of incorrectly completed reports regardless of which information item was incorrectly completed, they would use the np-chart; if they desired to calculate the proportion of nonconformances regardless of which information item was incorrectly completed, they would use the p-chart.) However, unlike the c-chart mentioned above, the u-chart can be used with either a constant or **variable** subgroup size. If the subgroup sizes vary more than 25% as demonstrated in our example below, individual control limits have to be calculated.

As with the other control charts, one should 1) Select the Data to be Analyzed, 2) Record the Data, 3) Do the Calculations, 4) Draw the Chart, and 5) Analyze the Chart.

## 1. Select the Data to be Analyzed

Before using any control chart, it is essential that the operational definition of the nonconforming characteristics be carefully identified in order to insure consistency in the collection process. In the example below, a high school chemistry teacher, working with her students, identified five principal discrepancies that resulted in incorrect laboratory reports being submitted. For this study we simply designated them "type 1" through "type 5." The discrepancies are scored in the same manner as shown for the c-chart above. Redoing the reports were not only a major cause of rework, but also for not submitting the reports in a timely fashion, both of which caused unhappy customers, namely, students, teacher, and parents. A group of students, several parents, and the teacher formed a task force to examine the root causes and what could be done to improve the quality of the initial submission of the reports. They decided to examine a random number of reports for 25 straight school days.

2.  Record the Data
    The data are recorded as shown in the completed u-chart below.

3.  Do the Calculations

3.1    The **Average Number per Unit** is calculated according to the formula:

$$\bar{u} = \Sigma c \div \Sigma n$$
$$= 192 \div 103$$
$$= 1.86$$

This value is placed in the placed maker "Avg."

3.2    The **Average Subgroup Size** is calculated according to the formula:

$$\bar{n} = \Sigma n \div k$$
$$= 103 \div 25$$
$$= 4.12$$

3.3    The **Subgroup Size Limits** are calculated:
$$>25\% = 4.12 \quad x \quad 1.25 = 5.15$$
$$<25\% = 4.12 \quad x \quad 0.75 = 3.09$$
Therefore, any proportion number in any subgroup that is less than 3.19 or greater than 5.15 will have to have their UCL and LCL's calculated separately. In our example shown below, please refer to subgroups #1, #7, #8, #11, #15, #16, #17, and #20.

3.4    The **Proportions** (u) for each subgroup are calculated according to the formula:
u = number in subgroup (c) ÷ subgroup size (n)

These figures are added to the chart as shown below.

3.5    The **Control Limits** are calculated according to the formulae:

$$\text{UCLu} = \bar{u} + 3\sqrt{\bar{u} \div \bar{n}}$$

$$= 1.86 + 3\sqrt{1.86 \div 4.12}$$

$$= 1.86 + 3\sqrt{0.4514}$$

$$= 1.86 + 3(0.6719)$$

$$= 1.86 + 2.02$$

$$= 3.88$$

$$\text{LCLu} = \bar{u} - 3\sqrt{\bar{u} \div \bar{n}}$$

$$= 1.86 - 2.02$$

$$= -0.16$$

$$\approx 0$$

3.6    The control limits for these subgroups that vary $\pm$ 25% are calculated separately. In our case this includes #1, #7, #8, #11, #15, #16, #17, and #20. For subgroups #1, #7, #15, and #17:

$$\text{UCLu} = 1.86 + 3 \quad u \div n$$

$$= 1.86 + 3 \quad 1.86 \div 3 \quad = 4.22$$

$$\text{LCLu} = 1.86 - 3 \quad u \div n$$

$$= 1.86 - 3 \quad 1.86 \div 3 \quad \approx 0$$

For subgroups #8 and #16:

$$\text{UCLu} = 1.86 + 3\sqrt{\bar{u} \div n}$$

$$= 1.86 + 3\sqrt{1.86 \div 2} = 4.75$$

$$\text{LCLu} = 1.86 - 3\sqrt{\bar{u} \div n}$$

$$= 1.86 - 3\sqrt{1.86 \div 2} \approx 0$$

For subgroups #11 and #20:

$$\text{UCLu} = 1.86 + 3\sqrt{\bar{u} \div n}$$

$$= 1.86 + 3\sqrt{1.86 \div 7} = 3.41$$

$$\text{LCLu} = 1.86 - 3\sqrt{\bar{u} \div n}$$

$$= 1.86 - 3\sqrt{1.86 \div 7} = 0.32$$

## 4. Draw the Chart

Do the scaling as described previously. In this case the largest proportion (u) is 8 and the ULCu is 1.86, therefore, take the 8 value and multiply it by 0.66 of the number of lines on your graph. In our case the number of lines is 30 and 0.66 of 30 is ≈ 20, therefore, 8 ÷ 20 = 0.4 or ≈ 0.5. Adjusting upward is done so that the dark lines have numbers whose multiples are easy to work with, *i.e.* 1, 2, 5, 10 etc. The completed chart is shown below:

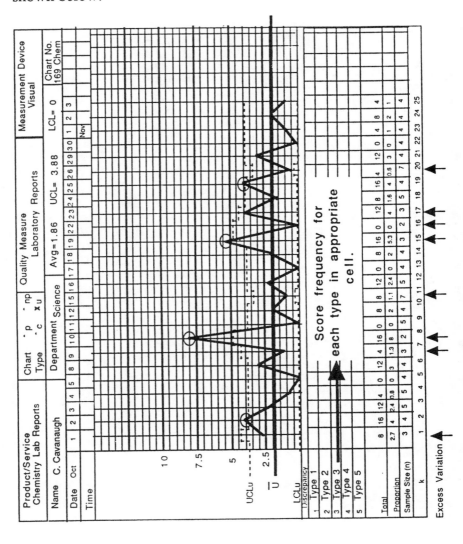

## 5. Analyze the Chart

The above chart indicates that the laboratory reporting system is not in control. On October 2, 10, 19 and 25 the number of errors exceeded the UCL which indicates special cause variation. The task force can begin to examine the reasons as to the variations.

# FLOW CHART

Although flow charting is one of the most useful tools in total quality management (TQM), it is probably the most under utilized in education. Flow charting is a way in which one can get a snapshot of each process within a system. As a result, a flow chart can demonstrate where non-value added work is performed. Of course, non-value added work adds to the cost of doing business, and in the case of education, this cost can be substantial.

When a flow chart is drawn and redundant processes are identified, a task force can easily generate a different flow chart showing how the processes within the system should be done. It is essential that when a flow chart of a system is drawn that everyone working within the system be involved in drawing it. There are many different types of flow charts, but we will describe two which we found to be useful in the academic units, namely, the **Deployment Flow Chart** and the **Process Flow Chart**.

## Deployment Flow Chart

**Procedure**

1. Definition of the System

Each system consists of a series of processes. However, it is not always clear where one system ends and another begins since many systems involve more than one process. Therefore, the task force should agree as to the starting and ending points they wish to study.

As with any universal visual tool, flow charting has a set of standardized symbols (Myron Tribus, 1989). They are shown as follows:

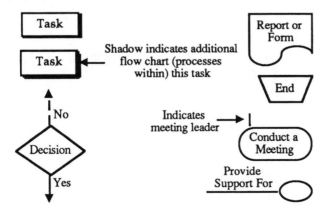

2. Drawing the Deployment Flow Chart

A deployment flow chart is useful when one wants to show the inter-relationships between the people and the tasks they actually perform while working within a system in order to generate either a service or a product.

The members of a task force should take it upon themselves to actually walk through each step in the system they are studying. As they do, they should inquire from the people performing each task what is actually involved. Copious notes should be taken along with sketches. Only after this is done should the members draw a deployment flow chart.

It should be mentioned that flow charts should not be drawn only when there are problems within a system. Instead, charts should be drawn for every task and process within all systems in order to root out non-value added work. In addition, if there are any changes within a system, its flow chart should be updated immediately for all to see.

The first thing that should be done in preparing the deployment flow chart is to enter the "people" coordinate horizontally. The boxes can contain either the particular person or his/her position or the particular department/unit that is performing a task. In the example below we will follow an actual deployment flow chart of class assignment in a social studies class.

Next the actual tasks and/or major steps are listed:

1. Prepare Assignment (Teacher)

2. Determine Options (Teacher and Group)

3. Analyze Options and Select Preferred (Group)

4. Approve Group Option (Teacher)

5. Research Assignment (Individual Students)

6. Compile Research (Group)

7. Outline Research Paper and Submit for Approval (Group)

8. Approve Outline (Teacher)

9. Write Subsections or Implement Project (Individual Students)

10. Approve Subsections (Group)

11. Combine Paper or Project Results (Group)

12. Approve Combined Effort (Group)

13. Submit Final Results (Group)

14. Approved? (Teacher)

15. Evaluate (Teacher and Group)

Using the symbols described above, draw the flow chart.

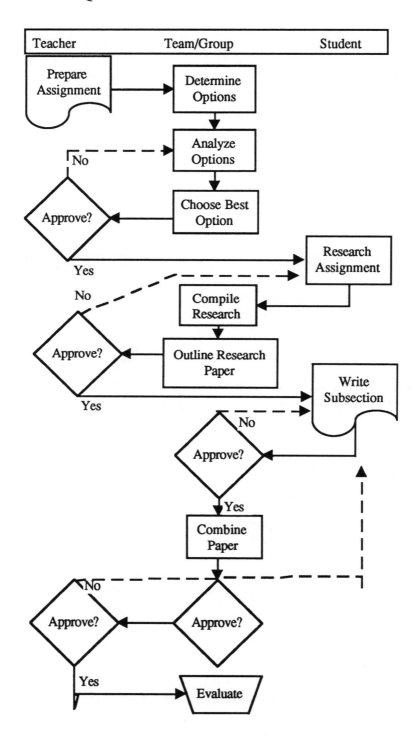

3. Record and Discuss the Results

Because the horizontal lines represent a customer-supplier relationship, the flow chart reveals the nature of the interactions. Examine the lines and try to determine if there is any non-value added work that can be reduced or eliminated. If there appears to be a breakdown in the system where someone is not supplying his customer with quality work try to examine the reason(s) why. Are there barriers or decision making delays that slow the flow?

A task force, after examining the system, recommended the revision shown on the next page which reduced the inspection time and empowered groups of students to make decisions about the member's work quality. As a result, the students worked harder, assignments were completed faster and results were excellent.

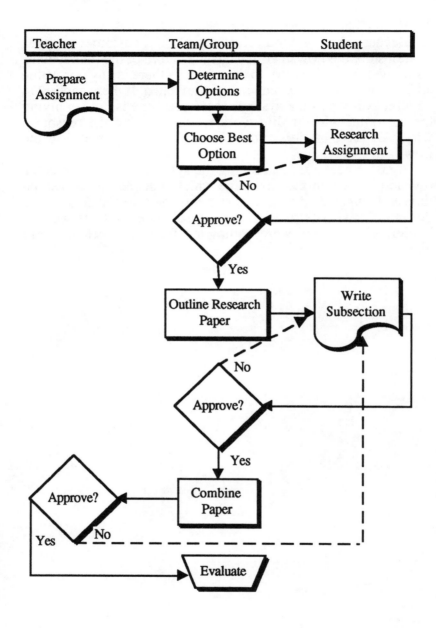

## <u>Process Flow Chart</u>

**Procedure**

1. <u>Statement of the Problem</u>

The process flow chart simply shows the major steps within a system and does not attempt to demonstrate the inter relationships between the people doing the tasks.  Like using any flow chart, the task force should agree to the starting and ending points of the system they wish to study.

2. <u>Drawing the Process Flow Chart</u>

The members of a task force should take it upon themselves to actually walk through each step in the system they are studying. As they do, they should inquire from the people performing each task what is actually involved. Copious notes should be taken along with sketches. Only after this is done should the members draw a process flow chart.

The first thing that should be done in preparing the process flow chart is to list the major steps in the system. Then using the standardized symbols shown below one should draw the flow chart.

Start / End        Task        Decision ?

Using the example in the aforementioned Deployment Flow Chart, one may have listed the  major steps as follows:

1.  Prepare assignment

2.  Determine options

3.  Choose best option

4.  Research assignment

5.  Outline paper

6.  Write subsections

7.  Prepare final paper

8.  Submit results    ☐

9.  Get approval    ◇

10. Evaluate    ☐

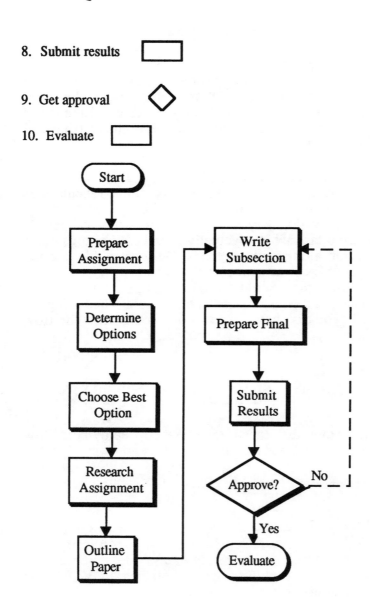

3.  <u>Record and Discuss the Results</u>
    By studying the flow chart the task force members may be able to recommend ways to better reduce redundant steps and improve the processes of the system.

# FORCE FIELD ANALYSIS

The **Force Field Analysis** tool was the product of federally funded research to change the meat buying habits of American housewives during the second world war. It was invented by Professor Kurt Lewin of the University of Iowa.

**Force Field Analysis** helps a task force to identify the perceived driving and restraining forces towards effecting a recommended change. Then, by increasing the forces driving the change, or by decreasing the forces inhibiting the change, or both, a task force can recommend actions to bring about the change successfully.

Actually the **Force Field Analysis** is much more useful when used with other TQI tools, *e.g.* the nominal group process, affinity diagram, and/or scenario builder. This is especially true if the recommended change is counter to the "tradition" of the classroom. Like the nominal group process, affinity diagram, and/or scenario builder, the **Force Field Analysis** involves the use of proper brainstorming procedures: a facilitator is selected, team members have an equal opportunity to express their ideas without criticism, and building upon the ideas of others is encouraged.

## Procedure
### 1. Statement of the Problem
Under the direction of the team leader (or the facilitator) the members of the task force should arrive at a statement of the precise desired change that will be made to management. To arrive at this statement it may be necessary to use other TQI tools such as the nominal group process (NGP) and the affinity diagram as previously explained.

For example, Mrs. Moore teaches second grade in a traditional school. Since she had heard from a teacher in another school that thematic units represented an effective teaching technique, she wanted to use it in her class. She realized there were some potential problems and established a task force to analyze the feasibility of such a change.

237

## 2. Recording the Suggestions

After brainstorming on the driving and restraining forces much like the procedure for the NGP, the task force, consisting of including herself, parents, the instructional support teacher and the principal recorded the following perceived driving and restraining forces.

**FORCE FIELD ANALYSIS**

**Recommended Change:   Infuse Thematic Units into Classroom**

| Driving Forces (+) | Restraining Forces (−) |
|---|---|
| | Alters the curriculum |
| Students respond enthusiastically to this approach | Teacher isn't knowledgeable about thematic units |
| | Requires the teacher to think about the curriculum differently and plan alternative activities |
| Interrelates many aspects of the curriculum | Teacher lacks the skill to create instructional materials for thematic units |
| | No incentive for teachers to try new ideas in their classes |
| Accommodates many different learning styles | School lacks resources for teachers to create materials |

3. <u>Discuss and Prioritize the Driving and Restraining Forces</u>

We recommend that the person who generated the idea give his/her rationale as to why s/he felt it was important. Then an open discussion should be conducted on each point, and, if possible, certain points could be combined under a single heading if the task force agrees.

After discussion and grouping of the driving and restraining forces, the task force should assign a value of relative importance to each point. The values could be determined much like the way we recommended in the nominal group process (NGP) where either a rank value or total points could be determined using a n-1 numbering system. (For example, in the restraining forces there are 6 separate items listed. Therefore, the group may wish to use the NGP technique and assign #5 to the most important perceived restraining force, #4 for the second most important, etc.)

In this case, the task force decided to use the NGP and the final ranking value, *i.e.*, #1 was considered the most significant driving/restraining force, #2 the second most important, etc. These values are placed along side of the comments and are shown below.

**FORCE FIELD ANALYSIS**

**Recommended Change:   Infuse Thematic Units into Classroom**

| Driving Forces (+) | Restraining Forces (−) |
|---|---|
| | Alters the curriculum (-5) |
| Students respond enthusiastically to this approach (+1) | Teacher isn't knowledgeable about thematic units (-1) |
| | Requires the teacher to think about the curriculum differently and plan alternative activities (-4) |
| Interrelates many aspects of the curriculum (+3) | Teacher lacks the skill to create instructional materials for thematic units (-6) |
| | No incentive for teachers to try new ideas in their classes (-2) |
| Accommodates many different learning styles (+2) | School lacks resources for teachers to create materials (-3) |

## 4. Recommending Steps to be Taken

After the driving and restraining forces are recorded, discussed, and prioritized the task force should begin to recommend steps that should be taken in order to effect the desired change. This should be done on the bottom of the form as shown below.

---

### FORCE FIELD ANALYSIS

**Recommended Change: Infuse Thematic Units into Classroom**

| Driving Forces (+) | Restraining Forces (–) |
|---|---|
|  | Alters the curriculum (-5) |
| Students respond enthusiastically to this approach (+1) | Teacher isn't knowledgeable about thematic units (-1) |
|  | Requires the teacher to think about the curriculum differently and plan alternative activities (-4) |
| Interrelates many aspects of the curriculum (+3) | Teacher lacks the skill to create instructional materials for thematic units (-6) |
|  | No incentive for teachers to try new ideas in their classes (-2) |
| Accommodates many different learning styles (+2) | School lacks resources for teachers to create materials (-3) |

RECOMMENDED ACTIONS:
1. The administration should provide funding for the teacher to attend a workshop on Thematic Units. (This would address the #1, #4, #5, and #6 ranked restraining forces and the #2 and #3 ranked driving forces.)
2. This teacher should be encouraged to implement Thematic Units and present her plans and outcomes before the entire faculty. (This would address the #2 and #5 restraining forces and all driving forces.)
3. Teachers who agree to share their Thematic Unit plans will receive money from the PTO for creating additional instructional materials. (This would address the #2 , #3 and #6 restraining forces and #1 and #3 driving forces.)
4. This teacher can become a lead teacher within the building, training colleagues in the use of Thematic Units. (This would address restraining forces #2,#4, #5, #6.)

# HISTOGRAM

The **Histogram** is a depiction of data on a bar graph which represents how often a class of data occurred. One of the main purposes of using a Histogram is to predict improvements in a system. The system must be stable, however, or the Histogram cannot be used to make predictions. If the system is unstable the Histogram might take different shapes at different times. Therefore, the Histogram is often used with a **Control Chart**.

A Task Force studying a system may gather statistical data about the system and then draw a Histogram to help them assess the current situation. Then, in order to test a theory, the Task Force may change one or more processes within a system and, after gathering additional statistical data and redrawing another Histogram, check to see if the modifications improved the system.

The Histogram is used when one wishes to analyze the variation within a system. One must have a set of either related attributes (counts) data or variables (measurements) data. Although we will describe how a Histogram is prepared and how the shape of the Histogram may vary, we will not do the actual calculation of the statistics. Instead, we refer the reader to any elementary statistics book for the actual calculations.

In the example that follows we have selected a case study from a seventh grade science class where the teacher wanted to have her students analyze their study habits and the relationship to their success rate in science. The class participated in discussions and agreed on possible factors affecting their school success and study habits. Each student agreed to monitor the amount of time s/he spent talking on the telephone for one month. They also agreed to keep track of the grades they received in science class during the month. At the end of the first month, the task force combined all data. The total number of minutes the class members spent talking on the telephone was 95,250. That represented 3,175 minutes per student for the month, or an average of 53 minutes per day for 30 days. The total number of minutes spent studying for the same period of time was 31,399. This meant that each student spent an average of 17 minutes studying science per day.

The task force recorded the data and made a Frequency Distribution chart. This was posted and the class discussed ways to improve their grades. At the end of the first month, the class agreed to cut the amount of talking on the telephone in half and use that time to study science. As before, each student again kept track of his/her time spent on the telephone and all science grades. The class wanted to see if making a small alteration in their daily habits would dramatically affect their science grade.

**Procedure**
1.  Select the Data to be Analyzed
    We have assumed that the Task Force or the individual studying a system has collected either the attribute data or the variable data. In our case study the students kept tract of both telephone time and grades received.

2.  Record the Data
    A frequency table is constructed similar to those shown below.

Frequency Distribution
Distribution of grades for Mrs. Appleton's seventh grade science class for November, 1991.
(Before reducing the time spent on the telephone.)

| Grade | Absolute Frequency | Relative Frequency % | Relative Cumulative % |
|-------|--------------------|----------------------|-----------------------|
| A     | 1                  | 3.33                 | 3.33                  |
| B     | 3                  | 10.00                | 13.33                 |
| C     | 6                  | 20.00                | 33.33                 |
| D     | 12                 | 40.00                | 73.33                 |
| F     | 8                  | 26.66                | 100                   |
| Total | 30                 | 100                  |                       |

Frequency Distribution
Distribution of grades of the students from Mrs. Appleton's science class for December, 1991 (After reducing the time spent on the telephone in half.)

| Grade | Absolute Frequency | Relative Frequency % | Relative Cumulative % |
|-------|--------------------|----------------------|-----------------------|
| A     | 6                  | 20.00                | 20.00                 |
| B     | 9                  | 30.00                | 50.00                 |
| C     | 13                 | 43.33                | 93.33                 |
| D     | 2                  | 6.66                 | 100                   |
| F     | 0                  |                      |                       |
| Total | 30                 | 100                  |                       |

### 3. Draw the Histogram

Draw the x-axis (horizontal) and the y-axis (vertical).  They should be of approximately of equal length and of sufficient size to best display your data.  Then draw a bar for each "Grade" with the corresponding "Frequency" for which it occurred.

The histograms  showing the distribution of grades of the students from Mrs. Appleton's science class from November, 1991 (before the self-imposed telephone restrictions) and from (after the self-imposed telephone restrictions) December, 1991 are shown below.

Distribution of grades from Mrs. Appleton's students during the month of November, 1991.

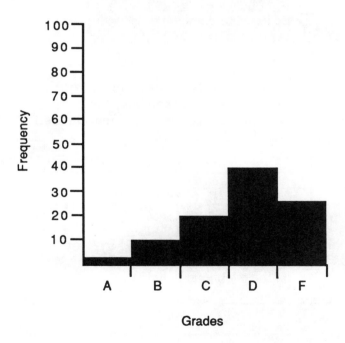

Grades

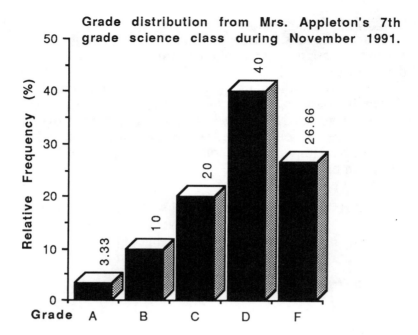

Grade distribution from Mrs. Appleton's 7th grade science class during November 1991.

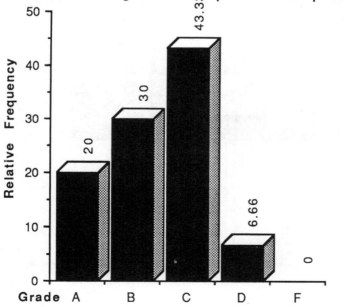

Grade distribution in Mrs. Appleton's 7th grade science class in December 1991. (After altering the time spent on the phone.)

## 4. Analyze the Shape of the Histogram(s)

Histograms have six common shapes, namely 1) symmetrical, 2) skewed right, 3) skewed left, 4) uniform, 5) random, and 6) bimodal. These are shown below.

### The Common Shapes of Histograms

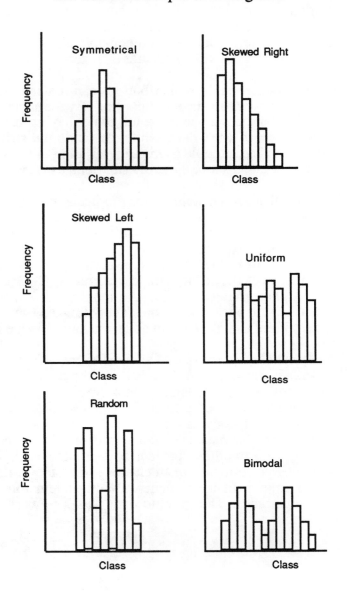

The symmetrical figure, called a bell-shaped curve, usually represents a "normal" distribution which indicates that the system under investigation is probably under control. Ideally the mean (average), mode, and median of the class data are equal and that 99.73% of total area under the curve is plus or minus 3 standard deviations.

Histograms can also trail off either to the right or left. Whereas the skewing to the right is known as a positive skew, the trailing to the left is known as a negative skew. These can occur when the data has values greater than zero, as in our case study.

The uniform and random distributions can indicate that the system under investigation is out of control. By the same token, a uniform distribution may be the result of not having sufficient number of classes in one's data, while the random distribution may result if one has multiple sources of variation in the system under study. In either case, these distributions usually provide little information.

The bimodal shaped histogram may indicate that the system under study is the result of several sources of data.

The first Histogram in our case study with Mrs. Appleton's science class is skewed left.

The skewed left is "negatively skewed," *i.e.,* it has a larger number of instances occurring with lower grades (C—F) and a few in the higher grades (A—B). As mentioned above, this skewed distribution occurs when the data within a system has a possible zero point and all the data collected have a value larger than zero.

The second Histogram is also skewed to the left, however, the class grades did improve. In this case one could make the case that the majority of students in Mrs. Appleton's class were able to achieve a grade better than "C" (93.3%) after making a slight change in their study habits.

After analyzing the data, these students decided to embark on a continuous improvement project to see how each could improve his/her performance in all classes. Next, they agreed to monitor the amount of time spent watching television while tracking their grades. The graphic data was a powerful tool indeed!

# NOMINAL GROUP PROCESS

This technique is a structured process which helps the group identify and rank the major problems or issues that need addressing. This technique is also good for identifying the major **strengths** of a department/unit/institution. The technique gives each participant an equal voice, a key element of the group process.

The example below is from Mr. Jones' Social Science class. The session was called by the teacher because of his concerns of a lack of quality in his classroom. Students, a representative number of parents and Mr. Jones participated in the process and were to arrive at a consensus as to the perceived problems and/or weaknesses that inhibited quality.

For the **Nominal Group Process** (NGP) it is recommended that each group have a facilitator that is not part of the task force/unit. The facilitator may have to encourage some members of the team who are reluctant to contribute/participate; likewise, the facilitator may have to restrain members who normally try to control such processes. All members need to feel comfortable with the process and comfortable in participating. Each facilitator will require a stopwatch during the workshop.

Each group should consist of 5 to 10 persons. Since large units will have several groups, it is possible, although unlikely, that each group may perceive different problems/weaknesses. If this should happen, the facilitator may have to review the results and plan another session for the entire unit before the final ranking can be assigned.

**Procedure**
1. Introduction to the Process (5 Minutes)
The facilitator provides instructions regarding the process but does not influence the group's decision. The facilitator keeps the group working within the time limits.

The facilitator tells the participants that the NGP allows them to explore areas systematically and to arrive at a consensus. The process consists of developing a list and ranking perceived problems. The results of the ranking are discussed, and the perceived problems which are the most important to the group are identified.

2. Presentation of the Question (15 Minutes)
The facilitator should direct the question to be considered to the group. For example, the facilitator, as in this case, might be

instructed to ask the group: "What do you consider to be the major problem of your unit that is affecting quality?"

The facilitator should repeat the question and then ask each participant to write short and specific 3 to 5 word answers for each perceived problem on **Form A** (see below). The facilitator should request that each member complete Form A silently and independently, reminding the participants that they have 5 minutes for this task. At the end of 5 minutes if it appears that several members have not finished, the facilitator should state that s/he will allow 2 additional minutes. If most members have already finished, the facilitator should not allow the extra time.

FORM A
Listing of Perceived Problems
What do you think are the major problems in your unit that inhibit quality?
Please use the form below and write out short but specific answers.

| Item # | Perceived Problem |
|---|---|
| 1 | |
| 2 | |
| 3 | |
| 4 | |
| 5 | |

## 3. Development of a Master List (20 Minutes)

While the group is developing their list of perceived problems, the facilitator should use an overhead and project **CHART I**.

At the end of the time allotted for listing the perceived problems of the unit, the facilitator should ask the participants to stop writing. Then in a round robin fashion, the facilitator will ask each to read aloud one of the perceived problems on his/her list. The facilitator will tell the participants that if they come to a problem on their list that has been given, they need not repeat it. If one item is phrased differently from another but appears to be the same, the facilitator will ask the group members to indicate by a show of hands if they think the items are the same. If a majority of the group feel the items are the same, the perceived problem will not be listed again; otherwise, both items will be listed. It may be necessary during this time for the facilitator to ask the participants not to speak out of turn. There should be **no discussion** of the list at this point. For a period of time the participants should not be influenced (to avoid coercion) by the opinions or remarks of others. This must be adhered to early in the process.  Otherwise, those less assertive members will not raise problems which they alone might perceive: for instance, that another member likes to control department meetings. As each perceived problem is given, the facilitator will record the item on the **CHART I**. The facilitator must **not** suggest categories or combinations. The items should be numbered and recorded as presented by the participants without editing, unless the item is too long, in which case the facilitator may try to shorten the phrasing of the perceived problem without changing the meaning.  If at the end of 20 minutes some group members have items that have not been presented, the facilitator will  ask each member to give the one **most important** perceived problem remaining on his/her list.

A sample of some of the initial results of the perceived problems that resulted from the NGP in Mr. Jones' Social Science class are shown below.

### Chart I
### Perceived Problems that Inhibit Quality in Mr. Jones' Social Science Class.

| Item # | Perceived Problem | Initial Value | Final Value | Final Rank |
|---|---|---|---|---|
| 1 | Class size too large | | | |
| 2 | Textbooks are out of date | | | |
| 3 | Classroom is in disrepair | | | |
| 4 | Students are tardy | | | |
| 5 | Too many students are absent | | | |
| 6 | Too many interruptions (announcements, etc.) | | | |
| 7 | Class periods are too short | | | |
| 8 | Teacher is unenthusiastic | | | |
| 9 | Teacher hasn't kept up new techniques & information | | | |
| 10 | Class activities are too routine (boring) | | | |
| 11 | Coercive, punitive discipline policy | | | |
| 12 | Students don't complete homework assignments | | | |
| 13 | Mr. Jones coaches football & uses class time to work out new plays | | | |
| 14 | Tests are too hard | | | |

### 4. Master List Item Clarification (15 Minutes)

The facilitator should point to each perceived problem on the master list and read the item aloud. The facilitator should ask if each item is understood. If an item is unclear, the facilitator should ask the individual who generated the item to address and clarify it. The facilitator should **not** attempt to either condense the list nor to permit the group to discuss the relative importance of the perceived problems at this point. Remember, the purpose of this step is **clarification.**

### 5. Initial Ranking of the Items (15 Minutes)

The facilitator should distribute **Form B** (see below) to each member of the group and should request that each member select and rank the **five (5)** most important perceived problems of the unit. The most important perceived problem should be assigned a #5; the next most important item should be assigned a #4; and so forth with the #1 being assigned for the least important. The participants then record their rankings on **Form B** whereupon the facilitator should collect the forms and tally the results on the master list giving each item an initial score.

Form B
Initial Ranking of Perceived Problems
Please refer to the master list (Chart I) that describes the perceived problems and indicate in the table below what you think are the five major problems.

| Item Number from the Master List | Initial Subjective Ranking Value |
|---|---|
|  | #5 (Most Important) |
|  | #4 |
|  | #3 |
|  | #2 |
|  | #1 (Least Important) |

Using the listings from our aforementioned example in Chart I, the members of the task force in Mr. Jones' class assigned the following values to the listed perceived problems.

Chart I
Perceived Problems that Inhibit Quality in Mr. Jones' Social Science Class.

| Item # | Perceived Problem | Initial Value | Final Value | Final Rank |
|--------|-------------------|---------------|-------------|------------|
| 1 | Class size too large | 7 | | |
| 2 | Textbooks are out of date | 23 | | |
| 3 | Classroom is in disrepair | 17 | | |
| 4 | Students are tardy | 40 | | |
| 5 | Too many students are absent | 20 | | |
| 6 | Too many interruptions (announcements, etc.) | 1 | | |
| 7 | Class periods are too short | 3 | | |
| 8 | Teacher is unenthusiastic | 29 | | |
| 9 | Teacher hasn't kept up new techniques & information | 31 | | |
| 10 | Class activities are too routine (boring) | 45 | | |
| 11 | Coercive, punitive discipline policy | 8 | | |
| 12 | Students don't complete homework assignments | 30 | | |
| 13 | Mr. Jones coaches football & uses class time to work out new plays | 27 | | |
| 14 | Tests are too hard | 35 | | |

## 6. Discussion of Initial Ranking (30 Minutes)

The facilitator should ask the participants to discuss the results of the ranking. The participants may wish to **elaborate, defend,** and to **dispute** the rankings. They may not add items. Items may be discussed even if they did not receive a high score. The members should be reminded that this is their opportunity to express opinions and to persuade others. The facilitator should attempt to keep the discussion orderly and to prevent anyone from dominating.

At this point similar items may be combined into a single category. In the above example a total of 14 separate items was eventually reduced to nine. These are shown below.

| | |
|---|---|
| Class size too large | Too many interruptions |
| Textbooks are out of date | Class periods are too short |
| Classroom is in disrepair | Teacher is unenthusiastic |
| Students are tardy | |
| Coercive, punitive discipline policy | |
| Students don't complete homework assignments | |

## 7. Break (20 Minutes)

The facilitator should encourage the participants to take a break and to move about, since it is rumored that if one sits too long, the blood drains from the brain to the lower extremities. Some members of the group may find this a welcome relief from the previous discussion (or debate, if that should occur). Others may want to take the discussion into the hallway. Likewise, the facilitator should devise innovative means to have the members return promptly after the break session is scheduled to end.

## 8. Final Listing and Ranking of Items (15 Minutes)

After the items have been discussed the facilitator should distribute a **copy of Form C** (see below) to all group members. The facilitator should request each member to rank the top five choices as before:  assign #5 to the one item they consider the most important; #4 to the second most important; etc.  At the end of the allocated time the facilitator should record the final values to each item on the master list.

Form C
Final Ranking of Perceived Problems
Please refer to the revised master list (Chart I) that describes the grouped perceived problems and indicate in the table below what you think are the five major problems.

| Item Number from the Master List | Initial Subjective Ranking Value |
|---|---|
|  | #5 (Most Important) |
|  | #4 |
|  | #3 |
|  | #2 |
|  | #1 (Least Important) |

The results of the Master List should be recorded and typed on **Form D** (see below). When this was done in Mr. Jones' class mentioned above, the following data were obtained.

Form D

Summary and Rank of the Perceived Problems that Inhibit Quality in Mr. Jones' Social Science Class

| Item # | Perceived Problem | Initial Value | Final Value | Final Rank |
|---|---|---|---|---|
| 1 | Class size too large | 7 | 0 | 9 |
| 2 | Textbooks are out of date | 23 | 17 | 5 |
| 3 | Classroom is in disrepair | 17 | 2 | 7 |
| 4 | Students are tardy | 40 | 29 | 4 |
| 5 | Too many students are absent | 20 | 0 | |
| 6 | Too many interruptions (announcements, etc.) | 1 | 32 | 3 |
| 7 | Class periods are too short | 3 | 5 | 6 |
| 8 | Teacher is unenthusiastic | 29 | 97 | 2 |
| 9 | Teacher hasn't kept up new techniques & information | 31 | 0 | |
| 10 | Class activities are too routine (boring) | 45 | 0 | |
| 11 | Coercive, punitive discipline policy | 8 | 1 | 8 |
| 12 | Students don't complete homework assignments | 30 | 110 | 1 |
| 13 | Mr. Jones coaches football & uses class time to work out new plays | 27 | 0 | |
| 14 | Tests are too hard | 35 | 0 | |

Below are the various charts and forms you will need to conduct the NGP in your class.

## Chart I
### Perceived Problems that Inhibit Quality in our Class

| Item # | Perceived Problem | Initial Value | Final Value | Final Rank |
|---|---|---|---|---|
| 1 | | | | |
| 2 | | | | |
| 3 | | | | |
| 4 | | | | |
| 5 | | | | |
| 6 | | | | |
| 7 | | | | |
| 8 | | | | |
| 9 | | | | |
| 10 | | | | |
| 11 | | | | |
| 12 | | | | |
| 13 | | | | |
| n | | | | |

## FORM A
### Listing of Perceived Problems.
What do you think are the major problems in this class that inhibits quality?
Please use the form below and write out short but specific answers.

| Item # | Perceived Problem |
|---|---|
| 1 | |
| 2 | |
| 3 | |
| 4 | |
| 5 | |

Form B
Initial Ranking of Perceived Problems.
Please refer to the master list (Chart I) that describes the perceived problems and indicate in the table below what you think are the five major problems.

| Item Number from the Master List | Initial Subjective Ranking Value |
|---|---|
|  | #5 (Most Important) |
|  | #4 |
|  | #3 |
|  | #2 |
|  | #1 (Least Important) |

Form C
Final Ranking of Perceived Problems
Please refer to the revised master list (Chart I) that describes the grouped perceived problems and indicate in the table below what you think are the five major problems.

| Item Number from the Master List | Initial Subjective Ranking Value |
|---|---|
|  | #5 (Most Important) |
|  | #4 |
|  | #3 |
|  | #2 |
|  | #1 (Least Important) |

Form D
Summary and Rank of the Perceived Problems that Inhibit
Quality.

| Item # | Perceived Problem | Initial Value | Final Value | Final Rank |
|--------|-------------------|---------------|-------------|------------|
| 1 | | | | |
| 2 | | | | |
| 3 | | | | |
| 4 | | | | |
| 5 | | | | |
| 6 | | | | |
| 7 | | | | |
| 8 | | | | |
| 9 | | | | |
| 10 | | | | |
| 11 | | | | |
| 12 | | | | |
| 13 | | | | |
| n | | | | |

# OPERATIONAL DEFINITION

An **Operational Definition** is a very precise statement of what is expected from process objectives. It is probable that most of the troubles within the classroom are the result of operational definitions which are imprecise or undefined. An operational definition is a prerequisite for collecting data, and it must be clearly understood by everyone, *e.g.* the members of the task force, teachers, students, etc.

Major problems arise in everyday events within schools because of unclear or undefined operational definitions. For example, students may want a clear definition of how their grades are going to be determined, including such simple and basic items as to what are they expected to know when they complete a course, how are they to be tested, and what are the classroom rules. Teachers are usually evaluated by the administration every year; never by students or parents. However, for most faculty, evaluation systems are not only statistically invalid but they also drive in fear (as do the tests most teachers give to students).

Operational definitions are used for **every** process that is trying to be improved. It is not necessarily right or wrong, but it must be **accepted by all members working on the system or process**. In addition, if the conditions change as one is examining the process the operational definition may change as well as any new measures added.

## Procedure:
1. Statement of the Problem
Before any characteristic of a system or process is examined, the actual problem or issue has to be clearly defined. This is best done in form of a question such as, "How can I increase the success rate of students identifying major bones in the body and give examples of three types of joints.

2. Identify the Criterion to be Applied to the Object or the Group
The criterion to be measured is the success rate of third grade students identifying the major bones of the body and giving examples of three types of joints.

3. Identify the Test
The actual testing method must be precisely described including the evaluation procedure. In this example, the student

must identify ten major bones of the body from numbered bones on a skeleton. In addition, they must name and give an example of three types of joints. (The students have previously been taught all major bones and joint types. They have participated in a variety of exercises using differing instructional modes to learn. There have been group activities utilizing the skeleton to experiment with types of joints.) Students will have the option to leave their seats and examine the skeleton closely as well as test out joint theories.

4. Describe the Decision Process

The decision process is what permits one to confirm or deny success. In this example, students will assess each other's answers using a scoresheet each group has developed and checked against a master sheet.

# PARETO DIAGRAM

The **Pareto Diagram** is a TQI tool that is used to identify the few significant factors that contribute to a problem and to separate them from the insignificant ones. It is based on the work of Vilfredo Pareto, an Italian economist (1848-1923) and was made popular by Joseph Juran in the 1940's. However, it was Alan Lakelin who came up with the 80/20 rule of the Pareto Diagram. The rule says that about 80 percent of the problem comes from about 20 percent of the causes.

The Pareto Diagram is a simple bar chart with the bars being arranged in descending order from left to right. Although many consider it a problem solving tool, it is really best for guiding a team to the problem areas that should be addressed first.

In the example below we have selected a case study from a high school auto shop where requests for repairs (known as "work orders") were not being completed in a timely fashion. Many of the repairs were not accomplished simply because the "work order" form was not completed correctly. The students and shop teacher identified six categories which attributed to the majority of errors, namely, 1) unclear requests, 2) principal's signature absent, 3) method of payment for parts not indicated, 4) date on which the work was to be performed was absent, 5) location of automobile not specified, and 6) work order request misfiled. The shop teacher appointed a task force and asked them to collect and analyze the data. As part of their study they used the Pareto Diagram which is shown below.

## Procedure

### 1. Select Categories to be Analyzed

The members of the task force should seek to identify those data that they need to collect to address a particular problem, such as time, location, number of defects, number of errors and to place them into a category. The number of categories should be kept to 10 or less.

### 2. Specify the Time period in Which the Data will be Collected

Obviously the time period that is selected will vary according to the system under study. It may be hours in the measuring the time it takes accounting to cut a check or years in case of testing an improvement theory. However, the time selection should be constant for all diagrams that are being compared.

In the above example, the shop teacher chose to compare the 6 categories over the past academic year.

## 3. Record the Data

A table is constructed and it has a category column and a frequency column as shown below.

| Category | # of Violations |
|---|---|
| Unclear requests | 130 |
| Principal's signature absent | 74 |
| Method of payment absent | 46 |
| Date to perform absent | 40 |
| Location of auto not identified | 38 |
| Work order misfiled | 32 |
| Total | 360 |

The frequency table is constructed which shows the category, frequency, relative percent, cumulative frequency, and cumulative percent.

| Category | Number Occurrences | Relative % | Cumulative Frequency | Cumulative % |
|---|---|---|---|---|
| Unclear request | 130 | 36.1 | 130 | 36.1 |
| No Principal's signature | 74 | 19.7 | 204 | 55.8 |
| Method of payment absent | 46 | 12.8 | 250 | 68.6 |
| Date to perform absent | 40 | 11.1 | 290 | 79.7 |
| Location of auto not identified | 38 | 10.6 | 328 | 90.3 |
| Work order misfiled | 32 | 8.9 | 360 | 99.2 |
| Total | 360 | 99.2% | | |

## 4. Draw the Graph

Draw the x-axis (horizontal). It should be long enough to best display your graph and it may vary from several inches to 6 or 7 inches. The width of each bar should be equal. It the case study we are examining the x-axis of 3.6 inches was selected and the scaling factor of 0.60 inch was selected to represent each of the categories.

Draw two vertical lines (y-axis) of equal length as shown below. They should be as long as the x-axis, if not longer. Again, they should be long enough to best display your graph.

Label and scale the axes. In this case study  the x-axis will represent the categories being compared, the y-axis on the left will represent the number of occurrences, and the right y-axis will represent cumulative percent.

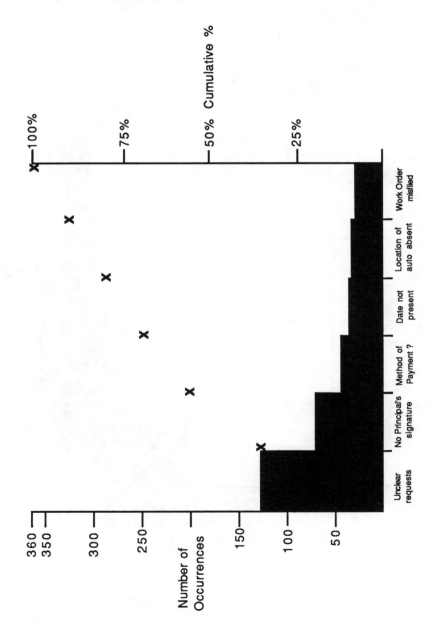

After the graph is drawn plot the cumulative frequencies and draw a line connecting the marks (**x**) as shown below.

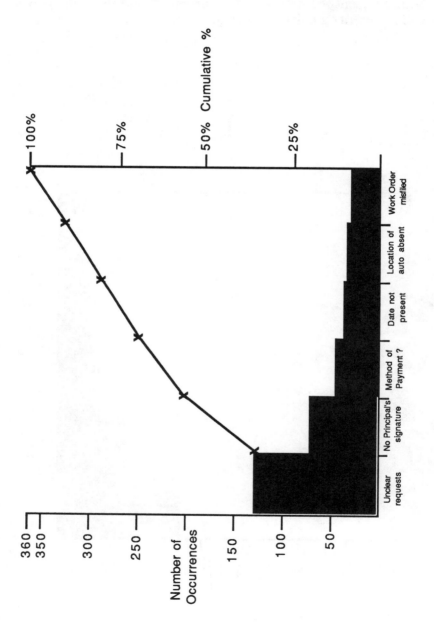

5.  Analyze the Diagram
    It is not unusual for 80 percent of the problem to be caused
by a few categories and the Pareto Diagram will easily
demonstrate this.  In the above example over 55 percent of the
occurrences were due to the first two categories.
    One must be careful when using this powerful tool.  It is true
the Pareto diagram can point out chunks of data that can be used
by a task force to analyze causes and then direct their efforts
towards a few categories, however, there are data that can not be
categorized easily.  Some data, without further analyses,  may
be misleading if they are too general.  The above data  could be
misinterpreted if the shop teacher simply concentrated on the
first two categories.

# RELATIONS DIAGRAM

The **Relations Diagram** is used as a planning tool. It is rarely used alone. Instead, when used with either the **Scenario Builder** and/or the **Affinity Diagram**, the **Relations Diagram** is a powerful tool to arrive at root causes and effects of a process or a problem.

When a task force uses the Relations Diagram to examine a complex problem over an extended period of time it will most likely be able to not only direct its efforts towards the major root causes of the problem(s) in an efficient manner, but it will also be able to constantly update and modify the necessary actions that might result from observed changes in the "system" under study.

**Procedure**

1. <u>Statement of the Problem</u>

Although it is possible to use the Relations Diagram by identifying a problem/issue and then stating it in a brief and specific manner, it is much more efficient to have examined a complex problem/issue with other tools before using the Relations Diagram. For example, we recommend that the task force first utilize one of the other tools such as the **Nominal Group Process** and/or the **Affinity Diagram,** to arrive at a consensus on the process/issue under investigation, then analyze the findings further with the Relations Diagram.

In this example, a high school drama class was attempting to establish a set design and construction shop. They determined that a team was the best way to work through the problem. Their school district could not underwrite such a project, however, the class was determined that the added capability such a shop would provide was worth examining. After doing an analysis with an Affinity Diagram, the team posted the following header cards to the question "What are the issues associated with us establishing a set design & construction shop?"

1. Get the support of parents.
2. Get the support of local business.
3. Demonstrate a need to the principal.
4. Get the support of the student body.
5. Develop and design a plan for the design & construction shop.
6. Prepare informational materials and programs
7. Develop and carry out a fund raising campaign.
8. Organize a volunteer effort to collect equipment and materials.

265

In order to examine the root cause and effects of issue, they next did a **Relations Diagram**.  This is shown below.

2.  <u>Recording the Perceptions</u>
    Place the header cards from the **Affinity Diagram** in a circular pattern around the problem/issue being examined as shown below.  This can be done using an overhead projector, but a large sheet of flip chart paper is usually better.

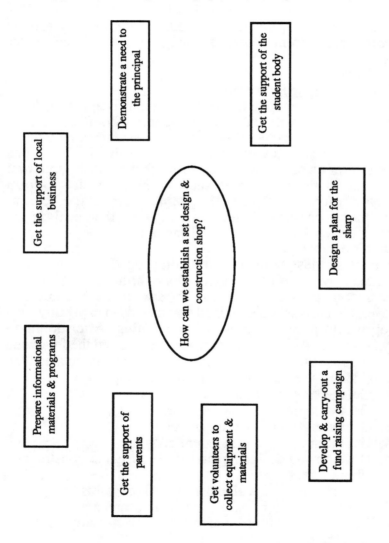

### 3. Demonstrate Interrelationships

One should ask if there is a "cause-and-effect" between the header groups. If a relationship exists, draw a line to connect the headers. An arrow is placed from the header that is a cause of something having an effect on the other header.

In the example below the task force decided that it was necessary to gain the support of the principal before going ahead with their plans. As a result, they drew arrows away from the cause and towards the header that it would effect or have influence over.

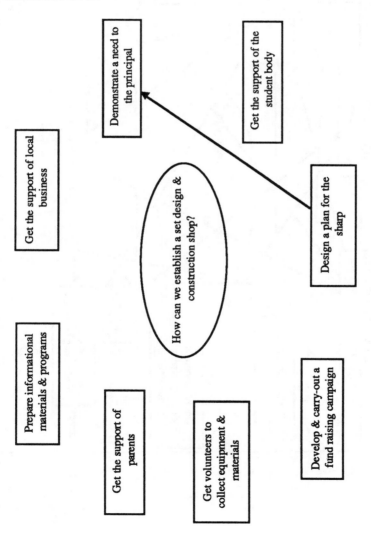

The inter-relations are continually examined until all headers are compared to each other. When this was done with the aforementioned example the following diagram was finally constructed.

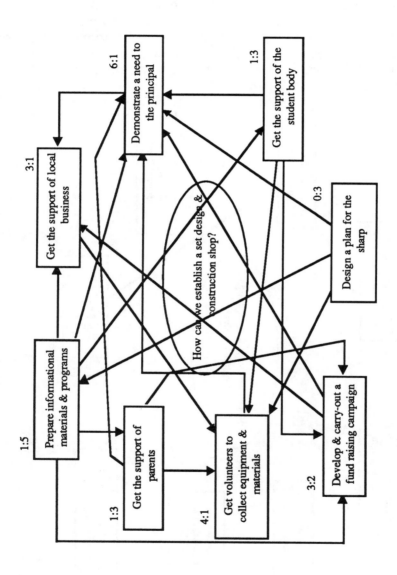

4. Analyze the Interrelationships

Count the number of arrows that are directed towards each header and the number that leave. Express this as the #Towards: #From. Write the numbers next to their respective headers as shown above.

The **root causes** are those headers that have the greatest number of arrows going **FROM**; the **root effects** are those headers having the greatest number of arrows going **TOWARDS**. In the above example the two root causes suggest that the task force should design and draw plans for the shop and develop informational materials and programs prior to going to the principal for his approval and support.

# RUN CHART

A **Run Chart**, also called a tier chart, is a line graph of data where the observed values can be either measurements (variables) or counts (attributes). The data is plotted on the vertical axis while the time is plotted on the horizontal axis.

One of main benefits of a run chart is to examine the functioning of a system over time. Similar data plotted together in a histogram may not reveal an important trend in the system that might require corrective action.

A run chart is constructed from data that is collected as the system is in operation. A run chart is often used by a task force as the initial tool in gathering information about the system under study. Usually more than 25 points are required for a valid run chart.

A run chart is a simple TQI tool and can be used with a wide variety of data. They are good for a single snapshot or for following trends. Various units within the school could make excellent use of run charts by posting good and poor trends for all to see and analyze. (Note: these charts should never be used as a threat or employees will refuse to offer their suggestions as how the system can be improved.) Depending upon the data the time factor can be seconds, minutes, hours, days, weeks, or years. Depending upon the data it may be possible to add the statistical upper control limits (UCL) and lower control limits (LCL) and make the run chart a "Control Chart."

## Procedure
### 1. Select the Data to be Analyzed
We have assumed that the Task Force or the individual studying a system has collected either the attribute (counts) data or the variables (measurements) data. In the case study below, Mrs. Salmon was interested in discovering the average amount of time it took her students to achieve mastery for each unit of study. She wanted to examine her assignments and teaching styles for each unit and was going to focus on those units where the students were having the most difficulty with mastery.

2. Record the Data
Record the data in the order which it was collected.


Average time (in days) to achieve mastery per unit

| Class period | Unit 1 | Unit 2 | Unit 3 | Unit 4 | Unit 5 | Unit 6 |
|---|---|---|---|---|---|---|
| #1    (8-8:50 AM) | 13 | 15 | 14 | 16 | 15 | 14 |
| #2    (9-9:50 AM) | 14 | 13 | 14 | 13 | 13 | 14 |
| #3 (10-10:50 AM) | 13 | 14 | 16 | 15 | 15 | 14 |
| #4 (11-11:50 AM) | 19 | 23 | 20 | 18 | 21 | 16 |
| #5 (12-12:50 PM) | 16 | 16 | 17 | 17 | 16 | 14 |
| #6    (1-1:50 PM) | 14 | 16 | 16 | 15 | 15 | 14 |

3. Draw the Graph
The first thing one has to do is to scale the chart and this will vary depending upon the type of data collected, *i.e.* variables or attributes.

In scaling for the variables data one starts by finding the largest and smallest values in the data. In our case the largest was 23 and the smallest was 13. The difference between these are determined (23-13=10). Then a rule of thumb is to divide the difference (10) by 66% of the number of lines on your graph paper. The chart paper used in our case study is shown below. It has 30 lines, therefore, 30 x 0.66= 19.8, or approximately 20. Therefore, 10 ÷ 20 is 0.5. Always rounding to the higher number each line will have an incremental value of 1.0.

Next the lines should be numbered from the middle of the chart. Since our values range from 13 to 23 minutes the value which is one half is 5 minutes. Since the center number is 5 minutes + 13 minutes or 18 minutes, we can set the center line at either 15 minutes or 20 minutes and assign an incremental value of one minute to the other lines.

Scaling for attributes data is identical to that of the variables scaling except the first line of the chart is assigned a value of zero and the increment values are added from the bottom up.

The data points are plotted on the graph paper as shown in and the points are connected with straight lines.

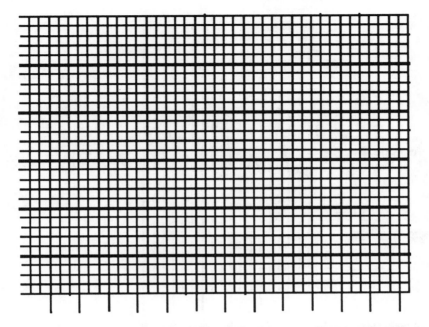

It should be mentioned that almost any chart paper can be used to plot the data of run charts and that the process of scaling would be the same.

The chart should be carefully labeled so that the results can be clearly understood by all members of the task force. An example of a completed run chart is shown below.

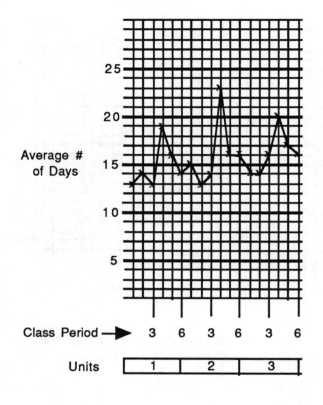

Average #
of Days

Class Period ➤    3    6    3    6    3    6

Units    1    2    3

4. Analyze the Chart

One should look for runs of 7 or more points showing increases or decreases as well as for other patterns.

In our case a pattern was discovered: students in "Period 4" took significantly longer to achieve mastery than students in all the other classes. Period 4 is just before lunch. Students may be tired, or hungry and distracted from their studies. (It could also be that Mrs. Salmon is tired and hungry and is not providing the necessary leadership.) She also discovered that the second period class averaged only 13.5 days to complete mastery in all the units. Her task now is to match this data with her teaching styles for the fourth and second periods. Based on that information, she will examine the learning styles of her students prior to making any adjustments in the class. Mrs. Salmon also will engage the students in the continuous improvement project, utilizing one or more of the other tools.

# SCATTER DIAGRAM

**Scatter Diagrams** are used to test the possible interrelationships of two factors. If a relationship appears to exist, the factors are said to be correlated. However, a cause-and-effect relationship can be verified only with the use of control charts.

A scatter diagram is a useful tool that can be used by action teams to analyze causes of poor processes or systems.

1. Select the Data to be Analyzed

In the following case study a teacher wanted to test whether the grade of the students in a fourth grade mathematics unit was related to the time they watched television (TV). The parents were asked, as part of their TQM contract, to record the amount of time in minutes that their child spent watching TV over a week and to submit this log to the teacher. At the end of the report period the teacher plotted the results.

2. Record the Data

| Student ID Number | Hours per Week Viewing TV | Math Grade in % |
|---|---|---|
| 001 | <1.0 | 96 |
| 002 | 2.5 | 98 |
| 003 | 14.0 | 60 |
| 004 | 21.0 | 72 |
| 005 | 21.0 | 56 |
| 006 | 2.5 | 88 |
| 007 | 3.0 | 83 |
| 008 | 7.0 | 86 |
| 009 | 8.0 | 71 |
| 010 | 3.0 | 91 |
| 011 | 3.0 | 86 |
| 012 | 18.0 | 60 |
| 013 | 21.0 | 56 |
| 014 | <1.0 | 93 |
| 015 | 10.0 | 75 |
| 016 | 9.0 | 76 |
| 017 | 10.0 | 77 |
| 018 | 2.5 | 92 |
| 019 | 6.0 | 70 |
| 020 | 7.5 | 73 |
| 021 | 2.5 | 99 |
| 022 | 14.5 | 60 |
| 023 | 9.0 | 77 |
| 024 | 8.5 | 69 |
| 025 | 4.0 | 80 |

### 3.  Draw the Diagram

The first thing one should do is scale the diagram so that both axes are approximately the same length.  The length of the axes should be long enough to accommodate the entire range of values and the entire length of each axis should be used. In our example the time per week the students watched TV ranged from less than 2.5 hours to 21 hours. The x-axis usually contains the data believed to be the influencing or independent factor while the y-axis contains the dependent or responding factor. In our example the teacher believed that the more the students watched TV the less they studied and, as a result, their grades suffered. Therefore, the independent factor is time watching TV and the dependent factor is the grade.

The diagram should be labeled, dated, and the points should be plotted.  The completed diagram is shown below.

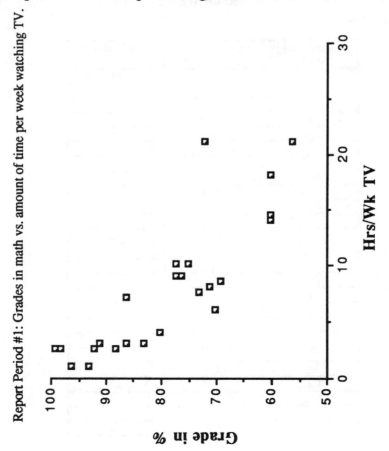

Report Period #1: Grades in math vs. amount of time per week watching TV.

4. <u>Analyze the Diagram</u>

Although it looks as if there might be a negative correlation between the amount of time the students watched TV and the grade that they received in the mathematics, there may be other factors that influenced the grades, such as the number of absences, etc. Clearly, however, the amount of time the students watch TV might be a possible root cause for poor grades in math.

# SCENARIO BUILDER

The **Scenario Builder** is a planning tool which quantifies roughly the outcomes that may result if one or more proposed changes to a system are implemented. It is useful for helping to analyze the most likely outcomes of an element of change on a complex system. It is a tool that asks "what if?" and concentrates the efforts of team members to propose most likely outcomes, both positive and negative. It is a powerful tool that combines many of the features obtained from an affinity diagram, the nominal group process, the force field analysis, and the systematic diagram. Like the **Affinity Diagram** it attempts to organize complex issues; like the **Nominal Group Process,** it forces the group into identifying and ranking the most likely effects that the proposed change may bring; like the **Force Field Analysis**, it concentrates on both the positive and negative driving and restraining forces and the action steps that should be taken to overcome the resistance of implementing the change; and, finally, like the **Systematic Diagram**, it helps to identify possible action items that are necessary in order to implement a broader goal.

The **Scenario Builder** should not be used until the task force members are familiar with the affinity diagram, the nominal group process, the force field analysis, and the systematic diagram. The **Scenario Builder** is **NOT** a replacement for the aforementioned tools, but it is a tool that one may wish to consider **IF** the situation under examination requires two or more of the tools for elucidation. Although the **Scenario Builder** requires a minimum of 3 hours of concentrated effort to complete, it still may save the task force many hours if, for example, three TQI tools are required to arrive at similar conclusions.

## Procedure
1. Spell out the recommended changes
In using the scenario builder, the group has defined the system that requires modification. In fact, the team members should have solidified the change(s) that must be implemented in order to improve the system.

The recommended change ("**C**") is placed in the middle of the hexagon (see Scenario Builder Figure). The task force members should assume that the appropriate recommendations will be accepted in order to implement the change.

2. Record the Perceptions
The task force members should list at least three beneficial outcomes of the proposed change, and, if possible, three

undesirable outcomes of the proposed change. The three beneficial outcomes should be listed in the squares labeled 1 through 3; the three undesirable outcomes should be listed in the squares 4 through 6. (Sometimes it is difficult and/or almost impossible to identify three truly unacceptable outcomes as a result of implementing improvements in processes or systems. However, the group should attempt to identify at least two undesirable outcomes.)

Following the above pattern, the group should label four scenarios that are likely to occur as a result of the outcomes identified in the squares labeled 1 through 6, and if possible, two should be positive and two should be negative scenarios. In any event, at least one should be either positive or negative.

The aforementioned pattern should be repeated with the triangles and the ellipsoids. At least one of the perceived outcomes should be either positive or negative at any of the levels.

Scenario Builder To Determine The Effect of Change

## 3. Score the Scenarios

Scoring of the scenarios can be done either as they are listed, or afterwards. But all six, first level scenarios should have at least a 70 percent perceived probability of occurring. To score the scenario builder the group assigns a number of +1 to +10 to any positive scenario that might occur if the change is implemented, and -1 to -10 to any negative scenario that might occur if the change is implemented. For example, the group may decide that a positive scenario A, identified and placed in square 1, would surely result if the change were effected and thus they assigned a value +10. The +10 means that the positive scenario would occur 100 percent of the time if the change were implemented and **IF** nothing were done to stop it. Likewise, a +3 should be assigned a value of 30 percent; +4, forty percent, etc. The group may decide that positive scenarios B and C should be assigned values of +7 and +5 respectively. Similarly, the task force might decide that negative scenario D would almost definitely occur (100% of the time) if the change were implemented, therefore, they would assign it a value of -10, whereas the negative scenarios E and F were only assigned values of -3 (30%) and -4 (40%) since they were less likely to occur if the change was implemented. If a **very positive** scenario would occur if the change is effected, and if its effect could not be altered, it should be assigned a value of +50. If a disaster would occur if the change is implemented, and if its effect could not be altered, it should be assigned a value of -50.

The values for the first level scenarios, 1 through 6, should be recorded on a scenario builder tally sheet as shown below. Likewise, the values for the second level scenarios, 1.1 through 6.4, should be recorded. Finally, the values for the third level scenarios, 1.1.1 through 6.4.3, should be recorded. The scoring guidelines for the scenario builder are shown in the following table.

| Positive Scenario | Negative Scenario | Would Likely Occur Percent of the Time | Effect Can Be Altered? |
|---|---|---|---|
| +1 | -1 | 10% | Yes |
| +2 | -2 | 20% | Yes |
| +3 | -3 | 30% | Yes |
| +4 | -4 | 40% | Yes |
| +5 | -5 | 50% | Yes, Requires Effort |
| +6 | -6 | 60% | Yes, Requires More Effort |
| +7 | -7 | 70% | Yes, Requires Much Effort |
| +8 | -8 | 80% | Yes, With Difficulty |
| +9 | -9 | 90% | Yes, But Unlikely |
| +10 | -10 | 100% | Not Likely |
| +50 | -50 | 100% | Never |

Scenario Builder tally sheet for estimating perceived effects of change on a process or a system and the prospect that a given event will occur.

| 1. ___ | 1. ___ | 1. ___ | 1. ___ |
|---|---|---|---|
| 1.1 ___ | 1.2 ___ | 1.3 ___ | 1.4 ___ |
| 1.1.1 ___ | 1.2.1 ___ | 1.3.1 ___ | 1.4.1 ___ |
| 1.1.2 ___ | 1.2.2 ___ | 1.3.2 ___ | 1.4.2 ___ |
| 1.1.3 ___ | 1.2.3 ___ | 1.3.3 ___ | 1.4.3 ___ |
| Total ___ | Total ___ | Total ___ | Total ___ |
| 2. ___ | 2. ___ | 2. ___ | 2. ___ |
| 2.1 ___ | 2.2 ___ | 2.3 ___ | 2.4 ___ |
| 2.1.1 ___ | 2.2.1 ___ | 2.3.1 ___ | 2.4.1 ___ |
| 2.1.2 ___ | 2.2.2 ___ | 2.3.2 ___ | 2.4.2 ___ |
| 2.1.3 ___ | 2.2.3 ___ | 2.3.3 ___ | 2.4.3 ___ |
| Total ___ | Total ___ | Total ___ | Total ___ |
| 3. ___ | 3. ___ | 3. ___ | 3. ___ |
| 3.1 ___ | 3.2 ___ | 3.3 ___ | 3.4 ___ |
| 3.1.1 ___ | 3.2.1 ___ | 3.3.1 ___ | 3.4.1 ___ |
| 3.1.2 ___ | 3.2.2 ___ | 3.3.2 ___ | 3.4.2 ___ |
| 3.1.3 ___ | 3.2.3 ___ | 3.3.3 ___ | 3.4.3 ___ |
| Total ___ | Total ___ | Total ___ | Total ___ |
| 4. ___ | 4. ___ | 4. ___ | 4. ___ |
| 4.1 ___ | 4.2 ___ | 4.3 ___ | 4.4 ___ |
| 4.1.1 ___ | 4.2.1 ___ | 4.3.1 ___ | 4.4.1 ___ |
| 4.1.2 ___ | 4.2.2 ___ | 4.3.2 ___ | 4.4.2 ___ |
| 4.1.3 ___ | 4.2.3 ___ | 4.3.3 ___ | 4.4.3 ___ |
| Total ___ | Total ___ | Total ___ | Total ___ |
| 5. ___ | 5. ___ | 5. ___ | 5. ___ |
| 5.1 ___ | 5.2 ___ | 5.3 ___ | 5.4 ___ |
| 5.1.1 ___ | 5.2.1 ___ | 5.3.1 ___ | 5.4.1 ___ |
| 5.1.2 ___ | 5.2.2 ___ | 5.3.2 ___ | 5.4.2 ___ |
| 5.1.3 ___ | 5.2.3 ___ | 5.3.3 ___ | 5.4.3 ___ |
| Total ___ | Total ___ | Total ___ | Total ___ |
| 6. ___ | 6. ___ | 6. ___ | 6. ___ |
| 6.1 ___ | 6.2 ___ | 6.3 ___ | 6.4 ___ |
| 6.1.1 ___ | 6.2.1 ___ | 6.3.1 ___ | 6.4.1 ___ |
| 6.1.2 ___ | 6.2.2 ___ | 6.3.2 ___ | 6.4.2 ___ |
| 6.1.3 ___ | 6.2.3 ___ | 6.3.3 ___ | 6.4.3 ___ |
| Total ___ | Total ___ | Total ___ | Total ___ |

4. Interpret the Scores

The team should examine the first level scenarios, labeled 1 through 6, and they should have values ±7, *i.e.* all should have a greater than 70 percent chance of occurring if the changes were implemented.

The task force should continue to build upon the **major** positive and negative scenarios through levels two and three. As before they should concentrate their efforts on only the scenarios with values of ±7 or greater.

5. Describe what will likely happen to each even and then what ACTION STEP needs to be taken to accentuate the positive and minimize the negative outcomes as well as the DESIRED OUTCOME

With the likely events of both positive and negative outcomes resulting in the implementation of the task force's recommendations to change a system being evaluated and quantified, action steps can now be identified to either recommend the change and to minimize the possible negative outcomes, or to, in fact, abandon the change as it might be disastrous to the classroom or school.

6. List and analyze any scenario that has a number greater than ±100

The scenarios that have a high score usually means that if the recommended changes were implemented and if the perceptions of the task force members were representative of the institutional culture, then the scenarios would take place.

7. Suggest what one or two systems should be improved to maximize the positive and minimize the negative

## Case Study

Here is an example of how the **Scenario Builder** was effectively used with students in a twelfth grade English class.

The students in Ms. Amie Mosier's twelfth grade English class were not doing well. A task force consisting of five students and Ms. Mosier was formed. After conducting a Nominal Group Process session with the class, they arrived at the conclusion that the students would learn more and do better quality work if the students could work cooperatively in groups.

Following the aforementioned directions:

1.  Spell out the recommended change(s)

The recommended change ("C") is: **Students will work in groups on all classroom assignments in order to receive better grades in English.**

2.  Record the Perceptions

The task force members should list approximately an equal number of beneficial outcomes and undesirable outcomes of the proposed change. These are shown below along with the scoring.

3.  Score the Scenarios

Scoring of the scenarios can be done either as they are listed, or afterwards. But all six, first level scenarios should have at least a 70 percent perceived probability of occurring. To score the scenario builder the group assigns a number of +1 to +10 to any positive scenario that might occur if the change is implemented, and -1 to -10 to any negative scenario that might occur if the change is implemented. If a **very positive** scenario would occur if the change is effected, and if its effect could not be altered, it should be assigned a value of +50. Likewise, if a disaster would occur if the change is implemented, and if its effect could not be altered, it should be assigned a value of -50. The aforementioned table was used and the following numbers were assigned to the scenarios if the recommended change ("C") is implemented: **Students will work in groups on all classroom assignments in order to receive better grades in English.**

1.  Students will get along well and will work effectively in the groups.  (+7)

    1.1    Students will realize the importance of group success.  (+7)

        1.1.1  Self esteem will rise because the group will be successful.  (+9)

        1.1.2  Students will bond with a different group of students.  (+6)

        1.1.3  Some will be frustrated because there will be less individual recognition.(-3)

    1.2    Students will achieve a quality group product.  (+8)

        1.2.1  Students will take pride in workmanship realizing they've produced a quality product.  (+10)

        1.2.2  Students will recognize excellence and know they can achieve it.  (+10)

        1.2.3  Students will be frustrated at the amount of work involved in achieving quality work.(-2)

1.3     Students will spend too much time chatting/gossiping and little time working on the assignment. (-2)

       1.3.1  Students will broaden their circle of friends. (+5)

       1.3.2  Students will practice better communication skills. (+5)

       1.3.3  Students will not achieve quality work because they will not focus on the assignment. (-8)

1.4     Students will broaden the assignment , causing them to be inefficient in their use of time. (-3)

       1.4.1  Students will become so enthusiastic they will continue to find new ways to explore the assignment. (+4)

       1.4.2  Students will learn many different off-shoots about the assignment, thus broadening their knowledge base. (+4)

       1.4.3  Students will not finish the assignment on time. (-6)

2.  After Ms. Mosier trains students in cooperative learning, groups will work effectively producing quality assignments. (+10)

2.1     Students will enjoy cooperative learning and will agree to work in groups. (+8)

       2.1.1  Students will become active learners and have fun in the classroom. (+8)

       2.1.2  Students will expand their friendships. (+7)

       2.1.3  Students will not focus on the assignment. (-3)

2.2     Students will feel good about being helpful to their classmates. (+50)

       2.2.1  Self-esteem will increase. (+10)

       2.2.2  Students will realize how working together increases success. (+10)

       2.2.3  Some students will do the work of others rather than helping them. (-7)

2.3     Training students will take up a great deal of class time. (-8)

       2.3.1  Ms. Mosier will consider this is important. (+10)

       2.3.2  Students will learn how to work cooperatively. (+7)

       2.3.3  Training will take away valuable class time, causing Ms. Mosier to feel stressed. (-8)

2.4    Students who are not in groups with their friends will not put all their focus and energy into accomplishing the assignment. (-5)

2.4.1    Students will get to know other students. (+5)

2.4.2    Factions within the classroom will begin to break down as students work together with others. (+4)

2.4.3    Some students will become angry and refuse to work together. (-7)

3.   Students will appreciate individual differences in their classmates and will recognize how each contributes to the success of the group. (+9)

3.1    Students will recognize that people learn differently. (+50)

3.1.1    Students will learn that some are "smart" in other subjects but "slow" in English. (+50)

3.1.2    Teaming will become more important than individual success. (+7)

3.1.3    Racial tension will be reduced as students work together. (+10)

3.2    Students will be frustrated with those who not contribute to the project. (-10)

3.2.1    Clicks will form within the group. (-10)

3.2.2    Hard feelings will result. (-10)

3.2.3    Racial tension will increase. (-10)

3.3    Leaders will evolve to direct the group. (-50)

3.3.1    All members of the group will develop significant leadership qualities. (+7)

3.3.2    Some of the leaders will become pushy. (-50)

3.3.3    Some students will ignore the leaders. (+10)

4.   Students will resist working together and will do individual projects within the group. (-8)

4.1    Students will work harder for their own gain than they otherwise would. (+3)

4.1.1    The quality of each person's work will be higher than normal. (+2)

4.1.2    Students will learn about independent study. (+3)

4.1.3    There will be an overlap among student's work. (-7)

    4.2      The group assignment will not be cohesive. (-7)
-     4.2.1  The individual parts of the assignment will good quality. (+3)
-     4.2.2  Students have will not learn to work cooperatively. (-10)
-     4.2.3  The group assignment will not be completed since the group will not tie it all together. (-9)

    4.3      Students will become angry because each thinks s/he is doing all the work. (-8)
-     4.3.1  Adrenaline will make all students work harder. (+2)
-     4.3.2  Some students will quit because they will feel unappreciated. (-4)
-     4.3.3  Groups will break apart because students will refuse to work together. (-9)

5. Some students will simply not participate in the group, and a few students will undertake responsibility for completing the group assignment. (-7)

    5.1      Some students will get the assignment done. (+3)
-     5.1.1  The assignment will be completed. (+3)
-     5.1.2  The goal of working together in a group will be achieved. (-10)
-     5.1.3  Students will be angry with other group members for not helping. (-8)

    5.2      There will be dissension between the students. (-10)
-     5.2.1  Natural tension will cause students to practice communication skills. (+2)
-     5.2.2  Students will break into factions...those working and those not. (-7)
-     5.2.3  Students will complain to Ms. Mosier that the assignment is unfair. (-8)

    5.3      Some students will not do any work. (-10)
-     5.3.1  Some students will relax. (+1)
-     5.3.2  Working students will be angry with those who are not. (-9)
-     5.3.3  Group goals will not being met since students will not learn to work together. (-10)

6. Tensions will be high since students will refuse to work with anyone other than their friends. (-8)

The task force entered the scores of each scenario into the table that follows.

Scenario Builder tally sheet for estimating perceived effects of change on a process or a system and the prospect that a given event will occur.

| | | | |
|---|---|---|---|
| 1. +7 | 1. +7 | 1. +7 | 1. +7 |
| 1.1 +7 | 1.2 +8 | 1.3 -2 | 1.4 -3 |
| 1.1.1 +9 | 1.2.1 +10 | 1.3.1 +5 | 1.4.1 +4 |
| 1.1.2 +6 | 1.2.2 +10 | 1.3.2 +5 | 1.4.2 +4 |
| 1.1.3 -3 | 1.2.3 - 2 | 1.3.3 -8 | 1.4.3 -6 |
| Total +26 | Total +33 | Total +7 | Total +6 |

| | | | |
|---|---|---|---|
| 2. +10 | 2. +10 | 2. +10 | 2. +10 |
| 2.1 +8 | 2.2 +9 | 2.3 -8 | 2.4 -5 |
| 2.1.1 +8 | 2.2.1 +50 | 2.3.1 +10 | 2.4.1 +5 |
| 2.1.2 +7 | 2.2.2 +10 | 2.3.2 +7 | 2.4.2 +4 |
| 2.1.3 -3 | 2.2.3 - 7 | 2.3.3 -8 | 2.4.3 - 7 |
| Total +30 | Total +72 | Total +11 | Total + 7 |

| | | | |
|---|---|---|---|
| 3. +9 | 3. +9 | 3. +9 | 3. +9 |
| 3.1 +50 | 3.2 -10 | 3.3 -50 | 3.4 ND |
| 3.1.1 +50 | 3.2.1 -10 | 3.3.1 +7 | 3.4.1 ___ |
| 3.1.2 +7 | 3.2.2 -10 | 3.3.2 -50 | 3.4.2 ___ |
| 3.1.3 +10 | 3.2.3 -10 | 3.3.3 - 9 | 3.4.3 ___ |
| Total +126 | Total -39 | Total -74 | Total ___ |

| | | | |
|---|---|---|---|
| 4. -8 | 4. -8 | 4. -8 | 4. -8 |
| 4.1 +3 | 4.2 -7 | 4.3 -8 | 4.4 ND |
| 4.1.1 +2 | 4.2.1 +3 | 4.3.1 +2 | 4.4.1 ___ |
| 4.1.2 +3 | 4.2.2 -10 | 4.3.2 -4 | 4.4.2 ___ |
| 4.1.3 -7 | 4.2.3 -9 | 4.3.3 -9 | 4.4.3 ___ |
| Total -7 | Total -31 | Total -27 | Total ___ |

| | | | |
|---|---|---|---|
| 5. -7 | 5. -7 | 5. -7 | 5. -7 |
| 5.1 +3 | 5.2 -10 | 5.3 -10 | 5.4 ND |
| 5.1.1 +3 | 5.2.1 +2 | 5.3.1 +1 | 5.4.1 ___ |
| 5.1.2 -10 | 5.2.2 -7 | 5.3.2 -9 | 5.4.2 ___ |
| 5.1.3 -8 | 5.2.3 -8 | 5.3.3 -10 | 5.4.3 ___ |
| Total -19 | Total - 30 | Total -35 | Total ___ |

| | | | |
|---|---|---|---|
| 6. -8 | | | |
| 6.1 ND | 6.2 ND | 6.3 ND | 6.4 ND |
| 6.1.1 ___ | 6.2.1 ___ | 6.3.1 ___ | 6.4.1 ___ |
| 6.1.2 ___ | 6.2.2 ___ | 6.3.2 ___ | 6.4.2 ___ |
| 6.1.3 ___ | 6.2.3 ___ | 6.3.3 ___ | 6.4.3 ___ |
| Total ___ | Total ___ | Total ___ | Total ___ |

4. <u>Interpret the Scores</u>
    4.1    <u>Examine the scores of the six, first level scenarios</u>

The team should examine the first level scenarios, labeled 1 through 6, and they should have values ±7, *i.e.* all should have a greater than 70 percent chance of occurring if the changes were implemented. All scenarios did have a score greater than ±7.

    4.2    <u>Build upon the second level scenarios that have a 70 percent chance or greater perceived probability of occurring</u>

The task force continued to build upon the **major** positive and negative scenarios through levels two and three. As before they concentrated their efforts on only the scenarios with values of ±7 or greater.

The task force, therefore, had to consider the following scenarios: 1.1, 1.2, 2.1, 2.2, 2.3, 3.1, 3.2, 3.3, 4.2, 4.3, 5.2, and 5.3.

5. <u>Describe what will likely happen to each event and then what ACTION STEP needs to be taken to accentuate the positive and minimize the negative outcomes as well as the DESIRED OUTCOME</u>

With the likely events of both positive and negative outcomes resulting in the implementation of the task force's recommendations to change a system being evaluated and quantified, action steps can now be identified to either recommend the change and to minimize the possible negative outcomes, or to, in fact, abandon the change as it might be disastrous to the organization.

SCENARIO 1: The students will get along well and work effectively in groups (+7) since they will realize the importance of group success (+7). Therefore self-esteem will rise because the group will be successful (+9) and this will cause the students to bond together (+6).

While working together to produce a quality "product (+8)," the individuals will take pride-in-workmanship (+10) and will recognize excellence and know they can achieve it (+10).

ACTION STEP: The task force will report its finding and recommendations back to the class.

DESIRED OUTCOMES: The students will realize that cooperative learning and teaming is the way things are done in real life situations.

SCENARIO 2: After Ms. Mosier trains the students in cooperative learning, groups will work effectively together (+10). After the training the students will enjoy working in groups (+8) as they will become active learners (+8). In addition, they will expand their friendships (+7). Group projects will make students feel good about helping their classmates (+50) and self-esteem will increase (+10). Students will realize the importance of group success, although some students may end up doing the work of others rather than showing them how the work should be done (-7).

Ms. Mosier knows that it will take time to train the students in TQI tools (-8) and that this time will come from regular class time (-8), but the training is very important (+10) if the students are to learn how to work as a team (+7).

ACTION STEP: Ms. Mosier will take time from the regular classes to teach the appropriate TQI tools which encourage teaming.

DESIRED OUTCOMES: The students will begin to work as a team and realize success in English.

SCENARIO 3: Students will appreciate individual differences in their classmates and will recognize how each contributes to the success of the group (+9). As a result students will recognize different learning styles (+50) and the differences in preferences for subjects (+50). Since teaming will become more important than individual success (+7), racial tension will be reduced as the students work together (+10).

The possibility exists that the students will become frustrated with those who do not contribute to the project (-10) and various subunits will result (-10) which will increase hard feelings (-10) and increase racial tension (-10).

As in any group project, leaders will emerge and direct the group project (-50). Actually, this may be a +50 if the leaders help the group to realize their own potential and don't become pushy (-50). Some students will totally ignore pushy leaders (+10).

ACTION STEP: Each group will have to constantly remind its members about the benefits of team work.

DESIRED OUTCOMES: The students will realize the importance of leadership in helping the group obtain success.

SCENARIO 4: Students will resist working together and will do individual projects within the group (-8). The group will not be cohesive (-7) since most students will not learn to work cooperatively (-1). As a result the group assignments will not be completed (-9). Students will become angry as each student will think that they are doing the majority of the work (-8) and the group will break apart because they will refuse to work together (-9).

ACTION STEP: Ms. Mosier must instill into the students the importance of teaming and how to use the TQI tools in order to achieve success.

DESIRED OUTCOMES: The students will learn the necessary skills to work together as a group.

SCENARIO 5: Some students will simply not participate in the group, and a few students will undertake responsibility for completing the group assignment (-7). (The task force members concluded that this scenario was so similar to #4 that it did not need to be discussed further since it would be resolved by the action step taken under scenario 4.)

SCENARIO 6: Tensions will be high since the students will refuse to work with anyone other that their friends (-8). No action step is recommended since this may fade after the work teams are formed and success is achieved.

6. List and analyze any scenario that has a number greater than ±100

The scenarios that have a high score usually means that if the recommended changes were implemented and if the perceptions of the task force members were representative of the institutional culture, then the scenarios would take place.

One scenario has a number greater than ±100 , namely 3.1, which reads:

> 3. Students will appreciate individual differences in their classmates and will recognize how each contributes to the success of the group. (+9)
> 3.1    Students will recognize that people learn differently. (+50)
>> 3.1.1   Students will learn that some are "smart" in other subjects but "slow" in English. (+50)
>> 3.1.2   Teaming will become more important than individual success. (+7)

3.1.3   Racial tension will be reduced as
students work together. (+10)

(It should be mentioned that before the end of the year Scenario 3 did occur!)

7. <u>Suggest what one or two systems should be improved to maximize the positive and minimize the negative</u>
After analyzing the results of the scenarios and the results that were obtained by the end of the school year, the action team decided that a major dysfunctional system was at the root of poor learning in their high school, namely, the students were not taught how to work together in order to obtain quality results. In a letter to the school board and the principal, the students suggested that a course in TQI procedures be taught at the ninth grade level, if not sooner.

# SYSTEMATIC DIAGRAM

The **Systematic Diagram** is used as a planning tool to determine the specific action steps that are necessary to accomplish a broader goal, especially if a number of people, departments, or units are involved. The **Systematic Diagram** is best used with an **Affinity Diagram** or a **Relations Diagram**.

## Procedure
1. Statement of the Problem/Goal
   We will build upon the example presented in the **Relations Diagram** section when a task force consisting of drama students and their teacher was attempting to establish a set design and construction shop. The goal is drawn on the left hand side of the paper. This can be done using an overhead projector or a large sheet of flip chart paper.

END

```
┌─────────────────┐
│ Establish a Set │
│   Design and    │
│  Construction   │
│      Shop       │
└─────────────────┘
```

2. Generate Levels of Events and Actions Necessary to Accomplish the Ends
   The first level of events and actions are usually broad, but as one moves from left to right the tasks become very specific as one level builds upon the other. In the example that follows the task force members know that if they are to accomplish their goal, they will ultimately require approval and support from the principal, parents, business community, and students. In order for that to occur, however, the task force recognized that it will need to develop a rationale, a design, and informational materials. The steps are incorporated in the completed Systematic Diagram below.

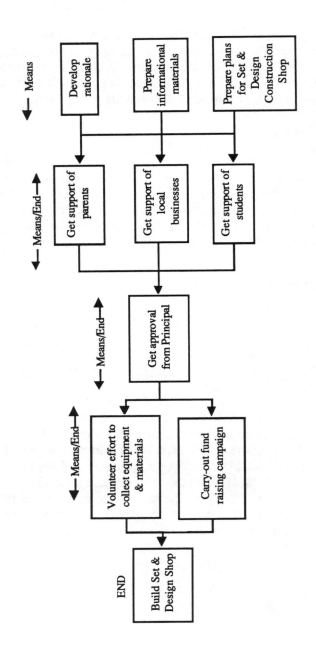

3. Analyze the Diagram and Assign Tasks

After the Systematic Diagram is completed the task force members should analyze their findings and discuss them with the rest of their class. Then specific tasks or action steps with specific time lines should be assigned. It is a good idea to post the Systematic Diagram with the names of the person(s) having the responsibility to accomplish a specific task (action).